The Best of
COOKING
Pleasures

VOLUME I

Cooking Club
of
America®

MINNETONKA, MINNESOTA

THE BEST OF COOKING PLEASURES—VOLUME I

Mike Vail
Vice President Product and Business Development

Tom Carpenter
Director of Book Development

Dan Kennedy
Book Production Manager

Jen Guinea
Book Development Coordinator

Jenya Prosmitsky
Book Design and Production

Laura Belpedio
Shari Gross
Book Development Assistants

Stafford Photography
Photography

1 2 3 4 5 6 7 8 / 03 02 01

ISBN 1-58159-135-7

Cooking Club of America
12301 Whitewater Drive
Minnetonka, MN 55343

Contents

Cranberry Sparkler, p. 143

WITH

The Best of

COOKING PLEASURES

VOLUME I

Some of your cooking certainly revolves around traditions—specific dishes and menus for certain occasions and events throughout the year. Tradition is comfortable and good, and certainly breeds success in the kitchen.

But cooking is also about adventure. Who among us would love our pastime as much if we didn't love to try new and exciting recipe ideas, cooking techniques and entertaining plans?

That's why we at the Cooking Club of America created *The Best of Cooking Pleasures—Volume I*. Here you will find the "best of the best" from the six issues of *Cooking Pleasures* magazine published in 2000. On the following pages are the most popular and exciting topics that came along, conveniently pulled together for you in one recipe-, idea-, technique- and picture-filled volume.

Perhaps you didn't save all your magazines throughout the year, or you joined the Club mid-way through. Maybe you just like the idea of having many of the year's articles—the best—together in one neat and easily-referenced place. Whatever your reasons, we hope you enjoy *The Best of Cooking Pleasures—Volume I* and use it to create great tastes now and for a long time to come.

Traditions last because they are good ideas. A tradition among many cooking magazine publishers is to create an "annual" volume like this, showcasing the year's ideas and presenting them in one beautiful volume. That's what we've done here—combining that old (and good) idea with the new excitement of great recipes and ideas from *Cooking Pleasures*.

It's time to enhance your old traditions and create some anew.

Caramelized Onion Focaccia, p. 22

Roast Pork with Pears and Sweet Onions, p. 61

Scallop Bundles, p. 113

Strawbery-Rhubarb Trifle, p. 80

Lemon-Rosemary Iced Tea, Oolong Peach Bloom, Green Tea-Cherry Cooler and Iced Chocolate Chai, p. 140

Linguine with Tomatoes, Basil and Brie, p. 131

Grilled Lobster with Shallot-Red Pepper Butter, p. 159

SOUPS, SALADS & BREADS

MEDITERRANEAN
STEWS

Chicken Stew with Garbanzo Beans and Squash

A culinary homage to Morocco's famed tagines—updated for American kitchens.

Text and Recipes by Kitty Morse

In Morocco, where I grew up, a tagine, or stew, is almost daily fare. These stews are exotically flavored combinations of meat, poultry or seafood, and seasonal vegetables or fresh or dried fruit. Tagine is also the name of the distinctive cooking pot capped with a conical lid in which the stew simmers over small charcoal braziers, called canouns, until the meat is reduced to fork tenderness.

Over the years, I've learned to adapt these recipes for my American kitchen, using readily available ingredients and basic cooking techniques. In summer, for instance, I love to make a stew of fresh vegetables lightly infused with lemon juice and fresh cilantro. This time of year, though, heartier dishes appeal to me. One of my favorite stews combines cooked baby carrots, beef and pitted prunes in a ginger sauce sweetened with honey. In Morocco, meat and fish are expensive, so they're used in minimal amounts. Because they're relatively inexpensive in the United States, these recipes call for more.

If you want to build a traditional Moroccan meal around a tagine, begin with an assortment of salads of cooked or raw vegetables. Then serve the stew, and follow it with couscous. End the meal with seasonal and dried fruits, honey-coated pastries and fresh mint tea.

1 large onion, finely chopped
1 red bell pepper, chopped
¾ teaspoon cinnamon
4 chicken thighs, skin removed
4 chicken legs, skin removed
¼ cup pearl barley
1 cup reduced-sodium chicken broth
¾ teaspoon salt
¼ teaspoon freshly ground pepper
1 (1-lb.) butternut squash, peeled, seeded, cut into ¾-inch pieces
1 (15-oz.) can garbanzo beans, drained, rinsed

1. Heat oven to 400°F. Heat oil in large heavy ovenproof pot or Dutch oven over medium heat until hot. Add onion, bell pepper and cinnamon; cook 6 to 7 minutes or until onion is very soft, stirring occasionally.
2. Increase heat to medium-high. Add chicken thighs and chicken legs; cook until lightly browned, 4 to 5 minutes, turning once.
3. Reduce heat to medium. Distribute barley around chicken; add broth, salt and pepper. Bring to a boil; remove from heat. Cover with foil, then with lid. Bake 30 to 35 minutes or until chicken is partially cooked.
4. Remove from oven; add squash and garbanzo beans around chicken. Cover and bake an additional 30 to 35 minutes or until squash is tender and chicken juices run clear.
8 servings

PER SERVING: 265 calories, 10.5 g total fat (2.5 g saturated fat), 19.5 g protein, 24.5 g carbohydrate, 45 mg cholesterol, 415 mg sodium, 5 g fiber

Chicken Stew with Garbanzo Beans and Squash

Garbanzos (chickpeas) are among the world's most ancient beans. Traces of garbanzos dating back 9,000 years were unearthed in Turkey. It isn't surprising that they figure prominently in a number of Mediterranean dishes.

2 tablespoons olive oil

Lamb and Bean Stew with Cumin

Think of this hearty bean stew as North Africa's answer to Texas chili. Remember to soak the dried beans overnight, or use the quick-soak method described.

Lamb and Bean Stew with Cumin

1   lb. (2 cups) dried navy
    beans
1   tablespoon olive oil
1½ lb. blade or shoulder arm
    lamb chops, bones
    removed, meat cut into
    ½-inch pieces
2   (14½-oz.) cans reduced-
    sodium chicken broth
2   medium carrots, cut into

    ½-inch slices
3   whole garlic cloves, peeled
2   bay leaves
2   small dried red chiles,
    seeded
2   teaspoons ground cumin
2   tablespoons tomato paste
1   (14.5-oz.) can diced
    tomatoes with roasted
    garlic, undrained

½   teaspoon salt
2   tablespoons chopped fresh
    cilantro

1. Soak beans overnight in generous
amount of water.* Drain beans; discard
soaking water.
2. Heat oil in large heavy pot or nonreactive Dutch oven over medium-high
heat until hot. Add lamb pieces in

3. Add beans, broth, carrots, garlic, bay leaves, chiles and cumin; mix well. Reduce heat to medium-low; cover and simmer 1 to 1½ hours or until beans are tender. (The older the beans, the longer they will take to cook.)

4. Remove and discard bay leaves and chiles. Stir in tomato paste. Add tomatoes and salt. Cover; simmer 15 minutes. Garnish with cilantro.

TIP *For quick-soak method, place beans in large pot. Cover with generous amount of water. Bring to a rolling boil; boil 2 to 3 minutes. Remove from heat. Cover; let stand 1 to 3 hours. Drain beans; discard soaking water.

8 (1¼-cup) servings

PER SERVING: 330 calories, 8.5 g total fat (2.5 g saturated fat), 24.5 g protein, 40 g carbohydrate, 35 mg cholesterol, 520 mg sodium, 10.5 g fiber

Baked Fish and Vegetable Stew with Charmoula Marinade

Charmoula is a popular Moroccan marinade used for seafood, lamb or vegetables. Although the cooking time may seem long for fish fillets, it is quite normal in Morocco to cook fish in this manner.

MARINADE
½ cup olive oil
¼ cup fresh lemon juice
2 tablespoons chopped Italian parsley
1 tablespoon chopped fresh cilantro
2 garlic cloves, minced
1 tablespoon paprika
2 teaspoons ground cumin
½ teaspoon salt
¼ teaspoon freshly ground pepper

STEW
1½ lb. fish fillets (halibut, sea bass or mahimahi), cut into 2-inch pieces

2 medium potatoes, peeled, thinly sliced
4 medium tomatoes, seeded, sliced
2 large carrots, cut diagonally into ¼-inch slices
1 red bell pepper, coarsely chopped
1 onion, thinly sliced
½ medium lemon, very thinly sliced
15 pitted cracked green olives* or kalamata olives
¼ teaspoon salt
¼ teaspoon freshly ground pepper

1. In large bowl, combine all marinade ingredients; mix well. Place fish pieces in glass baking dish; pour marinade over fish, turning to coat. Refrigerate 1 to 2 hours, turning occasionally.

2. Heat oven to 400°F. In nonreactive Dutch oven or 13x9-inch (3-quart) glass baking dish, layer potatoes, tomatoes, carrots, and half each of the bell pepper, onion and lemon slices.

3. Remove fish from marinade; reserve remaining marinade. Place fish over lemon slices. Top with remaining bell pepper, onion and lemon. Sprinkle with olives, salt and pepper. Spoon reserved marinade over top. Cover tightly with foil.

4. Bake 40 to 45 minutes (potatoes and carrots will be partially tender). Remove foil; bake an additional 20 to 25 minutes or until potatoes and carrots are very tender and fish flakes easily with fork. For extra "tang," sprinkle with additional lemon juice just before serving. If desired, garnish with additional chopped parsley or cilantro.

TIP *Cracked green olives are available in the ethnic food section of the grocery store or in Middle Eastern markets. The olives are cracked before they are cured to allow the brine to seep into them to remove any bitterness and to add flavor.

6 servings

PER SERVING: 365 calories, 21.5 g total fat (3 g saturated fat), 24 g protein, 20.5 g carbohydrate, 60 mg cholesterol, 660 mg sodium, 4 g fiber

Beef Stew in Honey Sauce

In Morocco, meat or fowl is often cooked with fresh or dried fruit in honey-sweetened sauces redolent of ginger or cinnamon. In this adaptation, the carrots give extra flavor and texture. All you need is a green salad to complete the meal.

2 tablespoons all-purpose flour
1 teaspoon ground ginger
¼ teaspoon freshly ground pepper
2 lb. boneless lean beef chuck roast, cut into 1½-inch pieces
2 tablespoons olive oil
2 cups baby carrots
4 to 4½ cups beef broth
1 cup pitted prunes
24 pearl onions, peeled*
2 tablespoons honey
¼ teaspoon salt
¼ cup blanched whole almonds, toasted**

1. Heat oven to 400°F. In large resealable plastic bag, combine flour, ginger and pepper; mix well. Add beef; shake to coat.

2. Heat oil in large heavy ovenproof pot or Dutch oven over medium-high heat until hot. Add beef in batches; cook 6 to 8 minutes or until browned.

3. Add carrots and 2 cups of the broth. Cover with foil, then with lid. Bake 1¼ to 1½ hours or until beef is almost tender.

4. Add prunes and onions. If stew seems dry, add ½ cup of the broth. Bake an additional 20 to 25 minutes or until beef is fork-tender.

5. With slotted spoon, transfer beef, carrots, prunes and onions to bowl; cover to keep warm. Place pot on top of stove; skim off any fat. Bring pan juices to a boil over medium-high heat. Add remaining 2 cups broth, honey and salt. Cook 5 to 10 minutes or until sauce slightly thickens, stirring occasionally to loosen any browned bits from bottom of pot.

6. Return beef mixture to pot; mix well. Cook until thoroughly heated. To serve, transfer stew to serving platter. Sprinkle with almonds.

TIPS *To peel pearl onions, place in boiling water and boil 3 minutes. Drain; rinse with cold water to cool. Cut off root end and squeeze opposite end (onion should pop right out of its skin).
**To toast almonds, heat oven to 350°F. Spread almonds on baking sheet; bake 5 to 8 minutes or until almonds are light brown.

5 (1-cup) servings

PER SERVING: 600 calories, 30 g total fat (9 g saturated fat), 45 g protein, 39 g carbohydrate, 110 mg cholesterol, 1070 mg sodium, 5 g fiber

North African Vegetable Stew

Fresh lemon juice adds a light tang to this Moroccan-style vegetable stew. You can use any combination of seasonal vegetables, and, if desired, serve it over rice or couscous.

2   tablespoons olive oil
2   medium onions, finely chopped

North African Vegetable Stew

2 cups loosely packed
	parsley sprigs
2 tablespoons fresh lemon
	juice
1 teaspoon paprika
1¼ cups reduced-sodium
	chicken broth
1 lb. small new potatoes,
	unpeeled
3 medium carrots, cut into
	1-inch pieces
2 small turnips, peeled,
	quartered
1 teaspoon seasoned salt
¼ teaspoon freshly ground
	pepper
1 (10-oz.) pkg. frozen baby
	lima beans
2 tablespoons coarsely
	chopped green olives
2 garlic cloves, minced

1. Heat oil in large heavy pot or nonreactive Dutch oven over medium heat until hot. Add onions; cook 8 to 10 minutes or until golden, stirring occasionally.
2. Meanwhile, in blender or food processor, combine parsley, lemon juice, paprika and ¼ cup of the broth; process until almost smooth.
3. Add parsley mixture to onions; mix well. Add potatoes, carrots, turnips, salt, pepper and remaining 1 cup broth. Reduce heat to medium-low; cover and cook 30 to 35 minutes or until potatoes are tender, stirring occasionally.
4. Add beans, olives and garlic; stir to mix. Cover; cook an additional 8 to 10 minutes or until beans are tender. If desired, garnish with additional chopped parsley.
4 (1⅓-cup) servings

PER SERVING: 315 calories, 8.5 g total fat (1.5 g saturated fat), 10.5 g protein, 52 g carbohydrate, 0 mg cholesterol, 935 mg sodium, 12 g fiber

Meatball and Vegetable Stew with Capers and Mint

Lamb, whether roasted, baked or stewed, is probably the most popular meat eaten in the Mediterranean. Ground lamb gives these meatballs a distinctive flavor, as do capers and mint, two ingredients that flavor many Tunisian dishes. If desired, serve this stew over hot couscous.

MEATBALLS
1 lb. ground lamb
3 tablespoons unseasoned
	bread crumbs
2 garlic cloves, minced
2 tablespoons chopped fresh
	mint or 2 teaspoons dried
½ teaspoon salt
¼ teaspoon freshly ground
	pepper
1 egg, beaten

STEW
1 tablespoon olive oil
1 large fennel bulb, fronds
	removed, bulb cut into
	large pieces
1 medium onion, coarsely
	chopped
2 garlic cloves, minced
1 (14.5-oz.) can diced
	tomatoes with roasted
	garlic, undrained
1 cup beef broth
2 tablespoons small capers
½ teaspoon freshly ground
	pepper
¾ cup frozen baby peas

GARNISH
	Chopped fresh mint

1. In large bowl, combine all meatball ingredients; mix with large spoon or hands until well blended. Shape mixture into about 3 dozen 1-inch balls.
2. Heat oil in large skillet over medium-high heat until hot. Add meatballs in batches; cook 10 to 12 minutes or until browned. Transfer meatballs to paper towels to drain; set aside.
3. In same skillet over medium-high heat, combine fennel, onion and garlic. Cook 8 to 10 minutes or until onion is lightly browned, stirring frequently.
4. Reduce heat to medium. Add meatballs, tomatoes, broth, capers and pepper. Cover; simmer about 20 minutes or until meatballs are no longer pink in center.
5. Stir in peas; simmer an additional 5 minutes. Garnish with mint.
6 servings

PER SERVING: 245 calories, 14 g total fat (5 g saturated fat), 16.5 g protein, 13.5 g carbohydrate, 85 mg cholesterol, 660 mg sodium, 3.5 g fiber

MEDITERRANEAN SPICE TRADITIONS

While Tunisians liberally lace many of their dishes with a hot sauce called harissa, Moroccans and Algerians rely on more subtle blends of spices to excite the palate. In addition to fresh herbs such as cilantro and parsley, caraway seed, anise seed and cumin seed are among the most common flavorings.

Ground cumin, a seasoning many might associate with Mexican cuisine, is often mixed with sweet paprika, herbs and lemon juice to make charmoula, a classic seafood marinade.

In Morocco, turmeric is usually paired with saffron, the world's most expensive spice, to imbue couscous or tagines with an exotic flavor and a prized golden color.

Ground cinnamon and ground ginger (fresh ginger is never used in North Africa) are often the surprise ingredients in a soup or a stew.

INDULGENCES

Three spas share their secrets for sensational soups.

Text by Jennifer Buege

P enance for holiday indulgence doesn't have to come at the price of flavor. Just ask these spa chefs: They've demonstrated that creamy soups—staples of the winter season—not only satisfy, but can be healthful fillers in a meal. For example, while Corn Chowder with Chipotle Chile, from Canyon Ranch in Tucson, Arizona, may be low in fat, its creamy texture and chile-spiked flavor make this soup a great appetizer, which is how it's often used at the spa. "We try to create the feeling of 'Wow, I can have a three-course meal here,'" says spa food coordinator Marilyn Majchrzak. The soup is not meant to be the meal but to add to the meal, she says.

Chef Robert McGarrigle of the Heartland Spa in Gilman, Illinois, also sees soups as a great way to get in a course that is low in fat and calories. His Potato-Leek Soup gets its creaminess from pureed russet potatoes and nonfat milk while maintaining the flavor appeal of a cream soup. Susan Witz, director of nutrition and yoga programs at the spa, says soups work well because they fill you up. "The message is to be satisfied," she says. "You should eat to satiety, not to fullness."

And while flavor is important, so is presentation, says Abby Rosado, director of Spa at Saddlebrook Resort in Wesley Chapel, Florida. The spa's recipe for Calabaza Soup with Rock Shrimp features pale pink shrimp in an orange squash puree flecked with green bell peppers.

Corn Chowder with Chipotle Chile

"Moderation, not deprivation," is the motto at Canyon Ranch, where the focus is on teaching people to cook and eat well.

1 dried chipotle chile
1 teaspoon olive oil
½ cup diced onion
2 teaspoons minced garlic
2 cups frozen corn
½ teaspoon chili powder
½ teaspoon cumin
1 (14½-oz.) can reduced-sodium chicken or vegetable broth
¾ cup evaporated skimmed milk
½ cup diced red bell pepper
½ cup diced green bell pepper
1 tablespoon chopped fresh cilantro
¼ teaspoon salt

1. Place chile in small bowl; cover with boiling water. Let stand 5 to 10 minutes or until soft. Drain. Cut chile in half; remove seeds and chop chile.
2. Place oil in large saucepan; sauté onion, garlic and chile over medium heat until onions are soft. Add corn, chili powder and cumin; sauté about 5 minutes, stirring frequently.
3. Add broth; simmer about 10 minutes, stirring occasionally. Stir in milk.
4. In blender or food processor, puree soup at low speed in batches until smooth. Return soup to saucepan. Add bell peppers, cilantro and salt. Cook over medium heat 5 minutes or until warm. If desired, garnish with additional diced bell pepper.
4 servings

PER SERVING: 150 calories, 2.5 g total fat (.5 g saturated fat), 9 g protein, 26 g carbohydrate, 0 mg cholesterol, 430 mg sodium, 3 g fiber

Excerpted from Great Tastes: Healthy Cooking from Canyon Ranch *by Canyon Ranch Staff (Canyon Ranch Enterprises).*

Calabaza Soup with Rock Shrimp

Spa Director Abby Rosado describes the food at the spa as "food for the soul." Presentation, nutrition and substance share equal rights in the recipes.

1 tablespoon olive oil
1 small onion, diced
¼ cup diced green bell pepper
1 teaspoon minced garlic
2½ cups reduced-sodium chicken or vegetable broth
⅛ teaspoon saffron threads, crushed

Corn Chowder with Chipotle Chile

2. Increase heat to medium-high. Add wine; bring to a boil, stirring and scraping up any brown bits from bottom of pan. Boil until wine is reduced to about 2 tablespoons.
3. Add potatoes, broth, salt and pepper; return to a boil. Reduce heat to low; simmer uncovered 20 to 25 minutes or until potatoes are tender.
4. In blender or food processor, puree soup at low speed in batches until smooth. Return soup to saucepan. Stir in milk. Heat until hot, stirring frequently. Do not boil.
6 servings

PER SERVING: 180 calories, 5 g total fat (.5 g saturated fat), 5 g protein, 29 g carbohydrate, 0 mg cholesterol, 905 mg sodium, 2.5 g fiber

3 cups cubed, peeled calabaza or butternut squash
½ lb. shelled, deveined uncooked medium rock shrimp*
¼ teaspoon salt
⅛ teaspoon freshly ground pepper

1. Heat oil in large saucepan over medium heat until hot. Add onion; sauté until translucent. Add bell pepper and garlic; sauté briefly. Add broth, saffron and squash; bring to a boil. Reduce heat to low; simmer 10 minutes.
2. Cool mixture slightly. In blender or food processor, puree soup at low speed in batches until smooth. Return soup to saucepan. Bring to a boil. Reduce heat. Add shrimp, salt and pepper; simmer 3 to 4 minutes or until shrimp turn pink.
TIP *½ lb. shelled, deveined uncooked medium shrimp can be substituted for the rock shrimp.
4 (1¼-cup) servings

PER SERVING: 165 calories, 5 g total fat (1 g saturated fat), 13 g protein, 18 g carbohydrate, 80 mg cholesterol, 545 mg sodium, 4 g fiber

Potato-Leek Soup

The chef at the Heartland Spa sees cooking healthfully as a "matter of attitude" for home cooks. The key is to look for foods naturally low in fat that you enjoy.

2 tablespoons olive oil
1½ cups chopped leeks
1 tablespoon minced garlic
½ cup dry white wine
4 medium russet potatoes, unpeeled, diced
4 cups vegetable broth
½ teaspoon salt
¼ teaspoon pepper
2 cups nonfat milk

1. Heat oil in large saucepan over medium heat until hot. Add leeks; sauté 2 to 3 minutes. Add garlic; sauté 2 to 3 minutes or until garlic is light brown, being careful not to let garlic burn.

BLENDING BASICS

One of the techniques used to create cream-style soups is to puree vegetables and liquids in a blender. There are two potential problems you may run into, however. Because a hot liquid is used, there is the possibility of being splattered with hot soup. Also, the soup can overflow if too much is added to the blender. To ensure safe blending, follow these steps:

1. Let the soup cool slightly before placing it in the blender; do not blend boiling soups.
2. Puree the soup in batches. Fill the blender only ⅓ to ½ full. If you fill the blender full, soup will erupt during blending.
3. Place the cover on the blender, then put a kitchen towel over the cover in case any soup spatters during blending.
4. First pulse the soup to release any steam buildup in the blender container, then fully blend it.
5. Return the soup to the saucepan and reheat before serving.

BEST-DRESSED
SALADS

Apple-Mustard Vinaigrette, Apricot-Ginger Dressing and Orange-Vinaigrette with Latin Flavors

Fruit juice provides the
foundation for lighter dressings.

Text and Recipes by Patsy Jamieson

No matter how creative the selection of ingredients, salads need to be coaxed to life with dressing. A simple vinaigrette dresses any number of salads with style. Vinaigrette can hardly be described as decadent, but when you consider the standard vinaigrette formula of three parts oil to one part vinegar, you can't help but wonder if there isn't some substitute for all that oil. Perhaps you have tried replacing some of the oil with water or chicken broth only to produce a sharp, thin dressing that refuses to cling to salad greens and forms a puddle on the bottom of the salad bowl.

There is a better technique for making lower-fat vinaigrettes: Use fruit juice or juice concentrates to replace some of the oil. Not only does it balance the dressing's acidity, but fruit juice contributes a fresh, lively flavor and has the body necessary to cling to greens. And the dressings are easy to make. Some can be blended by shaking them in jars; others are combined in a blender, which creates a creamy emulsion and eliminates the need to mince ingredients.

In addition to jazzing up your salads, the dressings that follow also make flavor-boosting marinades for grilled meat, poultry and fish. Now that's a recipe for carefree summer eating.

Orange-Miso Dressing

Miso, which is fermented soy bean paste, contributes body and richness to this dressing. There are several types of miso: Yellow (shiro) miso is mild and quite sweet; the darker colored red (aka) and dark brown (hatcho) misos are saltier and more intensely flavored. Miso can be found in Asian markets, health-food stores and some supermarkets in the refrigerated section. You can store miso in a covered container in the refrigerator almost indefinitely.

3 tablespoons red (aka) miso*

2 tablespoons boiling water
⅓ cup fresh orange juice
2 tablespoons sugar
3 tablespoons rice vinegar
3 tablespoons canola oil
1 tablespoon reduced-sodium
    soy sauce
2 (¼-inch-thick) slices fresh
    ginger, crushed
1 medium garlic clove,
    crushed

1. In small bowl, combine miso and boiling water; stir until smooth. Place in blender or food processor.
2. Add all remaining ingredients; process until blended. (*Dressing will keep, covered, in the refrigerator up to 4 days.*) Stir or shake before using.
TIP *If miso is unavailable, omit miso and boiling water. Increase soy sauce to 3 tablespoons and use 2 tablespoons packed brown sugar in place of sugar. Proceed as directed.
1 cup

PER TABLESPOON: 40 calories, 3 g total fat (0 g saturated fat), .5 g protein, 3.5 g carbohydrate, 0 mg cholesterol, 155 mg sodium, 0 g fiber

Apple-Mustard Vinaigrette

With a hint of sweetness that is balanced by grainy mustard, this dressing is good with both pungent greens, such as arugula and watercress, and more delicate ones, such as Boston and leaf lettuce. Finish off your salad with toasted walnuts or pecans. This vinaigrette is also useful as a marinade for pork or chicken.

⅓ cup finely chopped shallots
¼ cup frozen apple juice
    concentrate, thawed
¼ cup apple cider vinegar
¼ cup canola or olive oil
2 tablespoons water
2 tablespoons country-style
    (grainy) Dijon mustard
¾ teaspoon salt
¼ teaspoon ground pepper

In medium bowl, combine all ingredients; whisk until blended. (*Dressing will keep, covered, in the refrigerator up to 4 days.*) Stir or shake before serving.
1 cup

PER TABLESPOON: 40 calories, 3.5 g total fat (.5 g saturated fat), 0 g protein, 2.5 g carbohydrate, 0 mg cholesterol, 135 mg sodium, 0 g fiber

Apricot-Ginger Dressing

With a subtle kick of ginger, this fruity combo makes a great all-purpose dressing. It also works well as a marinade for chicken or lamb.

- ⅔ cup apricot nectar
- 3 tablespoons apple cider vinegar
- 3 tablespoons canola oil
- 1 teaspoon honey
- 3 (¼-inch-thick) slices fresh ginger, crushed
- 2 medium garlic cloves, crushed
- ¾ teaspoon salt
- ¼ teaspoon freshly ground pepper

In blender or food processor, combine all ingredients; blend until smooth. (*Dressing will keep, covered, in the refrigerator up to 4 days.*) Stir or shake before using.
1 cup

PER TABLESPOON: 30 calories, 2.5 g total fat (0 g saturated fat), 0 g protein, 2.5 g carbohydrate, 0 mg cholesterol, 110 mg sodium, 0 g fiber

Orange Vinaigrette with Latin Flavors

This spicy vinaigrette pairs well with assertive greens, such as escarole or chicory. Toss in some slivered sweet onion, and garnish the salad with toasted almonds. You also can use this dressing as a marinade for pork tenderloin or swordfish.

- ½ cup frozen orange juice concentrate, thawed
- ¼ cup extra-virgin olive oil
- 3 tablespoons sherry vinegar or red wine vinegar
- 2 tablespoons water
- 3 medium garlic cloves, crushed
- 1 teaspoon ground cumin
- 1 teaspoon paprika
- ¾ teaspoon salt
- ½ teaspoon freshly ground pepper

In blender or food processor, combine all ingredients; blend until smooth. (*Dressing will keep, covered, in the refrigerator up to 4 days.*) Stir or shake before using.
1 cup

PER TABLESPOON: 45 calories, 3.5 g total fat (.5 g saturated fat), .5 g protein, 4 g carbohydrate, 0 mg cholesterol, 110 mg sodium, 0 g fiber

SALAD

Here are some salad suggestions to pair with the vinaigrettes we've featured.

Apricot-Ginger Dressing

Warm Grilled Chicken Salad: Marinate boneless, skinless chicken breasts in a small amount of dressing. Grill the chicken breasts, basting with a little additional dressing, if desired. Grill Vidalia onion slices and strips of red bell pepper alongside the chicken. To serve, slice the breasts and add them, along with the grilled vegetables, to mixed greens; toss the salad with additional dressing.

Couscous Salad

Couscous Salad: Prepare couscous according to package directions, using olive oil rather than butter. Add chopped scallions, chopped fresh mint, chopped dried apricots and/or currants. Toss with the dressing and garnish with toasted pine nuts.

Orange Vinaigrette with Latin Flavors

Black Bean and Barley Salad: Combine drained, rinsed canned

SUGGESTIONS AND SOLUTIONS

black beans, cooked barley (or rice), chopped scallions, diced red bell pepper and chopped fresh cilantro; toss with the vinaigrette.

Jicama-Carrot Slaw: Combine grated jicama and carrots, and chopped fresh cilantro; toss with the vinaigrette.

Spinach and Garbanzo Bean Salad: Combine baby spinach, drained canned garbanzo beans, slivered red onion and sliced pitted black olives; toss with the vinaigrette.

Spinach and Garbanzo Bean Salad

Apple-Mustard Vinaigrette

Watercress, Pear and Roquefort Salad: Combine watercress sprigs and pear wedges; toss with the vinaigrette. Sprinkle with crumbled Roquefort (or Gorgonzola) cheese.

Beet and Arugula Salad: Toss wedges of cooked beets with a little vinaigrette. (If desired, marinate the beets in the vinaigrette in the refrigerator for up to 2 days.) Combine the beets and arugula; add additional vinaigrette and toss well. Sprinkle with crumbled goat cheese.

Green and Lima Bean Salad: Combine cooked green beans, cooked frozen baby lima beans and slivered red onion; toss with the vinaigrette. Taste and season with additional apple cider vinegar, if desired. Garnish with chopped fresh parsley.

Watercress, Pear and Roquefort Salad

Orange-Miso Dressing

Asian Cole Slaw: Combine shredded napa or green cabbage, grated carrots, slivered red pepper and chopped scallions; toss with the dressing. Sprinkle with chopped dry-roasted peanuts.

Grilled Vegetables: Grill a selection of vegetables, such as asparagus, eggplant, zucchini, bell peppers and red onions, until lightly charred and tender. Arrange on a platter and spoon the dressing over them. Sprinkle with toasted sesame seeds.

Asian Cole Slaw

FLATBREADS

Pita Bread with Greek Salad

Simple, rustic and satisfying, flatbreads from around the world are growing in popularity.

Text and Recipes by Lora Brody

Flatbreads are on the rise—a refreshing change from the puffy, air-filled loaves that have dominated breadbaskets and sandwiches for decades.

But flatbread is also ancient history. Using native grains and time-honored methods, people in many cultures feed their families every day with simple, nourishing flatbreads.

In the Sahara, nomadic people bake flatbread of barley flour and water in shallow sand pits, exactly as their forebears did.

In Mexico, home cooks shape tortillas by hand, using the same ingredients and methods passed down for generations.

On the streets of Bombay and Calcutta, men and women pat whole wheat dough into chapati, cook it on a griddle and use it as edible cutlery.

Each Passover, Jews celebrate their ancestors' escape from the pharaohs by eating matzo, a bread that never had a chance to rise during the Israelites' hurried departure from Egypt.

An internationally inspired array of flatbread is showing up in restaurants, supermarkets, bakeries, even school cafeterias. Home bakers, too, are finding these breads a simple, enjoyable alternative to the raised loaf. These recipes offer a variety of shapes, textures, flavors and cultural roots.

Pita Bread with Greek Salad

When using a baking stone, be sure to let it heat for at least 25 minutes or your pitas may not puff. Enjoy these pitas hot out of the oven, or allow them to cool before filling them with quick-to-fix Greek Salad.

1 cup plus 2 tablespoons warm water (110°F. to 115°F.)
1 tablespoon sugar
1 (¼-oz.) pkg. active dry yeast
3 to 3¼ cups all-purpose flour
1 teaspoon salt
2 tablespoons olive oil
  Greek Salad (recipe on page 25)

1. In small bowl, combine water, a pinch of the sugar and yeast. Let stand 5 minutes or until bubbles form. In large bowl, combine 3 cups of the flour, remaining sugar and salt. Add yeast mixture and oil; mix until soft dough forms, adding additional flour if necessary.

2. Turn dough out onto lightly floured surface; knead 5 to 6 minutes or until dough is smooth and very elastic. Cover; let rest 10 minutes. Knead an additional 5 minutes. Place in large greased bowl; cover and let rise in warm place until double in size, about 30 minutes.

3. Meanwhile, place oven rack in lowest rack position. Set baking stone on rack.* Heat oven to 450°F. Let baking stone heat 25 to 30 minutes before baking on it.

4. Gently punch dough to deflate; divide into 6 pieces. On lightly floured surface, roll each piece into a 7-inch round, about ¼ to ⅜ inch thick. With fingers, tuck ¼ inch of dough under edge; press flat to form narrow "hem." (This will help pita puff up in oven.) Place pitas on stone.

5. Bake 5 to 7 minutes or just until bottoms are light brown. Place pitas on wire rack and cover with clean towel to keep them soft. Cool completely. Serve with Greek Salad.

TIPS *If a baking stone is unavailable, use a heavy-duty baking sheet; let heat in oven 15 minutes before baking. If necessary, bake pitas in batches, letting stone or baking sheet reheat 5 to 10 minutes between baking.

Dough can be made in a food processor or in a bread machine on the dough cycle, following manufacturer's instructions. Follow directions above for shaping and baking.

6 pitas

PER SERVING: 300 calories, 5 g total fat (.5 g saturated fat), 7.5 g protein, 54 g carbohydrate, 0 mg cholesterol, 390 mg sodium, 2 g fiber

Caramelized Onion Focaccia

Caramelized Onion Focaccia

The subtle sweetness of caramelized onions gives this focaccia superb flavor. If you can't find Vidalia or other sweet onions, substitute large Spanish onions. You can caramelize the onions several days in advance and refrigerate them, bringing them to room temperature before adding them to the focaccia.

½ cup butter
6 sweet onions (about 2½ lb.), coarsely chopped
1 (¼-oz.) pkg. active dry yeast
1 cup warm water (110°F. to 115°F.)
2¾ to 3 cups all-purpose flour
1½ teaspoons salt
¼ cup plus 1 tablespoon olive oil

1. Melt butter in large heavy skillet or Dutch oven over medium heat. Add onions; stir to coat with butter. Cover; cook over medium heat 20 to 25 minutes or until onions are translucent. Uncover; cook over medium to medium-low heat 30 to 40 minutes or until onions are golden brown, stirring occasionally. Set aside.

2. Meanwhile, sprinkle yeast over 1/3 cup of the water; let stand 5 minutes or until bubbles form. In large bowl, combine 2¾ cups of the flour and salt. Add remaining ⅔ cup water and ¼ cup of the oil. Add yeast mixture; mix until soft dough forms, adding additional flour if necessary.

3. Turn dough out onto lightly floured surface; knead 10 minutes or until dough is soft and smooth. Place in large greased bowl; cover and let rise in warm place until double in size, about 1 hour.

4. If using baking stone, place on oven rack. Heat oven to 425°F. Grease 12-

inch round pizza pan or, if using baking stone, dust wooden pizza paddle with cornmeal. Punch dough to deflate. On lightly floured surface, roll dough into 12-inch round; place on pizza pan or wooden pizza paddle. Cover with clean cloth; let rise in warm place until nearly double in size, about 20 to 30 minutes.
5. When ready to bake, create deep dimples by pushing down dough with fingertips. Brush dough with remaining 1 tablespoon oil. Top dough with caramelized onions. Place baking sheet

in oven or slide focaccia onto baking stone.
6. Bake 15 to 18 minutes or until edges and bottom are golden brown.
TIP Dough can be made in a food processor or in a bread machine on the dough cycle, following manufacturer's instructions. Follow directions above for shaping and baking.
12 servings

PER SERVING: 275 calories, 15 g total fat (6 g saturated fat), 4.5 g protein, 31.5 g carbohydrate, 20 mg cholesterol, 345 mg sodium, 3 g fiber

Snap Sticks

For a dramatic presentation, stand these flat breadsticks on end in a tall, straight-sided vase.

  1 cup rye flour
  1 cup whole wheat flour
  1 cup all-purpose flour
  1½ teaspoons salt
  ¼ cup olive oil
  1 cup water
  ½ cup mixed seeds (anise, cumin, fennel, poppy or sesame seeds)
  1½ teaspoons kosher (coarse) salt
  2 teaspoons coarsely ground pepper

1. Heat oven to 475°F. In food processor, combine rye flour, whole wheat flour, all-purpose flour and salt; process to mix. Add oil. While processor is running, slowly add just enough of the water to form a soft, pliable dough. Process 90 seconds after dough has formed a ball. Divide dough into 3 pieces; cover.
2. Turn heavy-duty 15x10x1-inch baking pan upside down. Spray bottom (outside) with nonstick cooking spray. To keep pan from sliding around on work surface, place damp towel under pan.
3. Working with 1 piece at a time, roll dough with lightly floured rolling pin on outside bottom of pan to ¼-inch thickness. Sprinkle with ⅓ of the seeds, kosher salt and pepper. Continue rolling, pressing seeds and seasonings into dough until dough is as thin as possible. Roll from center toward edges to create a uniform layer. (Dough should almost cover pan.) With sharp knife, cut dough crosswise into ¾-inch strips. Do not move strips.
4. Place pan, still upside down, in oven. Bake 5 to 7 minutes or until strips are brown. (The thinner and browner the strips are, the crisper they will be.) Using long metal spatula, slide strips

Snap Sticks and Sourdough Rye Cracklebread

RECIPE
HOW-TO

CRACKLEBREAD AND SNAP STICK DOUGH

• When making Sourdough Rye Cracklebread or Snap Sticks, use the back of a baking sheet to roll out the dough. Doing so provides a flat surface without sides, which makes it easier to use a rolling pin to roll the dough paper thin. (The bread also bakes on the back of the sheet.)

• The dough should almost cover the entire surface of the pan. When rolling out the dough, it's okay if holes form, edges are uneven or if in some places the dough is thinner than in others. These traits will give the breads a nice rustic look.

onto wire rack to cool. Cool pan. Repeat with remaining dough. Cool strips completely. Store, uncovered, at room temperature.

TIP Sticks may become soft in humid weather. To crisp them, place in single layer on baking sheet; bake at 300°F. for 8 to 12 minutes.

45 sticks

PER STICK: 45 calories, 2 g total fat (.5 g saturated fat), 1 g protein, 6 g carbohydrate, 0 mg cholesterol, 235 g sodium, 1 g fiber

Sourdough Rye Cracklebread

This quick sourdough starter only takes an hour to make. It gives a light, slightly sour taste to these crackers.

SOURDOUGH STARTER
- ½ cup warm milk (110°F. to 115°F.)
- 1 teaspoon active dry yeast
- ⅓ cup all-purpose flour

BREAD
- 2 cups rye flour
- 1½ cups all-purpose flour
- 2 teaspoons salt
- 1 teaspoon freshly ground pepper
- 1 cup dark beer or water
- 3 tablespoons caraway seeds

1. Place milk in small bowl, add yeast; stir to dissolve. Stir in ⅓ cup all-purpose flour. Cover; let stand in warm place 1 hour.

2. Heat oven to 450°F. To prepare dough, combine rye flour, 1½ cups all-purpose flour, salt and pepper in large bowl. Add beer and sourdough starter; mix until dough forms. If dough is very soft, add additional 1 to 2 tablespoons flour.

3. Turn dough out onto floured surface. With floured hands, knead until dough is soft and smooth, about 5 minutes, adding additional flour if necessary. (Dough will be very sticky, but resist the urge to add a lot of flour. Add only enough to keep dough workable.) Place in large bowl; cover. Let rest 10 minutes.

4. Turn heavy-duty 15x10x1-inch baking pan upside down. Spray bottom (outside) with nonstick cooking spray. To keep pan from sliding around on work surface, place damp towel under pan.

5. Divide dough into 6 pieces; cover. Working with 1 piece at a time, flatten dough on outside bottom of pan; sprinkle lightly with flour. With lightly

floured rolling pin, roll dough to ¼-inch thickness. Roll from center toward edges to create a uniform layer.

6. Sprinkle dough with 1½ teaspoons caraway seeds. Continue to roll until dough is paper thin, spreading gently and evenly with fingers, if necessary, to make sure center is as thin as sides. (Don't worry if some holes form and edges are uneven.)

7. Place pan, still upside down, in oven. Bake 6 to 9 minutes or until deep golden brown, watching carefully to prevent burning. (Crackle-bread will not brown evenly.) Remove cracklebread from pan; cool completely. Repeat with remaining dough. Store at room temperature up to 1 week. Break bread into pieces to serve.

TIP Dough can be made in a food processor or in a bread machine on the dough cycle, following manufacturer's instructions. Follow directions above for shaping and baking.

6 rounds (about 80 small pieces)

PER PIECE: 20 calories, 0 g total fat (0 g saturated fat), 1 g protein, 4 g carbohydrate, 0 mg cholesterol, 60 mg sodium, .5 g fiber

Double Pesto Pizza

Whether you use homemade or store-bought pesto, you'll find this green-on-green pizza easy to make. Pesto livens up the crust and takes the place of tomato sauce.

CRUST
- 1 tablespoon active dry yeast
- 1¼ cups warm water (110°F. to 115°F.)
- 3 cups all-purpose flour
- ½ cup cornmeal
- 1½ teaspoons salt
- ¼ cup olive oil
- ⅔ cup plus 3 tablespoons pesto (recipe follows)

TOPPING
- ½ cup (2 oz.) freshly grated Parmesan cheese

1. Sprinkle yeast over ¼ cup of the water; let stand 5 minutes or until bubbles form. In large bowl, combine flour, cornmeal and salt. Add remaining 1 cup water and oil. Add yeast mixture; mix until well combined. Gradually mix in 3 tablespoons of the pesto.

2. Turn dough out onto lightly floured surface; knead 10 minutes or until dough is soft and smooth. Place in large greased bowl; cover and let rise in warm place until double in size, about 1 hour.

3. Meanwhile, if using baking stone, place on oven rack. Heat oven to 450°F. Grease 16-inch round pizza pan or 15x10x1-inch baking pan; dust with cornmeal. If using baking stone, dust wooden pizza paddle with cornmeal. Punch dough to deflate; place on lightly floured surface and roll into 16-inch round or to fit baking pan. Place dough on pan or wooden pizza paddle. Spread remaining ⅔ cup pesto over dough to within 1 inch of edge; sprinkle with cheese. Place baking pan in oven or slide pizza onto baking stone.

4. Bake 10 to 15 minutes or until crust is deep golden brown and cheese is melted.

TIP Dough can be made in a food processor or in a bread machine on the dough cycle, following manufacturer's instructions. Follow directions above for shaping and baking.

12 servings

PER SERVING: 320 calories, 18.5 g total fat (4 g saturated fat), 8.5 g protein, 30.5 g carbohydrate, 5 mg cholesterol, 510 mg sodium, 2 g fiber

Pesto

This pesto freezes beautifully. Store it in small plastic containers in the freezer and defrost at room temperature or in the microwave.

    3 cups fresh basil, stems
       removed
    ⅓ cup pine nuts, toasted*
    2 large garlic cloves, coarsely
       chopped
    ½ cup (2 oz.) freshly grated
       Parmigiano-Reggiano
       cheese
    ½ cup olive oil
    ½ teaspoon freshly ground
       pepper
    ¼ teaspoon salt

1. To prepare pesto, tear large basil leaves in thirds; place in food processor or blender. Add pine nuts and garlic; process until pureed.

2. Add cheese, oil, pepper and salt; process just until mixed.

TIP *To toast pine nuts, place in dry medium skillet. Heat over medium heat, stirring until pine nuts begin to brown. Watch carefully to prevent burning.

Greek Salad

    ¼ cup olive oil
    2 tablespoons red wine
       vinegar or balsamic
       vinegar
    ½ small red onion, thinly
       sliced (about 1 cup)
    1 (14-oz.) can quartered
       artichoke hearts, drained,
       coarsely chopped
   10 oz. pitted kalamata olives,
       drained (about 1⅓ cups)
    1 cup (4 oz.) crumbled feta
       cheese

1. In medium bowl, combine oil and vinegar. Rinse onion well under cold running water; drain. Add onion and all remaining ingredients; toss to combine.

2. To serve, cut each pita in half. Gently open each to form a pocket. Spoon salad into pita pockets. Serve immediately.

BAKING STONES

Why a stone: Many of the recipes here suggest using a baking stone. Doing so somewhat mimics the effects of baking in a clay-lined oven—the bread will have a crisper crust, particularly the bottom crust. Stones also distribute heat more evenly than baking sheets.

Choosing: Look for a stone that is made of thick, porous ceramic. The pores allow the stone to absorb heat; a thick stone shatters less easily than a thinner one and holds more heat.

Using: Place the stone in the oven on the lowest rack, leaving a 2-inch space around all sides of the stone to allow the heat to circulate. Heat the stone for 25 minutes before baking the bread.

Wear: After much use, a baking stone darkens and becomes harder. Although not necessary, you can clean it with a mixture of baking soda and water. Avoid using soap or detergent; the stone absorbs them and passes that taste to your breads.

—Jennifer Buege

ARTISAN
BREAD
at Home

Country French Bread

A French baker shares his secrets to making hearty country bread.

Text by Betsy Wray and Janice Cole; Recipe by Didier Rosada

A bread revival has been stirring in this country over the past several years. Artisan bread shops, featuring hearty loaves made with old-world techniques, have been growing in number. When we wanted to learn how to make a good crusty French loaf, the hallmark of the artisan bread shop, we went to the experts at the National Baking Center in Minneapolis, a school for professional bakers that is at the forefront of teaching old-world bread techniques. Baking instructor Didier Rosada, who studied in his native France and has worked in bakeries around the world, taught us to think anew about bread-making. In a nutshell: "The way you work with the four ingredients is the secret of bread, not the formula." If you follow Didier's techniques, modified here for the home baker, you too can turn out artisan loaves.

Country French Bread

- 1 lb. 5 oz./600 g (4½ cups) all-purpose flour
- 1 oz./30 g (5 tablespoons) rye flour
- 1 oz./30 g (¼ cup) whole wheat flour
- .45 oz./12.5 g (2½ teaspoons) salt
- .1 oz./2.5 g (¾ teaspoon) instant dry yeast
- 1 lb. .3 oz./462.5 g (2 cups) tepid water (75°F.)
  Cornmeal

1. In large bowl, stir together all-purpose flour, rye flour and whole wheat flour. Make a well in center of flour mixture; add salt and yeast. Pour 1¾ cups of the water into well. With fingers, mix water, salt and yeast until salt and yeast are dissolved.

2. Slowly begin mixing in flour from outside of well. Continue mixing in the flour and the remaining water until all flour is absorbed and a soft dough has formed. Dough should be shiny, moist and sticky. If dough seems dry, add 1 to 2 tablespoons water.

3. Turn dough out onto lightly floured surface. Knead dough by lifting dough up and throwing it out and down onto surface. Fold dough in half. Turn dough quarter turn; lift and throw again. Continue throwing, folding and turning 5 minutes. Let dough rest 2 minutes, then continue the kneading process an additional 2 to 3 minutes or until dough is smooth, soft and elastic. Dough will be sticky to begin with, but resist the urge to add extra flour. Dough will become less sticky during kneading process.

4. Shape dough into ball. Place in lightly floured large bowl; loosely cover with plastic wrap. Let rise 45 minutes.

5. Place dough on lightly floured surface. Press dough to flatten; stretch and fold dough to form into ball. Return to bowl; cover loosely. Let rise an additional 45 minutes.

6. Repeat process a third time; let rise a final 45 minutes.

7. Generously sprinkle wooden peel, baking sheet or cutting board with cornmeal. Divide dough in half; shape into loaves. Place on wooden peel. Cover with floured plastic wrap; let rise 1 hour 15 minutes to 1 hour 30 minutes or until loaves spring back when lightly touched, leaving a slight indentation.

8. Meanwhile, place baking stone on center rack in oven. Place bottom of broiler pan or heavy shallow roasting pan on bottom rack in oven, below baking stone. Heat oven to 450°F.

9. When dough has risen, sprinkle tops lightly with flour using fine sieve. With razor blade or very sharp knife, make ¼-inch deep decorative cuts on top of dough. Slide dough onto baking stone; immediately pour about ⅓ cup cold water into broiler pan. (There should be just enough water to cause steam for the first minute.)

10. Bake at 450°F. for 12 minutes. Reduce oven temperature to 425°F.; bake an additional 25 to 30 minutes or until breads are dark golden brown and bottoms sound hollow when tapped. Cool completely.
2 (16-slice) loaves

PER SLICE: 70 calories, 0 g total fat (0 g saturated fat), 2 g protein, 15 g carbohydrate, 0 mg cholesterol, 180 mg sodium, 1 g fiber

VARIATIONS

OLIVE BREAD: For two loaves, add 1¾ cups pitted whole Kalamata olives, patted dry, to dough after kneading process by pressing dough to flatten and placing olives in center. Fold dough over olives; cut in with pastry scraper, incorporating olives until evenly distributed. Add a little extra flour to compensate for the moisture in the olives. Continue with recipe as directed above.

WALNUT BREAD: For two loaves, add 2 cups coarsely chopped walnuts to dough after kneading process by pressing dough to flatten and placing walnuts in center. Fold dough over walnuts; cut in with pastry scraper, incorporating walnuts until evenly distributed. Continue with recipe as directed above.

Walnut Bread

STORING BREAD

Store your bread on the counter in a paper bag or in a bread basket covered with a towel for up to two days. If you must store it longer, freeze it. (To defrost it, let it come to room temperature on the counter, not in the refrigerator; then warm it in the oven.) Do not refrigerate bread; it actually gets stale faster in a 33°F. to 40°F. environment.

TECHNIQUE TIPS

Measuring ingredients: Baking is science and thus requires more accuracy and consistency than some other forms of cooking. Although most recipes for the home baker state ingredients in cup measurements, the most accurate way to measure is with a scale. Why? The weight of ingredients can vary depending on factors such as the moisture in the air, how much the ingredients settle in the cup and so on. That's why the recipe here states measurements in both weight and cups. If you own a scale, we recommend using it.

Water temperature: The temperature of the water used to make bread is critical. If it's too hot, it will kill the yeast. At 120°F., the yeast starts to die; it's completely destroyed at 140°F. Likewise, if the water is ice cold, the yeast won't ferment.

While most bread recipes instruct you to use water that is between 105°F. and 115°F., the recipe here calls for water that is 75°F. It's warm enough to activate the yeast but cool enough to ensure a slow fermentation, which is the key to good flavor and keeping quality. If you test the water with your hands, it will actually feel cool.

Mixing the dough: If you're comfortable doing so, mix the dough with your hand. Although this dough is softer, wetter and stickier than the traditional home-baked bread dough, resist the temptation to add more flour.

After mixing: The dough is soft, wet and sticky.

Kneading: The kneading method for Country French Bread is different than the traditional process. Instead of pushing the dough with the heels of the hands, Didier Rosada uses a

Kneading: Throw the dough down on the counter...

...then fold it in half, rotate one-quarter turn and repeat.

stretch-and-fold method that is best described as throwing and slapping the dough.

Once the dough is mixed, take the sticky mass, raise it through the air with both hands and slap it down on the counter. This process stretches the dough. On the counter, fold the dough in half, rotate it one-quarter turn and repeat the process. (Be careful not to use too

MAKING ARTISAN BREAD

After kneading: The dough is smooth and doesn't tear.

much flour on the counter or your hands; the dough will become too stiff.) Continue stretching and folding for about 5 minutes. Then let the dough—and your arms—rest for a couple of minutes. Resume the process for another 2 to 3 minutes. When you're done, the dough should be very smooth. When you pull on the dough, you should feel some resistance and it should not tear.

Risings: The rising step also is a bit different for this loaf than most bread recipes. The bread rises four times instead of the usual two. The longer, slower fermentation process is responsible for the loaf's excellent, well-developed flavor.

The temperature of the dough should be about 75°F. when you form it into a ball for the first rising. If it's cooler than this, put it in a warmer place; if it's warmer, put it in a cooler place. The room temperature should be a minimum of 70°F.

Use time, not dough size, as your guide for the risings. You won't notice a big change in dough size from one rising to the next.

Shaping: You have several options for shaping the loaf. Perhaps the simplest is a boule, French for "ball" and the word that is used to describe a round, white loaf. Once the loaf is shaped, let it rise on a baking sheet or wooden peel that has been generously sprinkled with cornmeal, to prevent sticking. (A peel is a large wooden board with a handle that's used to slide bread and pizza onto a baking stone in the oven.)

• **Boule:** After you've divided the dough, place the smooth side down on the counter. Fold the

Boule

outside edges into the center to create a ball. Flip over the ball so the tucked edges are on the bottom, and let it rise the final time.

• **Oblong loaf:** Place the smooth side of the divided dough down on the counter. Press the dough out slightly. Fold one side in; then fold the opposite side in. Using the heel of your

Oblong loaf

hand, press down the seam. Then fold the loaf on that seam. Place the loaf, fold side down, on the proofing surface.

• **Triangle:** Place the smooth side of the divided dough down on the counter. Portioning the round roughly into thirds, fold one-third of the circle in; then fold the next third in, creating a

Triangle

point at the top. Finally fold the bottom third in to finish the triangle shape. Press the folds to secure. Flip the loaf over so the seams are on the bottom.

Dusting and scoring: After the shaped dough has risen, dust the top with flour and score the top. Dusting the dough with flour is not essential but rather a tradition with rustic breads

such as this. You can simply use a sieve to sprinkle a little flour, or you can create a stencil and make a design.

Scoring the dough is *not* optional. It's necessary to allow moisture to escape the dough and help it achieve its proper shape. Bakers use several patterns for scoring, although you need not be elaborate. A simple cut down the center will do. Or try a tic-tac-toe pattern; a series of short, diagonal cuts; or several small Xs. Use a sharp razor blade or a lame, a double-edged blade mounted on a handle designed specifically for this purpose. Make the cuts at a 45-degree angle, about ¼ inch deep.

Baking: Two more deviations from basic bread-baking technique help this loaf achieve its rustic character: using a baking stone and adding steam in the oven. The stone, made of thick, porous ceramic, helps the loaf achieve a crisper crust and distributes heat more evenly than a baking sheet. Be sure to preheat the stone.

Many professional bakers have ovens that emit steam during the first minute or so of baking. The steam helps keep the crust from bursting, promoting better volume and crust. To somewhat mimic the action of these ovens, place a shallow pan in the bottom of the oven before preheating the oven. When the bread is ready to be baked, slide it onto the baking stone, then immediately pour about ⅓ cup of cold water into the pan. Try to do this whole process quickly so the oven is not open for more than a few seconds; you don't want to lose heat or steam.

Once the bread has baked the specified amount of time and it looks dark golden brown, there are a couple of additional ways to check for doneness: The bottom should be harder than the top crust, and you should hear a hollow sound when you tap the bottom of the bread.

Resist the temptation to eat the bread hot out of the oven! The flavor and texture will be better when it has completely cooled.

MAIN
DISHES

Poached Sea Bass on a Bed of Spring Vegetables

Enjoy the delicacies of the season when vegetables are at their tender best.

Text and Recipes by Georgeanne Brennan

It's always exhilarating to harvest spring vegetables from my garden. I love tasting the first asparagus, beans, peas and herbs because they bring bright new seasonal flavors to the table. Preparing them in the simplest ways allows their delicate flavor and tender texture to come forward, which is very different from the simmering stews and slow braises cooked during winter.

In the first flush of spring's warming weather, vegetables grow quickly, so it's important to catch them at their prime, before they become large and tough. Tiny, tender peas, picked at their sweetest, are very different than the large, starchy peas they become if left on the vine a few more days. The crisp, sweet spears of just-picked asparagus bear little resemblance to the woody stalks they turn into later. Even if you don't have a garden, take advantage of spring vegetables when they appear in the markets and buy them when they are at their very best.

Poached Sea Bass on a Bed of Spring Vegetables

The vegetables, sliced paper thin and sautéed only moments in butter and white wine, make a bed of spring flavors for the fish, which is covered with a tangle of fresh chervil and frisée.

- 2 tablespoons butter
- 6 baby carrots, thinly sliced
- 12 small young turnips, thinly sliced
- 3 baby or 1 small fennel bulb, fronds removed, thinly sliced
- 1¼ lb. sea bass or halibut fillets (1 inch thick), cut into 4 pieces
- ½ teaspoon salt
- ½ cup coarsely chopped fresh chervil
- ½ cup coarsely chopped frisée*
- ⅓ cup dry white wine

1. In nonstick skillet large enough to hold fish in a single layer, melt butter over medium heat. Increase heat to medium-high. Add carrots, turnips and fennel; sauté 3 to 5 minutes or until they soften and change color slightly.
2. Place fish over vegetables; sprinkle with salt. Cover; cook 4 minutes, turn-ing fish once.
3. Top fish with chervil and frisée; add wine. Reduce heat to low. Cover; cook an additional 1 to 2 minutes or until fish is opaque and just begins to flake and chervil and frisée have wilted but still retain their color.
4. Serve each fillet with a bed of vegetables on warm dinner plates.
TIP *Frisée often can be found in bulk mixed salad greens in some markets. It is pale yellow and resembles the inside leaves of curly endive.
4 servings

PER SERVING: 240 calories, 7.5 g total fat (4 g saturated fat), 29 g protein, 14.5 g carbohydrate, 90 mg cholesterol, 570 mg sodium, 5.5 g fiber

Sautéed Peas and Prosciutto

Young, early peas and prosciutto combine in this Mediterranean version of a classic spring dish.

- 2 tablespoons butter
- 2 tablespoons minced shallots
- 1 lb. fresh sugar snap peas
- ⅓ cup reduced-sodium chicken or vegetable broth
- 3 oz. thinly sliced prosciutto, cut into thin strips
- ⅛ teaspoon salt
- ¼ teaspoon freshly ground pepper
- 2 tablespoons minced fresh chervil

1. Melt butter in large skillet over medium-high heat. Add shallots; sauté 30 seconds.
2. Add peas and broth. Cover; cook 3 minutes or until peas are tender and liquid has evaporated, stirring occasionally.
3. Remove from heat; stir in prosciutto, salt and pepper. Sprinkle with chervil.
8 (½-cup) servings

PER SERVING: 70 calories, 4.5 g total fat (2.5 g saturated fat), 4 g protein, 4 g carbohydrate, 13 mg cholesterol, 160 mg sodium, 1.5 g fiber

GREEN HERBS

Green herbs are generally associated with spring because they flourish in the spring rains and warming days. They include chervil, chives, tarragon, cilantro, parsley, dill and lovage (a celery-like herb), as well as basil, which requires warmer weather.

• All green herbs are outstanding flavoring agents in salads. Chervil, parsley, cilantro and lovage can be used abundantly as leaves or sprigs.

• Once they have been cut, the storage life of green herbs is brief. Because their texture, appearance and flavor deteriorate quickly, use them shortly after harvest. Choose herbs with no signs of yellowing or slipperiness on the leaves and stems, an indication of aging. Wrap them in moist paper towels and put them in a plastic bag in the crisper section of the refrigerator to store them a few days.

• Since many green herbs are delicate, their flavor dissipates rapidly during cooking. For maximum impact, it is generally best to add them toward the end of cooking or just before serving.

• Rather than substituting a dried herb for a fresh one, it is better to substitute another fresh green herb. When dried, green herbs lose much of their character.

• Parsley usually can be substituted for either chervil or cilantro, and, although the flavor will be slightly different, the fresh taste of the green herb will prevail.

• Dill and tarragon also may be substituted for each other, as they are both intense and rather perfumed, though again the taste will be different.

Penne with Artichokes and Fresh Peas

The artichoke is a favorite springtime vegetable in the Mediterranean region, where it grows abundantly. It is used in a variety of ways, many of them as simple as this pasta dish.

- 8 oz. penne
- 1 tablespoon butter
- 3 tablespoons extra-virgin olive oil
- ½ cup chopped onion
- 1 cup shelled peas
- 1 (14-oz.) can artichoke hearts, drained, quartered
- 2 tablespoons dry white wine or water
- ¼ teaspoon salt
- ¼ teaspoon freshly ground pepper
- ½ cup chopped fresh Italian parsley
- ¼ cup (1 oz.) freshly grated Parmigiano-Reggiano cheese

1. Cook penne according to package directions.
2. While penne is cooking, in large skillet, heat butter and 1 tablespoon of the oil over medium heat. When butter is melted and oil is hot, add onion; sauté 2 to 3 minutes or until translucent.
3. Add peas and artichoke hearts; cook 3 to 4 minutes or until peas are crisp-tender. Add wine; bring to a boil over high heat, scraping up browned bits from bottom of skillet. Remove from heat; keep warm.
4. Drain penne thoroughly; place in serving bowl. Add vegetable mixture and juices from skillet; toss gently to mix. Add remaining 2 tablespoons oil, salt and pepper; toss to coat well. Add parsley and cheese; toss.
4 (1½-cup) servings

PER SERVING: 445 calories, 16.5 g total fat (4.5 g saturated fat), 15 g protein, 59.5 g carbohydrate, 15 mg cholesterol, 750 mg sodium, 8 g fiber

Radish, Green Onion and Herbed Goat Cheese Appetizer

This easy-to-prepare dish can be readily transported to picnics and parties. Serve it with crackers or raw vegetables.

- 8 oz. soft goat cheese
- 2 tablespoons milk
- ½ cup chopped radishes
- ½ cup chopped green onions
- ¼ cup chopped fresh Italian parsley
- ⅛ teaspoon salt

1. In medium bowl, combine cheese and milk; mix until creamy.
2. Stir in radishes, onions, parsley and salt. If necessary, add additional milk for ease in spreading.
1¼ cups

PER TABLESPOON: 35 calories, 2.5 g total fat (1.5 g saturated fat), 2 g protein, 1 g carbohydrate, 10 mg cholesterol, 55 mg sodium, 0 g fiber

Penne with Artichokes and Fresh Peas

Green and Yellow Bean Salad with Tomato-Basil Topping

Add oil; heat until hot. Sprinkle pork with ½ teaspoon of the salt and ½ teaspoon of the pepper. Brown pork in batches; set aside.

2. Melt butter in same Dutch oven over medium heat. Add leeks; sauté 2 to 3 minutes or until translucent.

3. Add wine; scrape up any browned bits in bottom of pan. Add broth, potatoes, turnips, carrots and remaining ½ teaspoon salt and 2 teaspoons pepper. Bring to a boil over medium-high heat. Reduce heat to medium-low; cover and simmer 10 to 12 minutes or until potatoes and carrots are tender.

4. Stir in peas, asparagus and browned pork. Return to a boil. Simmer an additional 6 to 7 minutes or until vegetables are tender and pork is no longer pink in center.

5. If a thicker stew is desired, scoop out 1 or 2 potatoes and a little broth; puree together in blender or food processor. Return mixture to stew. Stir in chives and tarragon.

6 (1⅔-cup) servings

PER SERVING: 430 calories, 14 g total fat (5 g saturated fat), 35 g protein, 42 g carbohydrate, 80 mg cholesterol, 815 mg sodium, 9.5 g fiber

Pork Tenderloin and Young Vegetable Ragout

Made with the first young vegetables of spring, this stew is a seasonal celebration of the garden. Unlike the long-simmering stews of winter, this one cooks quickly because the vegetables are immature and still very tender.

  2 tablespoons extra-virgin olive oil
  2 pork tenderloins (about 1½ lb.), cut into 1-inch pieces
  1 teaspoon salt
2½ teaspoons freshly ground pepper
  2 tablespoons butter

  4 leeks, coarsely chopped
  1 cup dry white wine
  3 cups reduced-sodium chicken broth
  6 small new potatoes, unpeeled, quartered
12 small young turnips, trimmed, leaving ½-inch greens
18 baby carrots
  1 cup shelled peas
18 asparagus spears, cut into 2-inch pieces
  ¼ cup minced fresh chives
  2 tablespoons minced fresh tarragon

1. Heat nonreactive Dutch oven or large pot over medium-high heat until hot.

Green and Yellow Bean Salad with Tomato-Basil Topping

Make this colorful salad to showcase the first young, tender beans of the season. Basil brings out the flavor of the beans, and tomatoes lend color and a welcome full-bodied taste.

VINAIGRETTE
  ¼ cup fresh lemon juice
  2 tablespoons finely chopped fresh tarragon
  1 teaspoon minced garlic
  ½ teaspoon sugar
  ¼ teaspoon salt
  ¼ teaspoon freshly ground pepper
1½ teaspoons olive oil
  ½ teaspoon Dijon mustard

SALAD
- ¾ lb. yellow wax beans
- ¾ lb. green beans

TOPPING
- 2 tomatoes, seeded, chopped
- ½ cup chopped fresh basil

1. In small bowl, combine all vinaigrette ingredients; stir until blended. Set aside.

2. Place yellow wax beans and green beans in steamer basket; place basket over boiling water. Cover and steam 8 to 12 minutes or just until beans are tender.

3. Place hot beans in large bowl. Pour vinaigrette over beans; toss well to coat. Let stand at room temperature up to 30 minutes before serving.

4. Meanwhile, combine tomatoes and basil. Just before serving, sprinkle tomato mixture over beans. Serve at room temperature.

8 servings

PER SERVING: 40 calories, 1 g total fat (0 g saturated fat), 1.5 g protein, 8 g carbohydrate, 0 mg cholesterol, 90 mg sodium, 3 g fiber

Roasted Asparagus with Lemon-Tarragon Vinaigrette

Roasting, a tasty alternative to steaming, brings out the natural sweetness of asparagus.

- 20 asparagus spears
- 2 tablespoons fresh lemon juice
- 2 tablespoons extra-virgin olive oil
- ¼ teaspoon salt
- ¼ teaspoon freshly ground pepper
- 2 tablespoons chopped fresh tarragon

1. Heat oven to 450°F. Place asparagus spears in shallow baking dish. Pour lemon juice and oil over asparagus; sprinkle with salt and pepper. Turn asparagus several times to coat.

2. Bake, uncovered, 12 to 18 minutes or until crisp-tender and color has darkened slightly, turning asparagus several times during baking.

3. Sprinkle with tarragon. Serve warm or at room temperature.

4 servings

PER SERVING: 85 calories, 7 g total fat (1 g saturated fat), 2.5 g protein, 4.5 g carbohydrate, 0 mg cholesterol, 150 mg sodium, 1.5 g fiber

Roasted Asparagus with Lemon-Tarragon Vinaigrette

GARLIC

POWER

Garlic-Parsley Stuffed Flank Steak

From mild to pungent, garlic's potency depends on how you use it.

Text and Recipes by Dana Jacobi

Garlic holds an important role in cooking throughout the world, but it's often a secondary one to other ingredients. Playing second fiddle isn't a bad gig, but garlic's a versatile little bulb, capable of taking the lead as well as performing solo. It just requires a little coaxing to reveal the breadth and depth of its talents, from its most powerful voice in the raw state to its mellow character when cooked. The secret lies in how you use it. Once you've learned how to handle garlic, you'll learn to appreciate it as a culinary star in the kitchen.

Garlic-Parsley Stuffed Flank Steak

The filling combines the flavors of a traditional Italian gremolata—parsley, garlic and lemon zest—with a kick of fresh chile. Its bright, clean flavors complement the richness of the meat.

BEEF
  1⅓ to 1½ lb. beef flank steak

MARINADE
  ½ cup fresh lemon juice
  3 tablespoons olive oil
  1 teaspoon salt
  ½ teaspoon freshly ground
      pepper

STUFFING
  6 garlic cloves
  ½ teaspoon salt
  3 tablespoons olive oil
  2 tablespoons minced
      jalapeño chile
  ¾ cup chopped Italian parsley

  2 teaspoons grated lemon
      peel
  ¼ teaspoon freshly ground
      pepper

1. Have butcher butterfly flank steak, or with knife cut steak horizontally in half, leaving one edge attached so steak opens like book.
2. In large resealable plastic bag, combine all marinade ingredients; mix well. Add steak. Seal bag; refrigerate 3 to 6 hours to marinate.
3. Meanwhile, place garlic on cutting board; sprinkle with ½ teaspoon salt. Mash garlic and salt together with side of chef's knife to form paste.
4. Heat 3 tablespoons oil in small skillet over medium heat until hot. Add garlic mixture; cook 1 minute or until garlic is fragrant and begins to soften. Add jalapeño; cook 10 seconds. Place in small bowl; set aside to cool. Add parsley, lemon peel and pepper.
5. Heat grill. Remove steak from marinade; discard marinade. Open steak;

spread stuffing over steak. Roll up steak (with the grain); secure with toothpicks every inch. Cut between toothpicks into 1-inch slices.
6. Place steak slices on gas grill over medium heat or on charcoal grill 4 to 6 inches from medium coals. Cook 10 to 14 minutes for medium-rare to medium, turning once. Remove toothpicks before serving.
4 servings

PER SERVING: 420 calories, 30.5 g total fat (8.5 g saturated fat), 31 g protein, 3.5 g carbohydrate, 90 mg cholesterol, 565 mg sodium, .5 g fiber

Chicken with 40 Cloves of Garlic

If you've ever had this classic dish, you know that what sounds like an overwhelming amount of garlic really isn't. The slow cooking of the whole cloves mellows the garlic's flavor. Our version is made with chicken breasts instead of a whole chicken and includes vegetables to make it a one-pot meal.

  1 tablespoon unsalted butter
  1 tablespoon extra-virgin
      olive oil
  4 chicken breast halves,
      bone-in with skin
  1 large carrot, cut into 1-inch
      pieces
  1 large leek (white portion
      only), cut into 1-inch
      pieces
  1 medium onion, cut into
      8 pieces
  1 small fennel bulb, fronds
      removed, cut into 1-inch
      pieces
  8 small red potatoes, halved
 40 garlic cloves, peeled
  ¼ cup dry white wine
  1 tablespoon chopped fresh
      rosemary
  1 teaspoon salt
  ¼ teaspoon freshly ground
      pepper

Garlic-Vegetable Soup with Pistou

GARLIC BROTH

    2 teaspoons extra-virgin
       olive oil
  ⅛ teaspoon salt
  ¼ cup chopped garlic
    4 cups water

SOUP

    1 teaspoon extra-virgin
       olive oil
    1 medium onion, chopped
  3½ cups garlic broth
    3 cups vegetable broth
    1 cup sliced (1 inch) green
       beans
    1 large tomato, seeded,
       chopped
    1 small zucchini, halved
       lengthwise, sliced (½ inch)
    1 bay leaf
    1 cup ditali (short macaroni
       tubes), small shell pasta
       or elbow macaroni
  ½ teaspoon salt
  ¼ teaspoon freshly ground pepper
  ½ cup Pistou (recipe follows)

1. Heat 2 teaspoons oil in medium saucepan over low heat until hot. Sprinkle with ⅛ teaspoon salt. Add garlic; sauté about 8 minutes or until soft, stirring occasionally.
2. Add water; bring to a boil, scraping up any browned bits. Reduce heat to low; simmer 30 minutes. Set aside.
3. Heat 1 teaspoon oil in large pot or nonreactive Dutch oven over medium-high heat until hot. Add onion; sauté about 3 minutes or until soft.
4. Add garlic broth, vegetable broth, green beans, tomato, zucchini and bay leaf. Bring to a boil. Add ditali, salt and pepper; cook 15 minutes.
5. Remove bay leaf. Ladle soup into bowls. Top each serving with 1 tablespoon Pistou.
5 (1⅓-cup) servings

PER SERVING: 175 calories, 5.5 g total fat (1 g saturated fat), 5.5 g protein, 26.5 g carbohydrate, 0 mg cholesterol, 850 mg sodium, 3 g fiber

1. In large pot or nonreactive Dutch oven, heat butter and oil over medium-high heat until butter is melted and hot. Add chicken; cook about 6 minutes or until browned, turning once. Remove chicken; place on plate.
2. Add carrot, leek, onion and fennel; cook about 3 minutes or until vegetables are lightly browned, stirring occasionally.
3. Add potatoes and garlic. Arrange chicken over vegetables. Pour wine over chicken. Sprinkle with rosemary, salt and pepper. Cover; bring to a boil over medium-high heat. Reduce heat to low; simmer 50 minutes or until chicken

juices run clear and garlic is soft.
4 servings

PER SERVING: 515 calories, 16.5 g total fat (5 g saturated fat), 35 g protein, 58 g carbohydrate, 85 mg cholesterol, 710 mg sodium, 7.5 g fiber

Garlic-Vegetable Soup with Pistou

This rich, full-flavored soup is the French version of minestrone. Instead of a base comprised completely of vegetable broth, however, we've replaced half of it with a homemade garlic broth. Make an extra batch of the tasty garlic broth.

ALL ABOUT GARLIC

Garlic is a food with personality. Depending on the variety and the way it's used, that personality can range from pungently assertive to downright mellow. Three basic varieties of garlic are most commonly available in the United States: the familiar white-skinned and strongly flavored American garlic; the somewhat milder, purple-tinged Mexican and Italian garlics; and the much milder, very large elephant garlic. Here are some tips for using the bulb.

Breaking up: To break up a bulb of garlic, insert your thumb at the top of the bulb and pull away the cloves, one or more at a time. Or place the entire bulb, root end up, on a cutting board. Press on it with the heel of your hand until the cloves begin to separate.

Peeling: Garlic is easily separated from its tight-fitting jacket using a knife. Place one or more cloves on a cutting board and press down on them firmly with the broad side of a heavy chef's knife. The skin will separate, leaving the clove partially crushed and ready to chop.

To peel several cloves, do what chefs do: Spread out the cloves on a cutting board and place a heavy skillet over them. Grasp the skillet on either side and lean quickly and heavily on it, pressing down.

To peel garlic leaving the clove intact, try a gadget called a garlic peeler, a piece of rubber tubing (pictured in photo at

left). When you roll a clove of garlic in the tube, the skin separates and the clove comes out clean.

Chopping: The more finely garlic is chopped or crushed, the stronger its flavor. A garlic press yields garlic with the most potent flavor: It releases the most oils from a clove because it ruptures the most cells. Some cooks believe it also makes the garlic taste bitter. Many chefs like the following method for mincing garlic:

Sprinkle ¼ to ½ teaspoon of salt from the recipe over the cloves. Smash the cloves with the broad side of a chef's knife to crush the garlic, then chop, working the salt into the garlic. The salt begins to break down the garlic's fibers, making it easier to blend into other ingredients. The salt also keeps the garlic from sticking to the knife or cutting board.

Using: Garlic is at its most pungent state when it is raw. Its assertive flavor lends character to such classic preparations as aïoli (a garlic mayonnaise) and pesto. Because its flavor strengthens as it sits, raw garlic should be used sparingly. Cooking garlic mellows its taste. For a strong garlic flavor in a cooked dish, mince the garlic and sauté it very briefly—20 to 30 seconds or until fragrant.

The longer garlic cooks, the more mild its taste becomes, as demonstrated in the dish Chicken with 40 Cloves of Garlic, where slow braising reduces the flavor of several bulbs of garlic to a mild, pleasant presence. When you roast garlic, its natural sugars caramelize, leaving cloves so mild and creamy that they can be spread on bread and mashed directly into potatoes.

Store heads of garlic in a dark, dry and cool place, preferably one that allows air to circulate. Although not essential, a covered clay garlic keeper (pictured in top photo) works well. Hanging garlic in a braid or keeping it in a bowl in a warm kitchen is fine for short periods but is not suitable for longer storage because it tends to dry out the garlic.

Pistou

Pistou, a term that refers both to this basil-garlic mixture and the French vegetable soup that is flavored with the paste, is very similar to Italian pesto. It's equally good in soup, over pasta or stirred into rice.

1¼   cups packed fresh basil
¾   cup Italian parsley
2   garlic cloves, coarsely
       chopped
¼   cup coarsely chopped
       tomato
2   tablespoons grated
       Parmigiano-Reggiano
       cheese
¼   teaspoon salt
⅛   teaspoon freshly ground
       pepper
4   teaspoons extra-virgin
       olive oil

1. In food processor, chop basil, parsley and garlic. Add tomato, cheese, salt and pepper; process until well blended.
2. With motor running, add oil; mix until smooth.
TIP Pistou freezes well.

Halibut with Roasted Garlic-Red Pepper Sauce

Garlic plays a more subtle role in a fabulous sweet-smoky pepper sauce that accompanies meaty halibut fillets. The garlic is roasted ahead of time, then pureed with red peppers that also have been roasted. The sauce works well with grilled chicken or other fish, too.

2   large red bell peppers
4   (6-oz.) halibut fillets
       (1 inch thick)
3   tablespoons plus
       2 teaspoons extra-virgin
       olive oil
¾   teaspoon salt
8   cloves Roasted Garlic
       (recipe follows)
1   teaspoon chopped fresh

      thyme
⅛   teaspoon freshly ground
       pepper
2   teaspoons sherry vinegar
       or red wine vinegar
       Fresh watercress or parsley
       for garnish

1. Place bell pepper over high heat on gas or electric burner. Cook, turning with tongs every 1 to 2 minutes, until skin is completely blackened. Place pepper in heavy plastic bag; close bag and let stand 15 minutes or until cool enough to handle. Remove from bag; peel blackened skin under running water. Slit pepper and remove veins and seeds; cut into 1-inch pieces.
2. Heat oven to 375°F. Line 15x10x1-inch pan with foil. Brush halibut with 2 teaspoons of the oil. Sprinkle with ½ teaspoon of the salt. Place halibut in pan. Bake 10 minutes or until fish just begins to flake.
3. Meanwhile, in food processor, combine bell peppers and garlic; puree. Add thyme, remaining ¼ teaspoon salt, pepper and vinegar. With motor running, add remaining 3 tablespoons oil.
4. Divide sauce onto individual plates. Place halibut in center of each plate. Garnish with watercress.
4 servings

PER SERVING: 290 calories, 14.5 g total fat (2 g saturated fat), 33 g protein, 5.5 g carbohydrate, 90 mg cholesterol, 580 mg sodium, 1.5 g fiber

Roasted Garlic

Roasting mellows garlic's flavor and softens its texture so that it can be blended into sauces, salad dressings, soups and stews—or even used as a spread on bread.

8   garlic cloves, skin on
½   teaspoon olive oil
⅛   teaspoon salt

1. Heat oven to 400°F. Place garlic in small bowl; add oil. Stir to coat garlic

thoroughly with oil. Place garlic in center of large square of foil. Sprinkle with salt. Bring 4 corners of foil up over garlic; seal by folding foil together.
2. Bake 45 to 60 minutes or until cloves are soft when pressed. (Roasted garlic can be stored in refrigerator 4 to 5 days.)
3. To use, cut root end off garlic cloves. Using fingers, squeeze garlic out cut end.
TIP Another method for roasting garlic is to slice off the top of one whole bulb of garlic, cutting it crosswise 1 inch below the tip. Drizzle oil over garlic; wrap in foil. Bake, following directions above. To use, squeeze until individual cloves pop out.

Goat Cheese and Caramelized Garlic Crostini

When entertaining, make the garlic and the cheese spread up to two days ahead to reduce last-minute pressure on you. Enjoy leftovers with soup for a light meal, or blend the cheese into a baked potato.

1   tablespoon extra-virgin
       olive oil
2   tablespoons water
1   bulb garlic, cloves
       separated, peeled
6   oz. soft goat cheese
½   teaspoon salt
½   teaspoon chopped fresh
       thyme
¼   teaspoon chopped fresh
       sage
¼   teaspoon chopped fresh
       rosemary
⅛   teaspoon freshly ground
       pepper
36   (¼-inch) slices baguette
3   tablespoons chopped
       walnuts
1   tablespoon chopped fresh
       chives

1. In small saucepan, heat oil and water until hot. Add garlic; cover and

cook over medium heat 4 minutes. Reduce heat to low; remove cover and cook 10 to 15 minutes or until garlic is deep brown on all sides, turning frequently. Remove garlic from skillet. (Caramelized garlic will keep 2 to 3 days in a tightly covered container in the refrigerator.)

2. In food processor, combine cheese and 8 cloves of the garlic; puree (save remaining garlic for garnish or another use). Add salt, thyme, sage, rosemary and pepper; process until well mixed. Place spread in small bowl. Cover with plastic wrap; refrigerate 1 to 4 hours to blend flavors.

3. When ready to toast bread, heat oven to 400°F. Place baguette slices in 15x10x1-inch pan. Bake 5 to 8 minutes or until slightly crisp. Set aside.

4. To serve, spread each toasted baguette slice with 1 teaspoon of the cheese mixture. Sprinkle with walnuts and chives; garnish with caramelized garlic, if desired.

36 crostini

PER CROSTINI: 30 calories, 2 g total fat (1 g saturated fat), 1 g protein, 2.5 g carbohydrate, 5 mg cholesterol, 70 mg sodium, 0 g fiber

Burst Cherry Tomatoes with Garlic and Herbs

Garden-fresh tomatoes are a treat on their own, but when you cook them with garlic and fresh herbs, the aroma and taste are irresistible. The key is to cook the tomatoes quickly over high heat so the outsides burst but the insides don't get too soft.

1 tablespoon extra-virgin olive oil
1 pint large cherry tomatoes
1 medium garlic clove, minced
1 tablespoon chopped fresh parsley
½ teaspoon salt
½ teaspoon chopped fresh thyme
¼ teaspoon finely chopped

Burst Cherry Tomatoes with Garlic and Herbs

fresh rosemary
⅛ teaspoon freshly ground pepper

1. Heat oil in medium skillet over high heat until hot. Add tomatoes; sauté 1 minute, rolling tomatoes constantly in skillet.

2. Reduce heat to medium. Add all remaining ingredients; mix well. Cook 2 minutes or until tomatoes just begin to soften and skins begin to crack, stir-ring constantly. (If tomatoes are small, reduce cooking time to 1 minute.)

4 servings

PER SERVING: 50 calories, 3.5 g total fat (.5 g saturated fat), 1 g protein, 4.5 g carbohydrate, 0 mg cholesterol, 300 mg sodium, 1 g fiber

THE
SAUTÉ
Way

Fillet of Beef with Tomatoes and Artichoke Hearts

Perfect this traditional method for cooking succulent meats and rich sauces.

Text and Recipes by William Rice and Jill Van Cleave

One of the best methods for cooking meat is also one of the fastest and most flavorful. Sautéing, a classic cooking technique, means "to jump" in French, and that's just what food does when you place thin slices of meat or poultry in a lightly oiled pan over high heat. When the meat hits the hot pan, it contracts, causing movement akin to a leap or jump.

This method produces meat that's crispy brown on the outside and moist on the inside. It's an exciting technique and, once mastered, is both efficient and fun. And after the meat has cooked, you have the foundation for making rich pan sauces to accompany it.

These recipes feature thin slices of boneless meats with sauces that are finished in the same pan. Larger, bone-in cuts of meat may also be sautéed, or seared, as a first step in a more lengthy cooking process such as braising or pan roasting. But first, learn to enjoy the heat of the kitchen as you master the art of tossing, turning, seasoning and saucing in rapid-fire succession.

Fillet of Beef with Tomatoes and Artichoke Hearts

Tender beef fillet is ideal for sautéing. Tenderloin does not need enrichment, so our pan sauce is a light reduction of wine, broth and tomatoes with a hint of mystery supplied by tarragon. Use ½ teaspoon of dried tarragon if fresh is unavailable. Artichokes garnish and complete the sauce.

- 4 (4 oz.) beef tenderloin steaks (¾ inch thick)
- ¼ teaspoon kosher (coarse) salt
- ¼ teaspoon freshly ground pepper
- 2 tablespoons vegetable oil
- ¼ cup finely chopped green onions
- ½ cup dry red wine
- ½ cup beef broth
- 1½ cups diced tomatoes
- 2 teaspoons chopped fresh tarragon
- ⅔ cup frozen artichoke hearts, thawed, drained

1. Sprinkle beef with salt and pepper. Heat large sauté pan over medium-high heat until hot. Add oil; heat until hot. Add beef; cook 4 minutes for medium-rare or until of desired doneness, turning once. Remove steaks from pan; place on plate.
2. Add green onions to pan; cook and stir 1 minute. Add wine; bring to a boil. Boil until liquid is syrupy, scraping up browned bits from bottom of pan. Add broth; bring to a boil. Stir in tomatoes and tarragon. Reduce heat to medium; cook 5 to 7 minutes or until tomato mixture thickens, stirring occasionally.
3. Stir in artichoke hearts. Return beef to pan; cook 1 minute to reheat, turning beef once.
4 servings

PER SERVING: 355 calories, 18.5 g total fat (5.5 g saturated fat), 37.5 g protein, 7.5 g carbohydrate, 95 mg cholesterol, 325 mg sodium, 2.5 g fiber

Chicken Breasts in Cider Cream

Chicken is the chameleon of the poultry world; it takes on whatever flavors are added to it. This versatility is useful because boneless breasts are one of the most popular meats to cook at home. In this French-style sauté, we salute the riches of Normandy with a sauce of cider and cream. Try using hard cider, a fermented apple juice, if you can find it. It is less alcoholic than wine and has a pleasant fruity taste and dry finish.

- 4 boneless skinless chicken breast halves
- ½ teaspoon sea salt
- ¼ teaspoon freshly ground pepper
- 1 tablespoon butter
- 1 tablespoon vegetable oil
- 2 tablespoons finely chopped shallots
- 1 tablespoon all-purpose flour
- ½ cup hard apple cider* or regular apple cider
- ½ cup whipping cream

Scaloppine with Spanish-Style Vinegar Sauce

1½ teaspoons fresh lemon juice
1 tablespoon chopped fresh
    parsley

1. Dry chicken with paper towels.
Sprinkle with salt and pepper.
2. In large skillet, heat butter and oil
over medium-high heat until butter is
melted and hot. Add chicken; cook 3 to
5 minutes or until brown, turning once.
Remove chicken from pan; place on
platter.
3. Reduce heat to medium. Add shallots; cook 30 to 60 seconds or until
softened. Stir in flour; cook and stir 1
minute. Add cider; stir until smooth,
scraping up browned bits from bottom
of pan. Stir in cream. Bring to a boil;
add lemon juice.
4. Return chicken to pan; reduce heat
to low. Cover; cook about 3 minutes or
until chicken juices run clear, turning
once. Sprinkle with parsley.
TIP *Hard apple cider is fermented
apple cider with 3 to 7 percent alcohol.
There are some excellent hard ciders
being produced today.

4 servings

PER SERVING: 310 calories, 19 g total fat (9 g saturated fat), 27
g protein, 7 g carbohydrate, 105 mg cholesterol, 285 mg sodium, .5 g fiber

Scaloppine with Spanish-Style Vinegar Sauce

*Scaloppine is an Italian term that refers
to a slice of meat, pounded thin, that is
floured and then sautéed. Any meat or
poultry prepared this way is lightning fast
to cook and will leave a residue of starch
to help thicken a pan sauce.*

8 veal scaloppine or thin
    turkey breast slices
    (about 1 lb.)
¼ cup all-purpose flour
1 tablespoon paprika
½ teaspoon sea salt
½ teaspoon freshly ground
    pepper
2 anchovy fillets, rinsed
3 tablespoons extra-virgin
    olive oil

1 teaspoon minced garlic
6 tablespoons sherry vinegar
    or red wine vinegar
⅔ cup reduced-sodium
    chicken broth

1. Dry veal with paper towels. In shallow dish, combine flour, paprika, salt
and pepper; mix well. Coat veal with
flour mixture, shaking off excess; place
in single layer on baking sheets.
2. Place anchovies on small plate;
mash with fork to form paste.
3. Heat large sauté pan over medium-
high heat until hot. Add 2 tablespoons
of the oil. Add veal in batches; cook 1
to 3 minutes or until browned, turning
once and adding additional 1 tablespoon oil as needed. Remove veal from
pan; place on plate.
4. Drain all but 1 tablespoon oil from
pan. Reduce heat to medium. Add garlic; cook 10 to 20 seconds or just until
fragrant. Increase heat to medium-high.
Add vinegar and anchovy paste. Bring
to a boil, scraping up browned bits
from bottom of pan. Boil until liquid is
reduced by half. Add broth; boil until
reduced by half.
5. Return veal to pan. To reheat, cook 1
minute or until no longer pink in center, turning slices once to coat with pan
juices.
WINE Two choices play up to the veal
(or turkey) without overwhelming it:
1997 Marqués de Cáceres Rioja from
Spain ($12) and 1996 Allegrini "La
Grola" Valpolicella ($15).
4 servings

PER SERVING: 225 calories, 14.5 g total fat (4 g saturated fat),
19 g protein, 5 g carbohydrate, 70 mg cholesterol, 270 mg
sodium, .5 g fiber

Marinated Lamb Leg Steak à la Grecque

*Lamb leg steaks are a delicious way to
enjoy lamb without having to roast an
entire leg. If leg steaks are not on display
in your market, ask the butcher to cut
them from a rolled boneless leg roast.*

The fresh tasting lemon, garlic and herb marinade tenderizes the meat for a quick sauté and reappears in a pan sauce that also contains chicken broth for intensified flavor.

2 (¾-lb.) lamb leg steaks
   (1 inch thick)
⅓ cup chopped fresh dill
⅓ cup chopped fresh parsley
¼ cup chopped green onions
4 teaspoons minced garlic
2 tablespoons fresh lemon
   juice
4 tablespoons extra-virgin
   olive oil
½ teaspoon kosher (coarse)
   salt
½ teaspoon freshly ground
   pepper
½ cup reduced-sodium
   chicken broth

Pork Tenderloin Medallions with Cranberries

1. Place lamb in shallow glass baking dish. In medium bowl, mix dill, parsley, green onions, garlic and lemon juice. Whisk in 3 tablespoons of the oil. Pour over lamb; turn lamb to coat all sides evenly. Cover; refrigerate 1 to 1½ hours to marinate.
2. Remove lamb from baking dish; scrape marinade from surface of lamb back into dish. Reserve marinade. Pat lamb dry with paper towels. Sprinkle with salt and pepper.
3. Heat large skillet over medium-high heat until hot. Add remaining 1 table-spoon oil; heat until hot. Add lamb; cook 6 minutes or until well browned, turning once. Remove lamb from skillet.
4. Add broth and reserved marinade to skillet. Bring to a boil, scraping up browned bits from bottom of skillet.
5. Return lamb to skillet; reduce heat to medium-low. Cover; cook about 3 minutes or until of desired doneness, turning once. Place lamb on cutting board; cover loosely with foil. Let stand 5 minutes.
6. Increase heat to medium-high; boil until pan juices are syrupy, about 2

minutes. Slice lamb thinly; pour reduced pan juices over lamb.
WINE Cabernet Sauvignon, with its ripe and robust flavors, is the choice here. Try 1998 J. Pedroncelli "Three Vineyards" Cabernet Sauvignon from Sonoma ($14) or 1987 Casa Lapostolle "Cuvée Alexandre" Cabernet Sauvignon from the Rapel Valley in Chile ($20).
6 servings

PER SERVING: 255 calories, 18.5 g total fat (4.5 g saturated fat), 19.5 g protein, 2 g carbohydrate, 65 mg cholesterol, 230 mg sodium, .5 g fiber

Pork Tenderloin Medallions with Cranberries

Pork tenderloin is a naturally tender cut of meat and does not require special treatment such as marinating or long, slow cooking. Hot and quick is the best method to obtain juicy, flavorful meat. Tenderloin should be cooked just until the center of the meat is still pink for the best

taste and texture. Here, a pan sauce is made by combining concentrates of cranberry juice and apple juice with port and dried cranberries. It provides a complementary sweet-sour flavor and attractive ruby color.

2 (¾-lb.) pork tenderloins
⅓ cup frozen cranberry juice
   concentrate, thawed
⅓ cup frozen apple juice
   concentrate, thawed
⅓ cup port or cranberry juice
⅓ cup water
1 tablespoon olive oil
1 tablespoon butter
6 garlic cloves, crushed
½ teaspoon kosher (coarse)
   salt
¼ teaspoon freshly ground
   pepper
3 tablespoons Dijon mustard
⅓ cup dried cranberries

1. Cut each tenderloin crosswise into 6 pieces. Place, cut side down, on

SAUTÉ PANS

The sauté pan is a frying pan, also called a sauteuse or sautoir. Use these guidelines when selecting a pan for sautéing.

• The classic sauté pan shape has a wide and flat bottom with straight sides and a long handle. The flat bottom spreads heat evenly and allows food to be cooked in a single layer. Straight sides keep splatters inside and create a tight seal when covered with a lid. A long handle helps keep hands away from intense heat. Sauté pans range in size from 8 to 14 inches in diameter with sides 2½ to 4½ inches high.

• A skillet also can be used for sautéing. Its sides slope or angle outward in a gentle curve. Skillets are not as deep as sauté pans and allow food to be tossed and moved around easily. Like the sauté pan, the skillet handle should be long and heat-resistant. The most practical sizes vary from 8 to 12 inches in diameter, although 6-inch omelet pans and 14-inch skillets are available.

• Choose the heaviest pan you are comfortable lifting. The high heat used in sautéing requires heavy-gauge metal construction that is highly conductive and capable of transmitting heat evenly. The best pans are copper lined with steel or tin; stainless steel constructed with bonded layers of metal; hard-anodized aluminum; and nonstick pans made of these same materials. Cast-iron and enameled cast-iron skillets are suitable as well, but avoid pans made of lightweight aluminum.

parchment paper or plastic wrap. Cover with second sheet of parchment; pound to ¼-inch thickness. In medium bowl, combine cranberry juice concentrate, apple juice concentrate, port and water. Set aside.

2. In large skillet, heat oil and butter over medium heat until butter is melted and hot. Add garlic; sauté 1 minute or until garlic begins to brown.

3. Add pork; sprinkle with salt and pepper. Cook pork, in batches if necessary, 2 to 3 minutes or until browned, turning once. Remove pork from skillet; place on platter. Discard garlic and pan drippings.

4. Return skillet to medium-high heat. Add cranberry juice mixture; bring to a boil, scraping up browned bits from bottom of skillet. Boil 2 to 3 minutes or until mixture reduces slightly. Whisk in mustard; boil until sauce is slightly thickened. Stir in cranberries. Add pork to sauce; cover. Reduce heat to low. Simmer 1 to 2 minutes or until pork is hot.

6 servings

PER SERVING: 270 calories, 9.5 g total fat (4 g saturated fat), 24.5 g protein, 22 g carbohydrate, 80 mg cholesterol, 320 mg sodium, .5 g fiber

SAUTÉ BASICS

Sautéing involves a series of simple steps done in quick succession in an uncovered skillet or frying pan. Just as in wok cooking, it is best to assemble all ingredients before beginning to cook.

1. Be sure the meat is of even thickness. Pieces can be flattened to achieve uniform thickness: Lightly brush the cut sides of the meat with water and place the meat, cut side down, between two pieces of parchment paper. (The water helps keep the paper from sticking to the meat.) Pound the meat with a meat pounder or the flat side of a meat mallet.

2. The meat should be dry. If it's wet or damp, it sizzles and steams but doesn't brown. Pat it dry with paper towels while heating the pan. If a marinade is used, scrape it off before drying the meat.

3. Heat the pan over medium-high heat until hot. (Some burners may need to be turned on high to obtain enough heat.) To tell if the pan is hot enough, place your hand over the pan. If you can feel heat being generated from the center of the pan (not just the outside edges), it's ready. Then add the fat to the pan. The fat must be hot, almost shimmering, before you add the meat. Use vegetable oil or olive oil, or a combination of oil and unsalted butter. If you use the combination of oil and butter, it must be added before the pan is heated. If you use only butter, it must be clarified or it will burn. (Clarified butter is butter that has been slowly melted to evaporate the water and separate the solids.)

4. Leave some space between pieces of meat; if you don't, heat becomes trapped underneath and the meat will steam rather than brown, causing juices to escape. Cook the meat in batches, if necessary.

5. Cook the meat until the first side is brown, then turn it using tongs or a spatula. Season the cooked side, if desired, while browning the second side. Generally, thin slices of boneless meat are done when browned on both sides, usually in 4 to 6 minutes. Keep the meat warm while deglazing the pan and making the sauce.

6. Deglazing the pan captures the rich cooking juices. Remove excess fat from the pan. Cooking over medium-high to high heat, add about ½ cup of wine, broth or water to the pan, and stir to scrape up browned particles that have adhered to the bottom. For a simple sauce, boil the liquid until it's reduced to a syrupy consistency, shaking the pan or stirring occasionally. Remove the pan from the heat, and stir in a tablespoon of butter. Season to taste.

OLIVES

MEDITERRANEAN GOLD

Orange-Fennel Marinated Olives

Discover this fruit's rich culinary potential.

Text and Recipes by Patsy Jamieson

More than any other ingredient, olives typify the cuisine of the Mediterranean region. Olives' distinctive and complex flavor, which combines all four of the primary tastes (acid, bitter, sweet, salty), is skillfully harnessed to enrich a variety of dishes, from appetizers to salads, breads to hearty stews. In some parts of the Middle East, they are even considered essential breakfast fare.

In North America, olives have not played a prominent role in cuisine. They are best known for transforming concoctions of gin and vermouth into martinis, or as garnishes for pizzas and salads. Recently, however, spurred by interest in the inherently healthful food of the Mediterranean and the increasing availability of various imported olives, American cooks are beginning to take advantage of the culinary potential of this versatile fruit.

Discover the magical qualities of olives with these Mediterranean-influenced dishes. As the Greeks would say, yamas (to our health)!

juice. Place in medium nonreactive bowl or jar. Cover; let stand at room temperature 1 hour to marinate, stirring occasionally. (Olives can be made up to 2 weeks ahead. Cover and refrigerate.) Serve at room temperature.

VARIATIONS Using the same method as above, try these variations:

LEMON-CORIANDER MARINATED OLIVES: 2 tablespoons extra-virgin olive oil; 4 garlic cloves, peeled; 2 strips lemon peel; 1 1/2 teaspoons coriander seeds, crushed; 1/2 teaspoon black peppercorns, crushed; 2 cups green olives (such as green cracked or picholine), rinsed; and 2 tablespoons lemon juice.

CUMIN-SPIKED MARINATED OLIVES: 2 tablespoons extra-virgin olive oil; 4 garlic cloves, peeled; 1 1/2 teaspoons cumin seeds, crushed; 1/2 teaspoon paprika; 1/8 teaspoon crushed red pepper; 2 cups assorted green and brine-cured ripe olives, rinsed; and 2 tablespoons lemon juice.

3 cups

PER 7 OLIVES: 40 calories, 4 g total fat (.5 g saturated fat), .5 g protein, 1.5 g carbohydrate, 0 mg cholesterol, 480 mg sodium, .5 g fiber

Olive and Roasted Red Pepper Appetizer Calzones

These mini-calzones, filled with intensely flavored dry-cured ripe olives, are truly addictive. The addition of cornmeal to the pizza dough gives a delightful crunch. This is the perfect way to show off the unique taste of olives!

DOUGH
- 1 1/2 cups all-purpose flour
- 1/2 cup yellow cornmeal
- 1 teaspoon salt
- 1/2 teaspoon sugar
- 1 (1/4-oz.) pkg. fast-acting dry yeast
- 2/3 cup very warm water (120°F. to 130°F.)
- 1 tablespoon olive oil

Orange-Fennel Marinated Olives

Marinated olives are one of the easiest— and classiest—hors d'oeuvres you can serve. Keep some on hand for an impromptu appetizer before serving one of the main dishes that follow. Seasoning possibilities are myriad.

- 3 tablespoons extra-virgin olive oil
- 2 1/4 teaspoons fennel seeds, crushed
- 12 (2x1/2-inch) strips orange peel
- 6 garlic cloves, halved lengthwise
- 3 cups mixed green and ripe olives
- 3 tablespoons fresh orange juice

1. Heat oil in medium skillet over medium-low heat. Add fennel seeds, orange peel and garlic; cook and stir 30 to 60 seconds or until fragrant. Add olives; cook and stir about 1 minute or until olives are warm but not hot.

2. Remove from heat; stir in orange

CRIMPING PASTRY

Press the edges of Olive and Roasted Red Pepper Appetizer Calzones with a fork to seal the pastries so they won't pop open while they bake.

FILLING

⅓ cup finely chopped purchased roasted red bell peppers
¼ cup dry-cured ripe olives, pitted, finely chopped
¼ cup (1 oz.) shredded mozzarella cheese
1 teaspoon chopped fresh rosemary
  Dash freshly ground pepper

GLAZE

1 egg
2 tablespoons water

1. Place flour, cornmeal, salt, sugar and yeast in food processor; pulse to mix. With motor running, gradually add ⅔ cup water and oil; process until dough forms a ball. Process 1 minute to knead.

2. Place dough in greased bowl. Cover; let rise in warm place 20 minutes. (Dough can be made up to 2 days ahead. Place in resealable plastic freezer bag; seal bag and refrigerate.)

3. In medium bowl, stir together all filling ingredients. (Filling can be made up to 2 days ahead. Cover and refrigerate.)

4. Heat oven to 375°F. Line 2 baking sheets with parchment paper. On lightly floured surface, roll out half of dough to ⅜-inch thickness. With 3½-inch round cutter, cut out 8 rounds. Pull away dough scraps; reserve.

5. In small bowl, beat egg and 2 tablespoons water. Brush rounds lightly with egg glaze. Place scant teaspoon filling just to one side of center of each round. Fold dough over to enclose filling. Crimp edges with tines of fork. Place calzones 2 inches apart on baking sheet. Brush tops lightly with egg glaze. With knife, make 3 slits in tops to allow steam to escape. Repeat with remaining half of dough, dough scraps and filling.

6. Bake calzones, 1 sheet at a time, 15 to 20 minutes or until light brown. Cool slightly on wire rack. Serve warm or at room temperature.

24 appetizers

PER APPETIZER: 55 calories, 1 g total fat (.5 g saturated fat), 1.5 g protein, 8.5 g carbohydrate, 5 mg cholesterol, 140 mg sodium, .5 g fiber

Penne with Eggplant and Olive Sauce

Olives play a supporting role in this simple pasta dish. They are mild, yet they contribute an extra dimension of flavor to the sauce and allow the meaty flavor of eggplant to shine through.

1 (28-oz.) can plum tomatoes, undrained

Penne with Eggplant and Olive Sauce

3 tablespoons olive oil
3 cups cubed (1 inch)
    eggplant (about ½ lb.)
1 cup chopped onions
4 garlic cloves, minced
⅛ teaspoon crushed red
    pepper
⅔ cup green olives (such
    as green cracked or
    manzanilla)
¼ teaspoon salt
¼ teaspoon freshly ground
    pepper
⅓ cup chopped fresh Italian
    parsley
1 lb. penne (tube-shaped
    pasta)
1 cup (4 oz.) crumbled feta
    cheese

1. Place tomatoes with juice in food processor; pulse until tomatoes are chopped but retain some texture. Set aside.
2. Heat 2 tablespoons of the oil in large skillet over medium-high heat until hot. Add eggplant; cook 5 to 7 minutes or until browned and tender, turning occasionally. Remove from skillet; set aside.
3. Reduce heat to medium-low; add remaining 1 tablespoon oil to skillet. Add onions; cook 3 to 5 minutes or until softened and lightly browned, stirring frequently.
4. Add garlic and red pepper; cook and stir 30 to 60 seconds. Add tomatoes; mix well. Increase heat to medium-high. Bring to a boil. Add eggplant, olives, salt and pepper; stir to mix. Reduce heat to medium-low; simmer, uncovered, 15 to 20 minutes or until eggplant is very tender and sauce has thickened. Stir in parsley.
5. Meanwhile, cook penne according to package directions. Drain; place in warm large bowl. Toss with sauce; sprinkle with cheese.
6 servings

PER SERVING: 475 calories, 14.5 g total fat (4.5 g saturated fat), 15 g protein, 71.5 g carbohydrate, 15 mg cholesterol, 1215 mg sodium, 6 g fiber

Provençale Beef Stew with Olives

Here is a robust make-ahead stew you can proudly serve to company. Accompany it with egg noodles and a good crusty bread to soak up the delicious sauce.

1 (3½-lb.) beef chuck roast,
    trimmed, cut into 1¾-inch
    pieces
1 (750-ml) bottle dry red wine
1 teaspoon black
    peppercorns, crushed
8 sprigs fresh thyme or
    1 teaspoon dried
8 fresh Italian parsley stems
    (reserve leaves for
    garnish)
2 (2x½-inch) strips orange
    peel
1 bay leaf
1 tablespoon olive oil
2 cups chopped onions
1 cup chopped carrots
4 garlic cloves, minced
1 (28-oz.) can plum tomatoes,
    drained
¼ teaspoon freshly ground
    pepper
⅔ cup niçoise olives, pitted
⅛ teaspoon salt, if desired
½ cup chopped fresh Italian
    parsley

1. In large glass baking dish or resealable plastic bag, combine beef, wine and peppercorns. Cover; refrigerate at least 2 hours or overnight to marinate.
2. Heat oven to 300°F. With butchers' twine and cheesecloth, tie thyme, parsley stems, orange peel and bay leaf together to make a bouquet garni. Set aside.
3. Drain beef, reserving marinade. Dry beef with paper towels. Heat oil in non-reactive Dutch oven over medium-high heat until hot. Brown beef in batches 2

Provençale Beef Stew with Olives

OLIVE BASICS

Despite their salty, pickled flavor when cured, olives are a fruit—they're members of the apricot and cherry family. They are distinguished from other fruits by their low sugar and high oil contents, and their characteristic bitter flavor. In the raw state, olives are positively inedible due to their extreme bitterness.

Curing: There are many ways to cure olives to remove the bitterness and render them palatable.

• Lye-curing is the quickest way to leach bitterness from olives. The fruit is treated with an alkaline solution, such as lye, wood ash or caustic soda. The olives are rinsed to remove all traces of the curing solution, then seasoned with a salty brine. This process produces mild-flavored olives. By international standards, they are called treated olives. Canned California green and black ripe olives are examples of this type of curing.

• Brine-curing removes bitterness by soaking olives in a salt-brine solution. It's a much longer process, but it creates olives with a much richer, more complex flavor. When olives are placed directly in brine without prior alkaline treatment, they are labeled untreated black olives. Niçoise, Kalamata and Greek-style ripe olives in brine are cured in this manner.

• Dry-curing is accomplished by layering olives with dry salt. Some dry-cured olives are treated briefly with an alkaline solution before salting, while others are packed directly in salt for curing. Some dry-cured olives are labeled oil-cured because they are rubbed with oil after curing. Dry-cured olives have an intense meaty—but not pickled—taste. You can identify dry-cured olives by their shriveled skin, deep black color and lack of brine. Popular varieties of dry-cured olives hail from Morocco, Gaeta in Italy,

Nyons in France and Thasos in Greece.

Color: Typically, green olives are picked once they have reached normal size but before they are ripe. The term "black olives" (or ripe olives) generally refers to olives that have been allowed to ripen before harvesting. However, California "ripe black" olives are harvested at an immature state and turn black through exposure to oxygen during processing.

Cooking with olives: The distinctive flavor of olives dissipates with prolonged cooking. Add them at the beginning of cooking in dishes with a brief cooking time, but wait until near the end of cooking to add olives to long-simmered dishes. You can reduce saltiness in brine-cured olives and help them blend with (rather than overpower) other ingredients in a recipe by soaking the olives in cold water for about 20 minutes or by blanching them briefly in boiling water before adding to the dish.

Pitting olives: You can purchase a tool resembling a hole punch that is designed for pitting olives and cherries, but it is effective only for pitting firm olives of a standard size, such as Kalamatas. The easiest way to pit all varieties of brine-cured olives is to rest the side of a chef's knife blade on the olive and gently tap the knife with your free hand. The olive will split open and you can then slip out the pit. To pit dry-cured olives, make a slit in the olive with a paring knife and then slip out the pit.

---

to 4 minutes or until well browned on all sides. Remove from Dutch oven; set aside.

4. Add onions and carrots to Dutch oven; cook 4 to 6 minutes or until softened and lightly browned, stirring frequently. Add garlic; cook and stir about 30 seconds. Add reserved marinade. Bring to a boil, stirring to scrape up any browned bits. Add beef, tomatoes, pepper and bouquet garni. Bring to a boil over medium-high heat.

5. Cover; bake 2½ hours or until beef is almost tender.

6. Add olives to stew; bake an additional 20 to 30 minutes or until beef is very tender.

7. With slotted spoon, transfer beef and olives to serving dish; keep warm. Discard bouquet garni. Skim fat from top of sauce with paper towels. If desired, boil sauce over high heat 5 to 10 minutes to intensify flavor and thicken slightly. Add salt. Pour sauce over beef and olives. (Stew can be made up to 2 days ahead. Cover and refrigerate. Reheat gently on stovetop before serving.) Garnish with parsley.

6 (1¼-cup) servings

PER SERVING: 550 calories, 30.5 g total fat (10.5 g saturated fat), 49 g protein, 15 g carbohydrate, 140 mg cholesterol, 485 mg sodium, 3.5 g fiber

Stuffed Chicken Breasts with Olives and Cheese

A simple stuffing of ripe olives and herbed cheese dresses up boneless chicken breasts admirably. The technique of first browning the chicken on the stovetop, then letting it finish cooking in the oven, ensures a moist, succulent result. Round out the meal with roasted red potatoes and steamed green beans.

- 4 boneless skinless chicken breast halves
- 3 tablespoons finely chopped Kalamata olives
- 3 tablespoons (1½ oz.) spreadable cheese with

garlic and herbs
2 teaspoons chopped fresh
 rosemary
2 teaspoons Dijon mustard
2 teaspoons lemon juice
1 teaspoon honey
½ teaspoon salt
½ teaspoon freshly ground
 pepper
1 tablespoon olive oil

1. Create a pocket by cutting a 3-inch horizontal slit in each chicken breast half. Place ¼ each of the olives and cheese in each pocket. Close pockets; secure with toothpicks. Place on plate; cover and refrigerate at least 30 minutes or up to 8 hours.

2. Heat oven to 375°F. In small bowl, combine rosemary, mustard, lemon juice and honey; mix well.

3. Sprinkle chicken with salt and pepper. Heat oil in large ovenproof skillet over medium-high heat until hot. Add chicken; cook 2 to 3 minutes or until lightly browned. Turn chicken; brush tops with rosemary mixture.

4. Place skillet in oven. Bake about 20 minutes or until chicken is tender and juices run clear. Remove toothpicks before serving.

4 servings

PER SERVING: 290 calories, 17.5 g total fat (5.5 g saturated fat), 29.5 g protein, 3 g carbohydrate, 90 mg cholesterol, 530 mg sodium, .5 g fiber

SELECTING OLIVES

Olives are frequently named for their place of origin, but some are labeled by the cultivar and still others are known by the method of curing used.

Inconsistencies abound. Olives are a seasonal, live (in a continuous fermentation process) product and vary considerably from batch to batch. If possible, sample olives before purchasing. Here is a brief list of some good choices for nibbling and cooking. If your grocery store doesn't carry these, check Italian or Greek specialty stores. Some delis also carry imported olives.

Green cracked: Most green olives are treated with lye, but you can find some that are cured using a traditional salt-brine method. A slit in the firm skin allows the brine to penetrate more quickly.

grown extensively in Spain and California.

Kalamata: From the region near the city of Kalamata in Greece, these almond-shaped ripe olives are slit, cured in salt brine and packed in vinegar.

Gaeta: A popular and flavorful olive from Italy, you will find both brine-cured and dry-cured olives labeled Gaetas.

Niçoise: This tiny, dark, brownish-purple olive from France is cured in brine. It has a somewhat tangy but delicate taste.

Picholine: Although associated with France, this variety is also produced widely in Morocco. It has a delightful fruity flavor.

Manzanilla: The ubiquitous martini olive, the manzanilla is almost always lye-cured. This variety is

LAMB
SAMPLER

Armenian Lamb Kabobs

Five inspired recipes showcase lamb's versatility.

Text and Recipes by Catherine Evans

When I put lamb on the menu for my spring cooking classes, those classes always sell out faster than others do. That tells me that many people are interested in learning how to cook this meat that is a bestseller in many restaurants but seldom served in American homes.

Why aren't more people preparing lamb at home? Perhaps my students had experiences like I did as a child. One of our special meals was roast leg of lamb. As was the custom at the time, my mother roasted the lamb to a uniform, well-done gray. The meat was always served with lots of gravy—because it was so dry. We thought it was a good dinner back then, but I wouldn't want to go back to those days.

Fortunately, we don't have to. Today, almost all lamb sold in stores is from animals less than a year old, and the meat is mild, tender and very tasty. Because of its tenderness, there's no reason to cook the lamb as long as my mother did, or as long as many old recipes suggest. The recipes here prove it—none cooks for more than half an hour; some cook in just 10 minutes!

Armenian Lamb Kabobs

My Armenian friends always cook kabobs in the manner described here: meat and each type of vegetable on separate skewers. This allows you to grill each ingredient to the right doneness. Serve the kabobs with grilled pita bread.

LAMB
- 1 cup plain yogurt
- ½ cup chopped onion
- ½ teaspoon paprika
- 2 garlic cloves, minced
- 1¼ lb. boneless leg of lamb, cut into 1½-inch pieces

SAUCE
- ¾ cup plain yogurt
- 1 teaspoon dried oregano
- ¼ teaspoon minced garlic

VEGETABLES
- 1 Japanese* or baby eggplant, cut into 1½-inch pieces
- 1 yellow bell pepper, cut into 1½-inch pieces
- 1 large onion, cut into 8 wedges
- 8 mushrooms
- 8 cherry tomatoes
- 2 tablespoons olive oil
- ¼ teaspoon salt

1. In large bowl, combine all lamb ingredients except lamb; mix well. Add lamb; stir to coat. Cover; refrigerate at least 1 hour or up to 12 hours.
2. Meanwhile, combine all sauce ingredients; cover and refrigerate.
3. When ready to grill, heat grill. Thread lamb onto 3 (12-inch) metal skewers; discard marinade. Thread each type of vegetable on separate 12-inch metal skewers. Brush vegetables with oil; sprinkle lamb and vegetables with salt.
4. Place kabobs on gas grill over medium heat or on charcoal grill 4 to 6 inches from medium coals. Cook lamb 10 to 12 minutes or until of desired doneness, turning once. Cook vegetables 4 to 12 minutes, turning once, removing vegetables when just tender.
5. Remove lamb and vegetables from skewers; arrange on large platter. Serve with sauce.

TIP *Japanese eggplants are long, slender eggplants that are deep purple in color. They are about one-fourth the size of the large purple eggplants usually found in the markets.

4 servings

PER SERVING: 385 calories, 18 g total fat (5 g saturated fat), 36 g protein, 19.5 g carbohydrate, 100 mg cholesterol, 275 mg sodium, 4.5 g fiber

Thai Lamb with Mint

The classic British combination of roast lamb and mint jelly is transformed here in an Asian stir-fry infused with generous amounts of fresh mint.

Thai Lamb with Mint

4 servings

PER SERVING: 290 calories, 15 g total fat (4 g saturated fat), 26.5 g protein, 12.5 g carbohydrate, 80 mg cholesterol, 410 mg sodium, 1.5 g fiber

Lamb Tagine

A traditional Moroccan tagine, or stew, simmers for a long time. This variation shortens the cooking time by using the tender leg portion of the lamb. Serve over quick-cooking couscous to soak up the fragrant juices.

1 tablespoon vegetable oil
1 onion, chopped
3 garlic cloves, minced
2 lb. boneless leg of lamb, cut into 1½-inch pieces
1 yellow summer squash
1 red bell pepper
1 green bell pepper
¼ lb. green beans
¾ cup reduced-sodium chicken broth
½ cup baby carrots
1 cup canned garbanzo beans, rinsed, drained
⅓ cup raisins
½ teaspoon ground cumin
¼ teaspoon salt
¼ teaspoon freshly ground pepper
⅛ teaspoon cinnamon
2 tablespoons water
1 tablespoon cornstarch

1. In large pot or nonreactive Dutch oven, heat oil over low heat until hot. Add onion and garlic; sauté 3 minutes. Stir in lamb; cover and cook about 10 minutes.
2. Meanwhile, cut squash, red bell pepper and green bell pepper into 1-inch pieces. Cut green beans into 2-inch pieces.
3. Add broth to lamb; bring to a boil. Layer squash, carrots, red bell pepper, green bell pepper, green beans, garbanzo beans and raisins over lamb. Sprinkle with cumin, salt, pepper and

1 tablespoon sugar
2 tablespoons fish sauce*
1 tablespoon water
2 teaspoons cornstarch
2 tablespoons vegetable oil
1 lb. boneless leg of lamb, thinly sliced
3 garlic cloves, minced
1 jalapeño pepper, seeded, chopped
1 red bell pepper, cut into thin strips
1 large onion, halved, cut into thin wedges
¾ cup chopped fresh mint

1. In small bowl, combine sugar, fish sauce, water and cornstarch; mix well. Set aside.

2. Heat 1 tablespoon of the oil in wok or large skillet over high heat. Cook lamb in batches 2 to 3 minutes or until brown. Remove lamb from wok; set aside.
3. Add remaining tablespoon oil to wok. Add garlic and jalapeño; stir-fry briefly. Add bell pepper and onion; stir-fry 2 to 4 minutes or until onion begins to soften.
4. Return lamb to wok. Cook until hot. Add fish sauce mixture to lamb; toss to coat. Bring to a gentle boil; cook until thickened. Stir in mint.
TIP *Fish sauce, also known as nam pla (Thailand) or nuoc mam (Vietnam), can be purchased in the Asian section of the supermarket or in Asian markets.

cinnamon. Cover and simmer 10 to 15 minutes or until lamb and vegetables are tender.

4. In small bowl, combine water and cornstarch; blend well. Add to lamb mixture; bring to a boil. Cook until thickened.

TIP For extra spice, serve with harissa, a Middle Eastern hot sauce flavored with cumin, garlic and coriander. It can be found in some supermarkets and specialty stores, or in Middle Eastern markets.

6 servings

PER SERVING: 360 calories, 13.5 g total fat (4 g saturated fat), 36.5 g protein, 22 g carbohydrate, 105 mg cholesterol, 260 mg sodium, 3.5 g fiber

Lamb Burgers

Fresh herbs add Mediterranean flavor to these tasty burgers. For juiciest texture, be careful not to overcook them.

BURGERS
- 1 lb. ground lamb
- 2 tablespoons minced fresh parsley
- 1 tablespoon minced fresh mint
- 2 teaspoons minced fresh oregano
- ¼ teaspoon freshly ground pepper
- 1 garlic clove, finely minced
- 2 tablespoons minced shallot
- 3 tablespoons red wine, if desired

TOPPING
- 4 sandwich buns, split
- 4 large slices tomato
- 4 sprigs fresh mint

1. In large bowl, combine all burger ingredients; mix well. Shape into 4 (4-inch) patties.*

2. Heat grill.** Place patties on gas grill over medium heat or on charcoal grill 4 to 6 inches from medium coals. Cook 10 to 12 minutes or until internal tem-

perature reaches 160°F., turning once.

3. Place patties in sandwich buns; top with tomato slices and mint sprigs.

TIPS *Ground meat has a better texture and flavor if it is not compressed too hard. Use just enough pressure so the meat holds together.

**To pan fry, sprinkle a small amount of salt in bottom of large nonstick skillet. Heat over medium-high heat until hot. Add patties; cook 8 to 10 minutes or until internal temperature reaches 160°F., turning once.

4 sandwiches

PER SANDWICH: 350 calories, 18 g total fat (7 g saturated fat), 22 g protein, 24 g carbohydrate, 70 mg cholesterol, 295 mg sodium, 1.5 g fiber

Grilled Marinated Leg of Lamb

Ask the butcher for a boneless leg of lamb that has been butterflied (split down the center), an ideal cut for grilling. The butterflied leg will be thicker in some parts, thinner in others, resulting in areas with varying degrees of doneness—a bonus if some of your guests like their meat more well done than others.

LAMB
- ½ boneless leg of lamb (sirloin half, about 2½ lb.)
- 4 garlic cloves, minced

MARINADE
- 1 cup red wine
- ¼ cup olive oil
- 2 tablespoons coarsely chopped fresh rosemary
- 1 tablespoon coarsely chopped fresh thyme
- ⅛ teaspoon freshly ground pepper
- ¼ teaspoon kosher (coarse) salt
- 2 tablespoons chopped onion

1. Trim lamb; make cuts through thick sections of meat to allow marinade to penetrate. Rub garlic on all sides of lamb.

2. In large resealable plastic bag, combine all marinade ingredients; mix well. Add lamb; seal bag. Refrigerate 6 to 12 hours, turning occasionally.

3. When ready to grill, heat grill. Remove lamb from marinade; discard marinade. Place lamb on gas grill over medium heat or on charcoal grill 4 to 6 inches from medium coals. Cook 25 to 35 minutes or until of desired doneness, turning once.

6 servings

PER SERVING: 310 calories, 15.5 g total fat (5 g saturated fat), 40.5 g protein, .5 g carbohydrate, 130 mg cholesterol, 125 mg sodium, 0 g fiber

ABOUT LAMB

Most of the recipes here call for boneless leg of lamb. One of the most versatile cuts of lamb, it can be sliced into strips for stir-frying, cut into chunks for kabobs or stew, butterflied for grilling, or ground for burgers. Here's what to look for in the market:

- Some of the large warehouse stores carry boneless leg of lamb in Cryovac vacuum packaging.

- You may also find leg of lamb rolled up and wrapped in netting. If you're using just part of the leg, unroll the lamb, cut off what you need, roll up the remaining meat and freeze it.

- Your market may carry frozen leg of lamb; defrost it in the refrigerator.

- If you can't find leg of lamb already boned, ask your butcher to bone it for you.

ROASTING
ON THE FAST TRACK

Roast Pork with Pears and Sweet Onions

Turn up the heat for juicy, crackly-skinned meat.

Text by Mary Caldwell; Recipes by Liz Clark

If you're one of those people for whom the crisp, irresistibly golden-brown skin of a perfectly roasted chicken is the best part of the entree, then quick roasting—cooking meat and poultry at a high heat—is for you. Wonderful things happen when you hike up the oven temperature past the more conventional 325°F. or 350°F. At 450°F., the intensity of the hot, dry air makes the surface moisture of food evaporate more quickly. It caramelizes sugars and browns fats very effectively, yielding a richly colored, crackly exterior that has an intensity of flavor unmatched by that of foods cooked at lower temperatures. Season with Mediterranean olives, fragrant herbs or an intriguing Indian-inspired blend of pungent and sweet spices, and the results are all the more enticing.

The other benefits of quick roasting? Well, it's quick! Depending on the food to be cooked, the technique can easily shave 15 to 30 minutes from preparation time. And it doesn't require constant monitoring, so you can assemble the rest of the meal while the entree cooks.

Roast Pork with Pears and Sweet Onions

The sweetness of pears and sweet onions complements this succulent roast pork. To complete the meal, serve a crisp green salad and crusty peasant bread.

- 2 tablespoons extra-virgin olive oil
- 1 (2-lb.) boneless center-cut pork loin
- ¼ teaspoon sea salt
- ¼ teaspoon freshly ground pepper
- 2 large sweet onions, cut into ¾-inch wedges
- 3 firm pears (Anjou or Bosc), unpeeled, cut into sixths
- 1 tablespoon chopped fresh rosemary

1. Heat oven to 450°F. Heat oil in shallow roasting pan or large ovenproof skillet.

2. Sprinkle pork with salt and pepper. Add pork and onions to pan; cook 6 to 8 minutes or until pork is browned on all sides.
3. Add pears and rosemary. Bake 35 to 40 minutes or until internal temperature reaches 155°F. Let stand 10 minutes before serving.
6 servings

PER SERVING: 400 calories, 22.5 g total fat (7 g saturated fat), 32 g protein, 17 g carbohydrate, 95 mg cholesterol, 155 mg sodium, 3 g fiber

Roast Chicken with Garam Masala

Garam masala is a northern Indian spice blend. There are many variations, but all contain both sweet and hot spices. You can purchase a blend, but if you mix it yourself, you can customize the flavors as we do here.

GARAM MASALA
- 1½ teaspoons cumin seeds
- 1½ teaspoons coriander seeds
- 1 teaspoon turmeric
- 1 teaspoon cinnamon
- ½ teaspoon whole cloves
- ½ teaspoon whole black peppercorns
- ¼ teaspoon freshly grated nutmeg
- ¼ teaspoon ground red pepper (cayenne)
- ¼ teaspoon cardamom seeds*

CHICKEN
- 4 chicken legs
- 4 chicken thighs

1. Heat oven to 450°F. Line 15x10x1-inch pan with foil. Place wire rack over foil; spray rack with nonstick cooking spray.
2. In blender or spice grinder, combine all garam masala ingredients; process until finely ground.
3. Rub chicken legs and thighs with garam masala, coating all sides. Place chicken on rack in pan; let stand at

Roast Salmon with Asian Glaze

room temperature at least 15 minutes to allow chicken to absorb spices.
4. Bake at 450°F. for 15 minutes. Reduce oven temperature to 425°F.; bake an additional 15 minutes or until juices run clear. Let stand 10 minutes before serving.
TIP *Cardamom can be purchased whole without the pods.
8 servings

PER SERVING: 140 calories, 8 g total fat (2.5 g saturated fat), 15 g protein, 1 g carbohydrate, 50 mg cholesterol, 50 mg sodium, .5 g fiber

Roast Salmon with Asian Glaze

To speed up preparation time, have the butcher remove the skin from the salmon for you. You can make the glaze a day

ahead of time and refrigerate it until you're ready to use it.

1   (2-lb.) salmon fillet, skin removed
2   tablespoons soy sauce
2   tablespoons Thai sweet chili sauce
1   tablespoon rice vinegar
1   tablespoon dark sesame oil

TECHNIQUE TIPS

Picking pans: The best pan for roasting is slightly larger than the food. There should be an inch or two between the food and the sides of the pan so hot air can circulate. If the pan is too large, the drippings will burn. Its sides should be low enough to allow the food to rise above the pan but high enough to accept a rack and minimize spatters. It should be made of a material that conducts heat evenly but doesn't react with acidic foods. Anodized aluminum, tempered glass and enameled cast iron work well. Cast iron pans work well when acidic foods aren't used. Lightweight aluminum pans may lead to scorching, especially at high temperatures, and they may impart an unpleasant tinny taste to dishes that contain acidic ingredients such as tomatoes.

Rack 'em up: In most cases, setting food on a rack allows the fat to drain off and the hot air to circulate all around the food for optimum browning. For the best mingling of flavors, however, skip the rack when cooking meat or poultry on a bed of ingredients such as onions, apples or potatoes.

Baste: In quick roasting, basting might inhibit development of the characteristic crisp exterior and would make a quick recipe unnecessarily labor-intensive.

Don't truss: When quick roasting, trussing poultry slows cooking and prevents the skin between the legs and the body from browning.

Check the temperature: Roasting times vary slightly depending on the thickness of the meat and the oven thermostat's accuracy. A meat thermometer eliminates guesswork, so you can cook to your taste and, more importantly, ensure that the meat's internal temperature is high enough to kill any bacteria that might be present.

Give it a rest: Let meat sit on the counter for 10 to 15 minutes before slicing. This gives the meat a chance to relax and allows the juices to flow back evenly throughout the meat. The meat will also continue to cook from the retained heat (the internal temperature will rise slightly as the meat rests).

2 garlic cloves, minced

1. Place salmon fillet in large shallow glass baking dish. In small bowl, combine all remaining ingredients; blend well. Pour mixture over salmon; turn salmon to thoroughly coat. Let stand at room temperature 15 minutes to marinate.

2. Meanwhile, heat oven to 450°F. Line

15x10x1-inch baking pan with foil. Place salmon on pan. Bake 12 to 18 minutes or until fish just begins to flake.

6 servings

PER SERVING: 190 calories, 8.5 g total fat (1.5 g saturated fat), 26 g protein, 1 g carbohydrate, 70 mg cholesterol, 155 mg sodium, 0 g fiber

Bistro Roast Chicken with New Potatoes and Green Olives

For a perfectly roasted chicken with moist flesh and a crisp, golden skin, don't truss it. You'll slow down the roasting time and prevent the leg skin from becoming crisp.

  1 (3½-lb.) whole chicken (free range, if available)
  1 lemon, halved
  1 large garlic clove, halved
  ½ teaspoon sea salt
  ½ teaspoon freshly ground pepper
 16 small new red potatoes, unpeeled
  1 cup pitted cracked green olives*
  4 garlic cloves, minced
  2 tablespoons extra-virgin olive oil
  2 teaspoons dried thyme

1. Heat oven to 450°F. Place rack in shallow roasting pan; spray with non-stick cooking spray.
2. Rub chicken inside and out with lemon halves; then rub with halved garlic clove. Place lemon and garlic halves inside chicken cavity. Sprinkle chicken inside and out with ¼ teaspoon each of the salt and pepper. Place chicken breast side down on sprayed rack in pan. Bake 20 minutes.
3. Meanwhile, quarter potatoes; place in large bowl. Add olives, garlic, oil, thyme and remaining ¼ teaspoon each of the salt and pepper; stir to coat thoroughly.
4. Remove chicken from oven. Place

chicken on plate; remove rack from pan. Spoon olives and potatoes into pan. Place chicken breast side up on top of olives and potatoes. Return to oven; bake an additional 20 to 25 minutes or until internal temperature reaches 180°F. Remove from oven; let stand 10 minutes before carving.
TIP *Cracked green olives are cracked before they are cured, allowing the brine to seep into the olive, removing bitterness and adding flavor. Spanish green olives can be substituted.

6 servings

PER SERVING: 580 calories, 21.5 g total fat (5 g saturated fat), 37 g protein, 59 g carbohydrate, 95 mg cholesterol, 885 mg sodium, 6 g fiber

Roast Rock Cornish Game Hens with Herbes de Provence

Coating the game hens with an oil and herb mixture keeps them moist while they roast.

  3 (24-oz.) Rock Cornish game hens, thawed
  ¼ cup extra-virgin olive oil
  1 tablespoon red wine vinegar
  3 garlic cloves, minced
  ¼ cup dried herbes de Provence*
  ½ teaspoon sea salt
  ¼ teaspoon freshly ground pepper

1. Heat oven to 450°F. To split game hens, place hen on cutting surface breast side up. Using kitchen shears, cut breast in half, starting from neck end. Turn hen over. With shears, cut down both sides of back bone; discard back bone or save for stock. Repeat with remaining game hens.
2. Place game hen halves in shallow glass baking dish. Add oil, vinegar, garlic, herbes de Provence, salt and pepper. Turn to coat hens evenly with mixture. Let stand 10 minutes.

3. Place rack in shallow roasting pan large enough to hold game hens in one layer. Place game hen halves skin side up on rack. With pastry brush, brush all of oil mixture over hens.
4. Bake 35 to 40 minutes or until golden brown and internal temperature reaches 185°F.
TIP *When adding herbes de Provence, rub mixture between fingers to slightly crush herbs and release volatile oils. Two teaspoons dried basil, marjoram, rosemary, sage and/or thyme can be substituted for the herbes de Provence.

6 servings

PER SERVING: 385 calories, 30 g total fat (7 g saturated fat), 26 g protein, 1 g carbohydrate, 150 mg cholesterol, 270 mg sodium, 0 g fiber

RECIPE
HOW-TO

SPLITTING GAME HENS

We suggest splitting the Roast Rock Cornish Game Hens because they'll cook faster and they're easier to eat.

To split a game hen for roasting, place the hen, breast side up, on a cutting surface. Using kitchen shears, cut the breast in half, starting from the neck end. Then turn over the hen and cut away the meat from both sides of the back bone, leaving two halves.

Bistro Roast Chicken with New Potatoes and Green Olives

Vegetables Grilled with Curried Oil and Mint Raita

Grilled foods showcase the flavors and textures of India.

Text and Recipes by Swati Elavia

Americans are discovering the foods of India and have begun to appreciate the complex palate of flavors that make up this highly developed cuisine. One of the most popular styles of Indian cooking is the traditional North Indian tandoori method, in which various spices are used to flavor food that is cooked at a very high temperature in a clay-lined oven, called a tandoor. The drum-shaped tandoor essentially bakes, broils and grills food. Dishes cooked this way acquire a spice-rich, earthy flavor.

While it's not practical to use a tandoor here, you can obtain similar results. The spice blends used in India are easily duplicated. And cooking food on a grill nearly duplicates the intense-heat cooking of the tandoor. Get a taste of India in your own backyard, at any time of year.

Vegetables Grilled with Curried Oil and Mint Raita

Although vegetables traditionally are cooked on the stove top in India, chefs and adventurous home cooks have started to grill them in a tandoor or on a conventional grill. Dijon mustard in the oil is reminiscent of Indian pickling spice.

CURRIED OIL
- 3 tablespoons butter
- 3 tablespoons vegetable oil
- 1 tablespoon yellow mustard seeds
- 4 teaspoons fennel seeds
- ¾ cup finely chopped onion
- 2 teaspoons ground cumin
- 2 teaspoons crushed red pepper flakes
- 1 teaspoon salt
- ⅓ cup fresh lime juice
- 3 tablespoons Dijon mustard

VEGETABLES
- 2 ears corn, husked, each cut into 4 pieces
- 2 medium zucchini, quartered
- 1 medium eggplant, cut crosswise into ½-inch-thick slices
- 1 medium yellow bell pepper, cut into 6 wedges
- 1 medium red bell pepper, cut into 6 wedges
- 8 asparagus spears

GARNISH
- Cilantro sprigs
- Mint Raita (recipe follows)

1. Melt butter in small saucepan over medium heat. Add oil; heat over high heat. Add mustard seeds; reduce heat to medium. Immediately cover to avoid splattering. Once popping noise stops, add fennel seeds; cook 30 seconds. Add onion; sauté 6 to 8 minutes or until light golden brown. Add all remaining curried oil ingredients; mix until well blended.
2. Heat grill. Arrange vegetables in single layer on ungreased baking sheet. Brush all sides of vegetables with half of the curried oil.
3. Place corn on gas grill over medium heat or on charcoal grill 4 to 6 inches from medium coals. Cook 5 minutes. Add remaining vegetables; cook an additional 6 to 8 minutes or until all vegetables are tender and lightly charred, turning once and brushing with curried oil after turning.
4. Place vegetables on platter. Garnish with cilantro sprigs. Serve immediately with Mint Raita.

6 servings

PER SERVING: 245 calories, 15 g total fat (4.5 g saturated fat), 7 g protein, 25 g carbohydrate, 16 mg cholesterol, 765 mg sodium, 5.5 g fiber

Mint Raita

- 1 teaspoon ground cumin
- 1 tablespoon chopped fresh mint
- 1 tablespoon chopped fresh cilantro
- ½ teaspoon salt
- ½ teaspoon sugar
- 1 (8-oz.) container nonfat plain yogurt

1. To toast cumin, place in dry small skillet. Cook over medium heat 30 to 60 seconds or until fragrant and slightly

Sea Bass in Cilantro-Coconut Chutney

olive oil; sprinkle with 2 teaspoons cumin and 1 teaspoon pepper. Place lamb chops on gas grill over medium heat or on charcoal grill 4 to 6 inches from medium coals. Cook 7 to 10 minutes for medium-rare to medium, turning once and brushing with glaze during last minute of cooking time. Remove lamb chops from grill; brush with glaze. Serve with remaining glaze. **4 servings**

PER SERVING: 415 calories, 19 g total fat (5 g saturated fat), 36 g protein, 26.5 g carbohydrate, 115 mg cholesterol, 530 mg sodium, 1.5 g fiber

Indian Shami Burgers

A combination of fresh and dried spices flavor this succulent burger. Other ground meats, such as lamb, can be substituted for the beef.

- 1 lb. lean ground beef
- ⅓ cup minced onion
- ¼ cup dry bread crumbs
- 2 tablespoons chopped fresh cilantro
- 1 tablespoon chopped fresh mint
- 1 tablespoon minced fresh ginger
- 1 tablespoon minced garlic
- 1 teaspoon salt
- 1 teaspoon garam masala*
- 1 teaspoon chopped jalapeño chile
- ½ teaspoon cayenne
- 2 tablespoons lime juice
- 4 sandwich buns or pita breads

1. In medium bowl, combine all ingredients except buns; mix well. Refrigerate up to 30 minutes.
2. Heat grill. Shape mixture into 4 (4-inch) patties. Place patties on gas grill over medium heat or on charcoal grill 4 to 6 inches from medium coals. Cook 8 to 10 minutes or until thoroughly cooked, turning once. Place patties on buns.

darker in color, stirring constantly.
2. Place cumin in medium bowl. Add all remaining ingredients; mix well. Serve at room temperature with grilled vegetables.

Cardamom Apple-Glazed Lamb Chops

The traditional glaze on these chops is a sweet-and-sour tamarind sauce with a hint of cardamom, but apple butter and spices are a great substitute in an American kitchen.

GLAZE
- ½ cup apple butter
- ½ cup red wine vinegar
- 4 teaspoons packed dark brown sugar
- 1 tablespoon minced fresh ginger
- 1½ teaspoons dried mint
- 1 teaspoon minced garlic

- 1 teaspoon minced jalapeño chile
- 1 teaspoon ground cumin
- 1 teaspoon ground cardamom
- ¾ teaspoon salt
- ½ teaspoon freshly ground pepper
- ¼ cup water

LAMB
- 8 lamb loin chops (1 inch thick)
- 2 tablespoons olive oil
- 2 teaspoons ground cumin
- 1 teaspoon freshly ground pepper

1. In small saucepan, combine all glaze ingredients; mix well. Bring to a boil over medium-high heat. Reduce heat to medium-low; simmer 8 to 10 minutes or until slightly thickened.
2. Heat grill. Brush lamb chops with

TIP *Garam masala is a blend of up to 12 spices, including cinnamon, cloves, cumin and pepper (see pg. 39). It is available in most grocery stores under the Spice Hunter brand or other commercial brands.

4 sandwiches

PER SANDWICH: 400 calories, 19 g total fat (7 g saturated fat), 26 g protein, 30.5 g carbohydrate, 65 mg cholesterol, 935 mg sodium, 2 g fiber

Royal Grilled Chicken

This dish combines the flavor of traditional Indian tikka spices and herbs—seasonings typically used with grilled meats—with the sharp taste of white cheddar.

MARINADE
- ½ cup chopped fresh cilantro
- ½ cup (2 oz.) shredded white cheddar cheese
- 1 tablespoon all-purpose flour
- 1 tablespoon minced fresh ginger
- 1 tablespoon minced garlic
- 1 tablespoon minced jalapeño chile
- 1 teaspoon white pepper
- 1 teaspoon ground cumin
- 1 teaspoon ground mace
- ½ teaspoon ground nutmeg
- ¼ teaspoon salt
- ¼ cup whipping cream
- 1 egg, beaten

CHICKEN
- 1¼ lb. boneless skinless chicken breast halves
  Vegetable oil for grilling

LIME BUTTER
- 2 tablespoons fresh lime juice
- 1 tablespoon butter

1. In medium bowl, combine all marinade ingredients; mix until smooth. Add chicken; rub marinade into chicken to thoroughly coat. Cover; refrigerate at least 3 hours or up to 6 hours.
2. Melt butter in small saucepan over medium heat. Add lime juice; mix well.
3. Heat grill. Lightly brush grill with oil. Remove chicken from marinade; discard any remaining marinade. Place chicken on gas grill over medium heat or on charcoal grill 4 to 6 inches from medium coals. Cook 6 to 10 minutes or until juices run clear, turning once and brushing with lime butter after turning. Remove chicken from grill; brush with lime butter.

4 servings

PER SERVING: 340 calories, 18.5 g total fat (9.5 g saturated fat), 36.5 g protein, 5.5 g carbohydrate, 155 mg cholesterol, 345 mg sodium, .5 g fiber

Sea Bass in Cilantro-Coconut Chutney

An exquisite cilantro-coconut chutney perfectly complements the buttery sea bass.

CHUTNEY
- 1 cup loosely packed chopped fresh cilantro
- ⅓ cup flaked unsweetened coconut
- 1 tablespoon minced jalapeño chile
- 1 teaspoon minced garlic
- 1 teaspoon minced fresh ginger
- 1 teaspoon cumin seeds
- 1 teaspoon sesame seeds
- ½ teaspoon salt
  Dash sugar
- ⅓ cup water
- 3 tablespoons fresh lime juice

FISH
- 4 (6-oz.) sea bass fillets
- 1 teaspoon vegetable oil
- ½ teaspoon freshly ground pepper

1. Heat grill. In blender, combine all chutney ingredients; blend until smooth. Reserve ⅓ cup chutney.
2. Brush sea bass fillets with oil; sprinkle with pepper. Coat top of each fillet generously with remaining chutney; place each on separate sheet of foil. Wrap foil around fish, keeping top of packet open.
3. Place packets on gas grill over medium-high heat or on charcoal grill 4 to 6 inches from medium-high coals. Cook 8 to 10 minutes or until fish just begins to flake, turning fish once. Serve with reserved chutney.

4 servings

PER SERVING: 220 calories, 8 g total fat (4.5 g saturated fat), 33 g protein, 4 g carbohydrate, 90 mg cholesterol, 440 mg sodium, 1.5 g fiber

RECIPE
HOW-TO

GRILLING FISH IN FOIL

In India, Sea Bass in Cilantro-Coconut Chutney would be cooked in banana leaves. The recipe has been adapted for grills by cooking the fish in foil. Cut foil pieces 6 inches larger than each fish fillet. Prepare the fillets as directed in the recipe; then place each fillet on a sheet of foil. Fold up the edges of the foil as shown but don't cover the fish. Leaving the top open prevents the fish from being steamed and allows it to absorb the flavors from the grill. Turn the fish in the foil once during cooking.

SWEETS

Triple Ginger-Pear Bread Pudding

Savor the flavors of the season in bread pudding.

Text and Recipes by Susan G. Purdy

When I was growing up, my mother could be counted on to serve a bowl of warm, custardy challah bread pudding studded with golden raisins to soothe my direst moments, whether from sorrows or sneezes. Of course, there were plenty of hugs and a few words of encouragement as well, but it is the scent of that soft, sweet pudding and its calming embrace that lingers in my taste memory. Bread pudding is still the family cure-all, and I make it for my daughter just as my sister makes it for her sons; it works every time.

While my mother occasionally tucked sliced apples or apricot preserves into her pudding, my own puddings wander farther afield because it's fun to discover different flavors and textures using a variety of breads and fruits. Following a basic recipe, you can showcase seasonal fruits and even transform this relatively humble family spoon food into a special party dessert. Whether you serve these dishes to family or guests, you're certain to start a new dessert tradition.

Triple Ginger-Pear Bread Pudding

Three forms of ginger (grated fresh, ground and crystallized) give surprising pizzazz to the mellow custard and sweet fruit flavor of this pudding. You can vary the quantity of each type of ginger to suit your own taste, or kick it up a notch if you wish. Peaches, nectarines or apricots can be substituted for the pears.

BREAD MIXTURE
- 6 cups lightly packed cubed (1½ inch) challah or Italian country bread
- 2 cups milk
- ⅓ cup sugar
- 1½ teaspoons ground ginger
- ½ teaspoon nutmeg
- 1 teaspoon vanilla
- ½ cup golden raisins

FRUIT
- 2 large Anjou, Bosc or Bartlett pears, peeled, cut into ¾-inch pieces (about 2 cups)
- 1 cup apricot preserves

CUSTARD
- 4 eggs, room temperature
- 1 cup whipping cream
- ¼ cup sugar
- ¼ cup finely chopped crystallized ginger
- 2 teaspoons grated fresh ginger
- ½ teaspoon ground ginger
- ½ teaspoon plus ⅛ teaspoon nutmeg
- ½ teaspoon salt

1. Heat broiler. Place bread in 15x10x1-inch pan. Broil 4 to 6 inches from heat 2 to 3 minutes or until golden, turning once. Watch carefully to prevent burning.

2. Heat oven to 350°F. Grease 2-quart glass baking dish. In large bowl, whisk together all remaining bread mixture ingredients except raisins. Stir in toasted bread and raisins. Let stand 3 to 5 minutes, stirring occasionally, until liquid is absorbed.

3. Add pears; stir gently to mix. Spread mixture evenly in baking dish. Spoon preserves over bread mixture.

4. In same large bowl, whisk eggs until mixed. Add all remaining custard ingredients; whisk until blended. Pour over bread mixture, making sure custard evenly coats bread. Sprinkle additional ⅛ teaspoon nutmeg over top.

5. Bake 65 to 70 minutes or until top is puffed and knife inserted in center comes out almost clean. Cool slightly on wire rack. Serve warm. Refrigerate leftovers.

12 servings

PER SERVING: 320 calories, 10 g total fat (5 g saturated fat), 6 g protein, 54.5 g carbohydrate, 105 mg cholesterol, 200 mg sodium, 2 g fiber

Chocolate Chip Bread Pudding

Chocolate Chip Bread Pudding

In this chocolate-lover's rendition of classic "bread and butter" pudding, chocolate chips replace the raisins traditionally scattered over buttered, toasted slices of crustless bread baked in a yolk-rich egg custard. The secret to extra flavor is to butter the bread and toast it to a rich golden color.

BREAD MIXTURE
- ¼ cup unsalted butter, softened
- 10 slices (½ inch) firm white bread, crusts removed
- 1 cup semisweet chocolate chips
- 2 cups milk
- ¼ cup sugar
- 1 teaspoon vanilla
- ¼ teaspoon ground nutmeg
- Dash salt

CUSTARD
- 3 eggs, room temperature
- 2 egg yolks, room temperature
- 1 cup whipping cream
- ⅓ cup sugar
- ½ teaspoon vanilla
- ¼ teaspoon plus ⅛ teaspoon nutmeg
- ¼ cup semisweet chocolate chips

1. Heat broiler. Generously butter one side of each bread slice; cut each slice diagonally twice to make 4 triangles. Place, butter side up, in 15x10x1-inch pan. Broil 4 to 6 inches from heat 2 to 3 minutes or until toasted, turning once. Watch carefully to prevent burning.
2. Heat oven to 350°F. Butter 2-quart oval glass baking dish. Arrange bread, buttered side up, in overlapping layers in baking dish. Sprinkle with 1 cup chocolate chips.
3. In large bowl, whisk together all remaining bread mixture ingredients.

Roasted Banana Bread Pudding with Bourbon-Praline Sauce

Pour over bread in dish. Let stand 3 to 5 minutes or until liquid is absorbed, stirring occasionally.
4. In same large bowl, whisk eggs and egg yolks until mixed. Add all remaining custard ingredients except ⅛ teaspoon nutmeg and chocolate chips. Whisk custard until blended. Pour over bread mixture, making sure custard evenly coats bread. Sprinkle with ⅛ teaspoon nutmeg and ¼ cup chocolate chips.
5. Bake 50 to 60 minutes or until top is puffed and knife inserted in center comes out almost clean. Cool slightly on wire rack. Serve warm. Refrigerate leftovers.

12 servings

PER SERVING: 310 calories, 19 g total fat (10.5 g saturated fat), 6 g protein, 32.5 g carbohydrate, 125 mg cholesterol, 165 mg sodium, 1.5 g fiber

Roasted Banana Bread Pudding with Bourbon-Praline Sauce

Baked in individual ramekins, this flavorful warm dessert can be served in its dish or unmolded onto a dessert plate. The contrast between the mildly sweet banana flavor and the intense praline sauce is dazzling and transforms the humble pudding into a party show-stopper. Serve with softly whipped cream, if desired.

BREAD MIXTURE
- 4 cups lightly packed cubed
  (¾ inch) challah or
  French bread
- 5 firm ripe bananas
- 1½ cups milk
- ⅓ cup packed light brown
  sugar
- 1 teaspoon cinnamon
- ½ teaspoon nutmeg

CUSTARD
- 3 eggs, room temperature
- 1 cup whipping cream
- ⅓ cup packed light brown
  sugar
- 1 tablespoon bourbon or
  dark rum, if desired
- 1 teaspoon vanilla
- ¼ teaspoon salt
- 2 teaspoons sugar

SAUCE
- ½ cup coarsely chopped
  pecans
- 2 tablespoons unsalted butter
- ½ cup packed dark brown
  sugar
- ½ cup whipping cream
- 2 tablespoons milk
- 2 tablespoons cornstarch
- 1 tablespoon bourbon or
  dark rum, if desired
- 1 teaspoon vanilla
  Dash salt

1. Heat broiler. Generously butter 8 (½-cup) ovenproof ramekins or custard cups. Place ramekins in large shallow pan; ramekins should not touch each other.

2. Place bread in 15x10x1-inch pan. Broil 4 to 6 inches from heat 2 to 3 minutes or until golden brown, turning once. Watch carefully to prevent burning.

3. Heat oven to 425°F. Lightly butter 8-inch square baking pan. Set 1 banana aside for garnish. Peel remaining 4 bananas; place in pan. Bake at 425°F. for 10 to 12 minutes or until soft and slightly browned.

4. Reduce oven temperature to 350°F. Place 2 baked bananas in medium bowl; mash with fork. Let remaining 2 baked bananas cool slightly; cut into ¼-inch slices. (Bananas are very soft but can be sliced.) Place 3 or 4 slices in bottom of each ramekin.

5. In large bowl, whisk together all remaining bread mixture ingredients except reserved banana. Whisk in mashed bananas. Stir in toasted bread. Let stand 4 to 5 minutes or until liquid is absorbed, stirring occasionally.

6. In separate large bowl, whisk eggs until mixed. Add all remaining custard ingredients except 2 teaspoons sugar; whisk until blended. Spoon scant ⅓ cup soaked bread mixture into each ramekin, filling nearly to top; do not pack. Pour custard over bread mixture in each ramekin. Sprinkle with 2 teaspoons sugar.

7. Place ramekins in large shallow pan; fill pan with hot water to about ⅓ way up sides of ramekins. Bake at 350°F. for 45 minutes or until tops are puffed and knife inserted in center comes out clean. Remove puddings from water bath; place on wire rack to cool slightly.

8. Meanwhile, to prepare sauce, place pecans and butter in heavy medium saucepan. Cook over medium heat 4 minutes or until nuts are toasted, stirring frequently. Add ½ cup dark brown sugar and ½ cup cream; stir until smooth. In small bowl, blend 2 tablespoons milk and cornstarch. Stir cornstarch mixture into sauce. Increase heat to medium-high; cook until mixture comes to a boil, stirring constantly. Boil 2 minutes or until thickened, stirring constantly. Remove from heat; stir in 1 tablespoon bourbon, 1 teaspoon vanilla and dash salt. Serve warm. (Store sauce, covered, in refrigerator. If too thick after reheating, stir in 1 to 2 tablespoons milk.)

9. Diagonally slice reserved banana. Serve puddings warm in ramekins, topped by warm sauce and garnished with banana. Or to unmold, run knife around sides of each ramekin; top each

with dessert plate and invert with sharp downward motion. Turn puddings right side up onto plate. Refrigerate leftovers.
8 servings

PER SERVING: 520 calories, 26 g total fat (12.5 g saturated fat), 8 g protein, 66.5 g carbohydrate, 150 mg cholesterol, 220 mg sodium, 3 g fiber

Apple-Raisin-Honey Bread Pudding with Maple Sauce

This delicious pudding will remind you of the flavors of fall and the comfort of childhood. It is guaranteed to cure the blues. For a sophisticated finish, serve it warm, with a scoop of vanilla ice cream and a dollop of warm maple sauce made with pure maple syrup.

BREAD MIXTURE
- 5 cups lightly packed cubed
  (1½ inch) Italian country
  bread
- 2 cups milk
- ¼ cup honey
- 2 tablespoons sugar
  Dash salt
- ½ cup raisins
- 2 medium McIntosh apples,
  peeled, sliced
  (about 2 cups)

CUSTARD
- 3 eggs, room temperature
- 1 cup whipping cream
- ⅓ cup honey
- ¼ cup sugar
- 1 teaspoon vanilla
- ¾ teaspoon cinnamon
  Dash salt
- 1 teaspoon nutmeg

SAUCE
- ¼ cup water
- 2 teaspoons cornstarch
- ½ cup whipping cream
- ½ cup pure maple syrup
- ⅛ teaspoon cinnamon

1. Heat broiler. Place bread in 15x10x1-

inch pan. Broil 4 to 6 inches from heat
1 to 2 minutes or until golden brown,
turning once. Watch carefully to prevent
burning.

2. Heat oven to 350°F. Grease 2-quart
glass baking dish. In medium bowl,
whisk together all remaining bread
mixture ingredients except raisins and
apples. Stir in toasted bread and raisins.
Let stand 3 to 5 minutes or until liquid
is absorbed, stirring occasionally. Add
apples; stir gently to mix. Spoon into
baking dish.

3. In large bowl, whisk eggs until
mixed. Add all remaining custard ingredients except nutmeg. Add ¾ teaspoon
of the nutmeg; whisk custard until
blended. Pour over bread mixture, making sure custard evenly coats bread.
Sprinkle with remaining ¼ teaspoon
nutmeg.

4. Bake 55 to 65 minutes or until top is
puffed and knife inserted in center
comes out almost clean. Cool slightly
on wire rack. Serve warm with sauce.

5. Meanwhile, to prepare sauce, in
small bowl blend water and cornstarch
until smooth. In small saucepan, cook
½ cup cream, syrup and ⅛ teaspoon
cinnamon over medium heat until hot,
stirring often. Stir in cornstarch mixture. Bring to a boil. Boil 2 to 3 minutes
or until thick enough to coat back of
spoon, stirring constantly. Serve warm.
(Store sauce, covered, in refrigerator. If
too thick after reheating, stir in 1 to 2
tablespoons milk.) Refrigerate leftovers.
12 servings

PER SERVING: 295 calories, 12 g total fat (7 g saturated fat), 5
g protein, 45 g carbohydrate, 90 mg cholesterol, 155 mg sodium, 1 g fiber

Toasted Pecan-Pumpkin Bread Pudding

*This homey pudding made with toasted
pecans combines all the taste of a well-
spiced pumpkin pie with the rich texture
of a satisfying bread pudding. If you have
leftover pumpkin bread, try it in place of
the challah.*

BREAD MIXTURE
- 6 cups lightly packed cubed (1½ inch) challah or Italian country bread
- 1½ cups chopped pecans
- 2 cups milk
- ¼ cup packed brown sugar
- 1 teaspoon cinnamon
- ½ teaspoon ground ginger
- ½ teaspoon ground allspice
- ½ teaspoon nutmeg
- ⅛ teaspoon ground cloves
- 1 teaspoon vanilla

CUSTARD
- 4 eggs, room temperature
- 1 (15-oz.) can pumpkin
- 1 cup whipping cream
- ½ cup packed brown sugar
- 1½ teaspoons cinnamon
- 1 teaspoon ground ginger
- 1 teaspoon nutmeg
- ½ teaspoon salt
- ¼ teaspoon ground cloves

1. Heat broiler. Place bread in 15x10x1-
inch pan. Broil 4 to 6 inches from heat
60 to 90 seconds or until toasted, turning once. Watch carefully to prevent
burning.

2. Heat oven to 350°F. Spray 2-quart
glass baking dish with nonstick cooking
spray. Spread pecans on baking sheet.
Bake 7 to 9 minutes or until lightly
toasted, stirring occasionally. Cool.

3. In large bowl, whisk together all
remaining bread mixture ingredients.
Stir in toasted bread. Let stand 3 to 5
minutes or until liquid is absorbed, stirring occasionally. Stir in 1 cup of the
pecans. Spread mixture evenly in baking dish.

4. In same large bowl, whisk eggs until
mixed. Add all remaining custard ingredients; whisk until blended. Pour over
bread mixture, making sure custard
evenly coats bread. Sprinkle with
remaining ½ cup pecans.

5. Bake 60 to 70 minutes or until top
is puffed and knife inserted in center
comes out almost clean. Cool slightly
on wire rack. Serve warm.

Refrigerate leftovers.
12 servings

PER SERVING: 330 calories, 20 g total fat (6 g saturated fat), 7
g protein, 32.5 g carbohydrate, 105 mg cholesterol, 190 mg
sodium, 3 g fiber

REHEATING BREAD PUDDING

To reheat cold pudding in the oven,
add a splash of milk for moisture and
bake at 325°F. for 10 to 15 minutes
or until warm throughout. To reheat
an individual portion of pudding in
the microwave, partially cover the
pudding with plastic wrap (don't let it
touch the pudding surface) and heat
on high for about 1 minute 20 seconds. Test the temperature in the
center and repeat for a few seconds
longer if needed.

DREAM
CAKES

Espresso and Cream Cake

Airy, delicate sponge cakes set
the stage for elegant desserts.

Text and Recipes by Lisa Saltzman

I grew up thinking there was only one style of cake—the moist, rich butter cake my mother made for birthdays and holidays. When I entered cooking school in Paris, I was surprised to discover a whole new genre I had never experienced—sponge cakes. In France, they are considered the only cake worth learning to make—a perfect foundation upon which a variety of fresh fruits, buttercreams and other fillings rest.

A sponge cake has a light, airy texture and contains no chemical leavening. Where a butter cake is leavened by baking powder and the air beaten into the creamed butter, the sponge cake's leavening is provided completely by air beaten into the eggs. It contains a small amount of butter, added for texture rather than flavor. The result is an extremely versatile cake that can be used as a base for trifles, mousse cakes, jelly rolls and classic buttercream cakes—perfect desserts for entertaining.

Espresso and Cream Cake

This cake is pastry-cart elegant but actually very simple to make. The smooth flavor of espresso, softness of whipped cream and crunch of toasted hazelnuts create a heavenly combination.

CAKE
1 Coffee Sponge Cake
   (recipe follows)

SUGAR SYRUP
¼ cup sugar
¼ cup water
1 tablespoon hazelnut liqueur
   or cold coffee

ESPRESSO CREAM
3 cups whipping cream
6 tablespoons sugar
4 teaspoons instant espresso
   coffee powder
1½ teaspoons vanilla

GARNISH
½ cup finely chopped toasted
   hazelnuts

1. Prepare Coffee Sponge Cake. Slice cake horizontally into 3 layers. Set aside.
2. To prepare sugar syrup, in small saucepan, combine ¼ cup sugar and water. Bring to a boil, stirring until sugar dissolves. Stir in liqueur; cool.
3. In large bowl, combine all espresso cream ingredients; beat at medium speed until soft peaks form. (Do not overbeat or cream will have a grainy appearance.)
4. To assemble cake, place one layer on 9-inch cardboard round or cake platter. Brush with sugar syrup. Spread 1½ cups espresso cream over cake. Place second cake layer on espresso cream. Brush with sugar syrup. Spread with 1½ cups espresso cream. Top with third cake layer; brush with sugar syrup. Cover cake; refrigerate at least 20 minutes. Refrigerate remaining espresso cream.
5. Reserve 1 cup espresso cream for

HAZELNUT GARNISH

To apply the hazelnut garnish on the Espresso and Cream Cake, hold the frosted cake (which has been placed on a cardboard round, removable tart pan bottom or plate) in one hand. With the other hand, scoop up some of the chopped nuts and lightly press them into the frosted sides. Rotate the cake as you work. Place a dish below the cake to catch any nuts that fall so you can reuse them.

Strawbery-Rhubarb Trifle

decorating; frost cake with remaining espresso cream. Press hazelnuts around sides of cake.

6. Place reserved 1 cup espresso cream in pastry bag fitted with small star tip. Pipe rosettes around top of cake. Refrigerate until ready to serve. Store in refrigerator.

12 servings

PER SERVING: 435 calories, 29.5 g total fat (14 g saturated fat), 6 g protein, 39 g carbohydrate, 145 mg cholesterol, 45 mg sodium, 1 g fiber

Coffee Sponge Cake

    4 eggs, room temperature,
      separated

    1 cup sugar
    3 tablespoons warm whole
      milk
    1 tablespoon instant espresso
      coffee powder
    ½ teaspoon vanilla
    1 cup sifted cake flour
    ½ teaspoon cream of tartar
    2 tablespoons unsalted butter,
      melted, cooled

1. Heat oven to 350°F. Spray 9x2-inch round pan with nonstick cooking spray. Line pan with parchment paper; spray paper and lightly flour.

2. In large bowl, combine egg yolks and ½ cup of the sugar; mix well. Place bowl over saucepan of barely simmer-

ing water (bowl should not touch water). Whisk egg mixture constantly 1 to 2 minutes or until sugar is dissolved and mixture is warm to the touch. Remove from heat.

3. Beat mixture at medium-high speed 5 minutes or until mixture is thick enough to hold a 3-second ribbon. Meanwhile, in small bowl, combine milk, espresso coffee powder and vanilla. Reduce speed to medium; slowly add milk mixture, beating until combined. Gradually sift and fold flour into yolk mixture; fold until thoroughly combined.

4. In another large bowl, beat egg whites at medium speed just until frothy. Add cream of tartar. Increase speed to medium-high; beat until soft peaks form. Gradually add remaining ½ cup sugar, beating until stiff peaks form. Fold ¼ of egg whites into batter to lighten mixture. Gently and quickly fold in remaining egg whites until combined.

5. Place butter in medium bowl. Add large spoonful of batter to butter; whisk until well mixed. Fold mixture back into batter. Pour batter into pan, gently spreading evenly.

6. Bake 20 to 30 minutes or until toothpick inserted in center comes out clean and cake springs back when lightly touched. Cool on wire rack 20 minutes. Run small knife around edge of pan to loosen cake; turn cake out onto wire rack. Remove paper; cool completely.

Strawberry-Rhubarb Trifle

This luscious strawberry dessert combines the best qualities of an English trifle, with its sponge cake and fresh fruit, and an Italian tiramisu, using mascarpone and liqueur to soak the cake.

CAKE
    1 Vanilla Sponge Cake
      (recipe follows)

FILLING
    1 lb. rhubarb, sliced

(about 3½ cups)
1½ cups sugar
6 cups sliced fresh
   strawberries
1 tablespoon Grand Marnier
   liqueur or orange juice
8 oz. mascarpone cheese,*
   softened
1 cup whipping cream
⅓ cup powdered sugar

SUGAR SYRUP
2 tablespoons sugar
2 tablespoons water
1 tablespoon Grand Marnier
   liqueur or orange juice

1. Prepare Vanilla Sponge Cake. Slice cake horizontally in half. Set aside.
2. In medium saucepan, combine rhubarb and ½ cup of the sugar; cover and cook over medium heat 10 to 15 minutes or until tender. Remove cover; cook an additional 5 to 10 minutes or until mixture is thickened, stirring constantly. Remove from heat. Refrigerate until cool.
3. Meanwhile, prepare sugar syrup. In small saucepan, combine 2 tablespoons sugar and water. Bring to a boil, stirring until sugar dissolves. Remove from heat. Stir in 1 tablespoon liqueur; cool.
4. Using potato masher, crush 3 cups of the strawberries. In large bowl, combine crushed strawberries, remaining 3 cups sliced strawberries, remaining 1 cup sugar and 1 tablespoon liqueur; mix gently. Set aside.
5. In another large bowl, beat mascarpone at medium speed until smooth. Gradually add cream and powdered sugar; beat at medium speed until stiff peaks form.
6. Generously brush both sides of each cake layer with sugar syrup. Cut cake into 1-inch cubes.
7. To assemble dessert, spoon about ¼ of mascarpone cream over bottom of 13-cup glass bowl. Place ⅓ of cubed cake over mascarpone cream. Spoon ⅓ of rhubarb mixture over cake layer; top with ¼ of mascarpone cream and ⅓ of

the strawberry mixture. Repeat layers twice. Cover; refrigerate up to 3 hours. Store in refrigerator.
TIP *Mascarpone is a rich Italian-style cream cheese. It can be found in the deli or dairy section of grocery stores or specialty markets. If unavailable, substitute cream cheese.
12 servings

PER SERVING: 420 calories, 17 g total fat (10 g saturated fat), 5.5 g protein, 63 g carbohydrate, 120 mg cholesterol, 90 mg sodium, 2.5 g fiber

Vanilla Sponge Cake

4 eggs, room temperature,
   separated
1 cup sugar
3 tablespoons warm whole
   milk
½ teaspoon vanilla
1 cup sifted cake flour
½ teaspoon cream of tartar
2 tablespoons unsalted butter,
   melted, cooled

1. Heat oven to 350°F. Spray 9x2-inch round cake pan with nonstick cooking spray. Line pan with parchment paper; spray paper and lightly flour.
2. In large bowl, combine egg yolks and ½ cup of the sugar; mix well. Place bowl over saucepan of barely simmering water (bowl should not touch water). Whisk egg mixture constantly 1 to 2 minutes or until sugar is dissolved and mixture is warm to the touch.
3. Beat mixture at medium-high speed 5 minutes or until mixture is thick enough to hold a 3-second ribbon. Reduce speed to medium; slowly add milk and vanilla, beating until combined. Gradually sift and fold flour into yolk mixture; fold until thoroughly combined.
4. In another large bowl, beat egg whites just until frothy. Add cream of tartar; beat until soft peaks form. Gradually add remaining ½ cup sugar, beating until stiff peaks form. Fold ¼ of egg whites into batter to lighten mix-

ture. Gently and quickly fold in remaining egg whites until combined.
5. Place butter in medium bowl. Add large spoonful of batter to butter; whisk until well mixed. Fold mixture back into batter. Pour batter into pan, gently spreading evenly.
6. Bake 25 to 35 minutes or until cake springs back when lightly touched and starts to shrink away from sides of pan. Cool in pan on wire rack 20 minutes. Run small knife around edge of pan to loosen cake; turn cake out onto wire rack. Remove paper; cool completely.

Triple Chocolate Mousse Cake

A delicious twist on a classic dessert, this cake is made with three chocolate mousses: semisweet, white and milk chocolate. Make the sponge cake the day before or early in the morning so there's time to chill the assembled cake 2 to 4 hours before serving.

CAKE
1 Chocolate Sponge Cake
   (recipe follows)

SUGAR SYRUP
⅓ cup sugar
⅓ cup water
1 tablespoon dark rum
   or orange juice

FILLING
1½ cups whipping cream
3 oz. semisweet chocolate,
   chopped
2 tablespoons dark rum or
   orange juice
3 oz. white chocolate,
   chopped
4 tablespoons water
3 oz. milk chocolate, chopped
1½ teaspoons instant espresso
   coffee powder

GLAZE
3 oz. semisweet chocolate,
   chopped

¼   cup unsalted butter, cut up
1½ teaspoons corn syrup

1. Prepare Chocolate Sponge Cake. Slice cake horizontally into 4 layers. Set aside.
2. To prepare sugar syrup, in small saucepan, combine sugar and ⅓ cup water. Bring to a boil, stirring until sugar dissolves. Stir in 1 tablespoon rum; cool.
3. In large bowl, beat cream at medium-high speed until soft peaks form. Refrigerate while melting chocolates.
4. In medium microwave-safe bowl, melt 3 oz. semisweet chocolate and 2 tablespoons rum in microwave on high 40 to 60 seconds. Stir until smooth; cool just to room temperature.
5. In separate medium microwave-safe bowl, melt white chocolate and 2 tablespoons of the water in microwave on high 30 to 60 seconds. Stir until smooth; cool just to room temperature. In separate medium microwave-safe bowl, melt milk chocolate, espresso coffee powder and remaining 2 tablespoons water in microwave on high 30 to 60 seconds; cool just to room temperature.
6. Add ⅓ of whipped cream to each bowl of melted chocolate; fold until well mixed.
7. To assemble cake, place bottom cake layer in 9-inch springform pan. Brush generously with sugar syrup. Spread semisweet chocolate mixture on cake layer. Place second cake layer over semisweet chocolate mixture; brush with sugar syrup. Spread milk chocolate mixture on cake. Top with third cake layer; brush with sugar syrup. Spread with white chocolate mixture. Top with final cake layer; brush with sugar syrup. Gently press to even cake layers. Cover; refrigerate 2 to 4 hours.
8. Meanwhile, make glaze. In an-other medium microwave-safe bowl, combine all glaze ingredients. Microwave on high 1 minute or until almost melted. Stir until smooth. Let stand until thickened but still pourable.
9. Pour glaze onto center of chilled cake; spread glaze over top. (Use as few strokes as possible to spread glaze; the more you spread the glaze, the duller the final result well be.) Refrigerate until ready to serve. Just before serving, remove sides of springform pan; smooth sides of cake, if necessary. Store in refrigerator.

16 servings

PER SERVING: 360 calories, 21.5 g total fat (12.5 g saturated fat), 5 g protein, 40 g carbohydrate, 120 mg cholesterol, 45 mg sodium, 2 g fiber

Chocolate Sponge Cake

6   eggs, room temperature, separated
1¼ cups sugar
¼   cup hot water
1   teaspoon vanilla
¾   cup sifted cake flour
½   cup sifted unsweetened cocoa
¾   teaspoon cream of tartar
¼   cup unsalted butter, melted, cooled

1. Heat oven to 350°F. Grease 9-inch springform pan; sprinkle with flour. Line pan with parchment paper.
2. In large bowl, combine egg yolks and ½ cup of the sugar; mix well. Set bowl over saucepan of barely simmering water (bowl should not touch water). Whisk egg mixture constantly 40 to 60 seconds or until sugar is dissolved and mixture is warm to the touch.
3. Beat egg mixture at medium-high speed 5 minutes or until mixture is

Triple Chocolate Mousse Cake

thick and 3-second ribbon forms. Reduce speed to medium; slowly add water and vanilla, beating until combined. Gradually sift and fold flour and cocoa into yolk mixture; fold until thoroughly combined.

4. In another large bowl, beat egg whites at medium speed just until frothy. Add cream of tartar; beat at medium-high speed until soft peaks form. Gradually add remaining ¾ cup sugar, beating until stiff peaks form. Fold ¼ of egg whites into batter to lighten mixture. Gently and quickly fold in remaining egg whites until combined.

5. Place butter in medium bowl. Add large spoonful of batter to butter; whisk until well mixed. Fold mixture back into batter. Pour batter into pan, gently spreading evenly.

6. Bake 35 to 40 minutes or until cake springs back when lightly touched and begins to shrink away from sides of pan. Cool in pan on wire rack 20 minutes. Run small knife around edge of pan to loosen cake; remove sides of springform pan. Turn cake out onto wire rack; remove base and paper. (Cake may sink slightly during cooling. If this happens, simply press edges down to even cake.)

Orange Cassata

For best results, frost the cake in two stages. First apply a thin layer of frosting, called a crumb coat, to seal in crumbs and smooth its shape. Chill the cake for 5 to 10 minutes, then finish frosting it.

CAKE
1 Orange Sponge Cake (recipe follows)

SUGAR SYRUP
2 tablespoons sugar
2 tablespoons water
1 tablespoon Grand Marnier liqueur or orange juice

FILLING
1 (15-oz.) container whole

milk ricotta cheese*
3 tablespoons sugar
3 tablespoons Grand Marnier liqueur or orange juice
2 tablespoons whipping cream
2 oz. semisweet chocolate, chopped
⅓ cup coarsely chopped Candied Orange Peel (recipe follows)

FROSTING
6 oz. semisweet chocolate, chopped
⅓ cup cold coffee
½ cup unsalted butter, softened, cut up

1. Prepare Orange Sponge Cake. Slice cake crosswise to create 3 equal layers.
2. To prepare sugar syrup, in small saucepan, combine 2 tablespoons sugar and water. Bring to a boil, stirring until sugar dissolves. Stir in 1 tablespoon liqueur.
3. Brush both sides of each cake layer with sugar syrup. Set aside.
4. In large bowl, beat ricotta cheese at medium speed until smooth. Add 3 tablespoons sugar, 3 tablespoons liqueur and cream; beat until mixed. Stir in 2 oz. chocolate and candied orange peel.
5. To assemble cake, place one layer on serving platter. Spread with half of filling. Top with second cake layer and remaining half of filling. Top with third cake layer. Cover; refrigerate while preparing frosting.
6. In medium bowl, combine 6 oz. chocolate and coffee. Place bowl over saucepan of barely simmering water (bowl should not touch water). Heat until melted and smooth, stirring occasionally. Remove from heat. Slowly add butter, stirring until melted. Refrigerate until of spreading consistency.
7. If necessary, trim sides of cake until even. Frost with frosting. Refrigerate until ready to serve. Store in refrigerator. Let stand at room temperature 15 minutes before serving.

TIP *Whole milk ricotta cheese is a necessity for this dessert. Low-fat ricotta cheese tends to be very grainy and detracts from the desired creamy texture.
12 servings

PER SERVING: 490 calories, 30 g total fat (18 g saturated fat), 8 g protein, 48.5 g carbohydrate, 140 mg cholesterol, 70 mg sodium, 1.5 g fiber

Orange Sponge Cake
4 eggs, room temperature, separated
1 cup sugar
3 tablespoons warm whole milk
1 tablespoon grated orange peel
½ teaspoon vanilla
1 cup sifted cake flour
½ teaspoon cream of tartar
2 tablespoons unsalted butter, melted, cooled

1. Heat oven to 400°F. Spray 15x10x1-inch pan with nonstick cooking spray. Line pan with parchment paper; spray paper and lightly flour.
2. In large bowl, combine egg yolks and ½ cup of the sugar; mix well. Place bowl over saucepan of barely simmering water (bowl should not touch water). Whisk egg mixture constantly 1 to 2 minutes or until sugar is dissolved and mixture is warm to the touch. Remove from heat.
3. Beat egg mixture at medium-high speed 5 minutes or until mixture is thick enough to hold a 3-second ribbon. Reduce speed to medium; slowly add milk, orange peel and vanilla, beating until combined. Gradually sift and fold flour into yolk mixture; fold until thoroughly combined.
4. In another large bowl, beat egg whites at medium speed just until frothy. Add cream of tartar. Increase speed to medium-high; beat until soft peaks form. Gradually add remaining ½ cup sugar, beating until stiff peaks form. Fold ¼ of egg whites into batter to lighten mixture. Gently and quickly

MIXING IS KEY

The key to making sponge cake is volume—whipping the eggs to their maximum volume and maintaining that volume as much as possible as you add other ingredients. Follow these suggestions for perfect cakes.

Warming the egg yolks

Warm eggs: Warm the egg yolks and sugar before beating by placing the mixing bowl over a pan of barely simmering water. Whisk the mixture constantly for 1 to 2 minutes to warm the yolks and dissolve the sugar. To be certain the sugar has dissolved, rub a small amount of egg between your fingers. The mixture should feel smooth rather than grainy. Warming the egg yolks relaxes the protein in the eggs, speeds the beating process and aids in developing better volume.

Three-second ribbon: Beating the egg yolks to the proper consistency is crucial. For best results, use the three-second ribbon test. Once the beaten yolks have lightened in color and tripled in volume, test them by lifting the whisk and letting the mixture fall back onto the surface of the batter in a ribbon. If it holds its shape for three seconds or more, it is thick enough. If the ribbon disappears quickly back into the batter, continue to beat until it attains a three-second ribbon.

Folding technique: An improper folding technique can easily deflate the volume of the eggs. To fold in the cake flour, sift ⅓ of the flour directly onto the surface of the beaten egg yolk mixture. Using a rubber spatula, cut through the center of the batter down to the bottom of the bowl. Hold the spatula flat against the bowl, scoop along the side of the bowl and fold over the top of the batter. Continue in this circular motion until the batter is fully blended. Repeat this procedure until all the flour is incorporated. To fold the egg whites into the batter, lighten the batter by stirring in a quarter of the beaten whites, then gently but quickly fold in the remaining whites.

Melted butter: The weight of melted butter can cause the butter to sink to the bottom of the bowl or deflate the delicate batter. To avoid problems, place the melted butter in a medium bowl. After the egg whites have been folded into the batter, add a large spoonful of batter to the butter. Whisk the mixture until thoroughly blended. Then carefully fold the butter mixture into the batter.

Three-second ribbon

fold in remaining egg whites until combined.
5. Place butter in medium bowl. Add large spoonful of batter to butter; whisk until well mixed. Fold mixture back into batter. Pour batter into pan, gently spreading evenly.
6. Bake 10 to 12 minutes or until cake springs back when lightly touched and starts to shrink away from sides of pan. Cool in pan on wire rack.

Candied Orange Peel

1   orange
¾   cup sugar
½   cup water
1½ tablespoons corn syrup

1. With vegetable peeler, peel orange in long strips. (Avoid the bitter white pith below the peel.)
2. Place peel in small saucepan; cover with water. Bring to a boil. Reduce heat to low; simmer 10 minutes to soften peel. Drain; set peel aside.
3. In same saucepan, combine ½ cup of the sugar, ½ cup water and corn syrup. Bring to a boil; boil 2 minutes or until sugar is dissolved. Add orange peel. Reduce heat to low; simmer 15 to 20 minutes, stirring occasionally.
4. Drain orange peel. Place remaining ¼ cup sugar in small bowl; add peel and toss. Candied peel can be stored in airtight container in refrigerator several weeks.

Lime Roulade

A roulade can be one of the simplest, yet most elegant, cake preparations. It is light, uncomplicated and refreshing. Served with fresh fruit, it is an ideal ending to any meal.

CAKE
1   Lime Sponge Cake
    (recipe follows)

FILLING
2   eggs

3 egg yolks
⅓ cup fresh lime juice
⅓ cup sugar
6 tablespoons unsalted butter, cut up
2 tablespoons milk
¼ cup loosely packed grated lime peel

TOPPING
1 cup fresh raspberries
1 cup fresh blueberries
4 tablespoons sugar
⅓ cup whipping cream
1 teaspoon vanilla

1. Prepare Lime Sponge Cake. Set aside.
2. In medium bowl, whisk eggs and egg yolks together. Set aside.
3. In medium saucepan, combine lime juice, ⅓ cup sugar and butter; heat over medium heat until butter is melted. Stir in milk. Slowly pour ½ cup of the hot lime juice mixture into beaten egg mixture, whisking constantly.
4. Slowly pour egg mixture into juice mixture in saucepan, whisking constantly. Cook over medium heat, stirring constantly, until mixture thickens and just coats a spoon. Do not allow mixture to boil. (If desired, use a candy thermometer to test the temperature; the filling should be 185°F.) Stir in lime peel. Pour into medium bowl. Press sheet of plastic wrap directly onto warm filling; poke several holes with knife to release steam. Refrigerate 30 minutes or until chilled.
5. Unroll cake; spread filling over cake, leaving 1 to 2 inches on one long side uncovered. Starting with opposite long side of cake, roll gently but snugly, leaving 1-inch "lip" unrolled at end. Place roulade on platter; cover with plastic wrap and refrigerate at least 1 hour or up to 8 hours.
6. Meanwhile, toss raspberries and blueberries with 3 tablespoons of the sugar. Let stand 15 to 30 minutes.
7. Before serving, combine cream, remaining 1 tablespoon sugar and

vanilla in small bowl; beat until soft peaks form. Fill pastry bag fitted with star tip with whipped cream. Using circular motion, pipe decorative border along "lip" of cake. Slice ends of roulade diagonally. Serve with berries. Store in refrigerator.
10 servings

PER SERVING: 355 calories, 16.5 g total fat (9 g saturated fat), 6.5 g protein, 46.5 g carbohydrate, 225 mg cholesterol, 50 mg sodium, 1.5 g fiber

Lime Sponge Cake

4 eggs, room temperature, separated
1 cup sugar
3 tablespoons warm whole milk
1 tablespoon grated lime peel
½ teaspoon vanilla
1 cup sifted cake flour
½ teaspoon cream of tartar
2 tablespoons unsalted butter, melted, cooled
Powdered sugar

1. Heat oven to 400°F. Spray 15x10x1-inch pan with nonstick cooking spray. Line pan with parchment paper; spray paper and lightly flour.
2. In large bowl, combine egg yolks and ½ cup of the sugar; mix well. Place bowl over saucepan of barely simmering water (bowl should not touch water). Whisk egg mixture constantly 1 to 2 minutes or until sugar is dissolved and mixture is warm to the touch.
3. Beat mixture at medium-high speed 5 minutes or until mixture is thick enough to hold a 3-second ribbon. Reduce speed to medium; slowly add milk, lime peel and vanilla, beating until combined. Gradually sift and fold flour into yolk mixture; fold until thoroughly combined.
4. In another large bowl, beat egg whites just until frothy. Add cream of tartar; beat until soft peaks form. Gradually add remaining ½ cup sugar, beating until stiff peaks form. Fold ¼ of

egg whites into batter to lighten mixture. Gently and quickly fold in remaining egg whites until combined.
5. Place butter in medium bowl. Add large spoonful of batter to butter; whisk until well mixed. Fold mixture back into batter. Pour batter into pan, gently spreading evenly.
6. Bake 10 to 12 minutes or until cake springs back when lightly touched and starts to shrink away from sides of pan.
7. Meanwhile, place clean towel on surface; sprinkle with powdered sugar.
8. Remove cake from oven. Turn cake out onto towel; remove paper. Roll cake with towel starting at long edge. Let stand until cool.

RECIPE HOW-TO

ROLLING LIME SPONGE CAKE

For a sponge cake to be flexible enough for rolling, it must be thin and moist. Immediately after baking, turn the cake pan upside down onto a thin, lint-free kitchen towel that has been sprinkled with powdered sugar. Remove the pan and parchment paper, then roll the cake gently but tightly in the towel. The towel helps the cake retain moisture as it cools, and the powdered sugar prevents the cake from sticking to the towel. Cool the cake in the towel. Once the cake is cooled, unroll the cake and remove the towel. Then spread the filling over the cake and roll it up again.

TEMPTATIONS OF THE
TART

Cranberry-Grape Tart with Walnut Pastry

Showcase the season's luscious fruit in one-crust pastries.

Text and Recipes by Carole Walter

When fruits finally ripen and appear in markets, I become single-minded—single-crust minded, that is. For me, there's no better way to enjoy the season's sweet bounty than in a tart. Unlike pies, which are often double-crusted, tarts are made with exposed tops, allowing the fruit to strut its stuff. The single crust requires less effort—it can be free form or pressed into a tart pan. Tarts contain less fruit, reducing the risk of soggy crusts. And they're easy to serve, making them fitting choices when you're entertaining.

Showcase your favorite fruit in these stunning desserts. They're easier than pie!

to ¾-inch overhang. Fold overhang inside pan. Remove excess dough at corners; press gently to seal dough. Refrigerate while preparing filling.
5. In large bowl, combine cranberries and grapes.
6. In small bowl, stir together ¾ cup sugar, cornstarch and ⅛ teaspoon salt. Sprinkle over fruit; stir gently to blend. Spoon mixture into dough-lined pan. (Fruit will be slightly higher than top of pan.)
7. Bake 50 minutes. Place strip of foil loosely over fruit; bake an additional 20 minutes or until edges are golden brown. Remove from oven; let stand 10 minutes. In small saucepan, heat jelly over low heat until melted. Brush over hot tart. Refrigerate until cool.
TIP *A 9-inch round tart pan can be used. Baking time may need to increase 5 to 10 minutes.
8 servings

PER SERVING: 305 calories, 12.5 g total fat (5 g saturated fat), 3.5 g protein, 48 g carbohydrate, 15 mg cholesterol, 110 mg sodium, 2 g fiber

Cranberry-Grape Tart with Walnut Pastry

Grapes provide a wonderfully sweet counterpoint to tart cranberries in this delectable tart. The walnut crust is unforgettable!

PASTRY
- 1⅓ cups all-purpose flour
- ⅓ cup finely chopped walnuts
- 2 teaspoons sugar
- ¼ teaspoon salt
- ¼ cup unsalted butter, chilled, cut up
- 2 tablespoons shortening, chilled, cut up
- 4 to 5 tablespoons ice water

FILLING
- 2 cups fresh cranberries
- 1½ cups seedless red grapes
- ¾ cup sugar
- 4 teaspoons cornstarch
- ⅛ teaspoon salt
- 1 tablespoon red currant jelly

1. In large bowl, combine flour, walnuts, 2 teaspoons sugar and ¼ teaspoon salt; mix well. With pastry blender or fingertips, work in butter and shortening until a mixture of coarse crumbs and some pea-size pieces form.
2. Sprinkle water 1 tablespoon at a time around edge of bowl. Stir with fork until moist crumbs form.
3. Press together to form dough. All crumbs should adhere to dough and clean the bowl. If not, add a few drops of water. Shape into 5x3-inch rectangle. Dust lightly with flour; cover with plastic wrap. Refrigerate at least 1 hour.
4. Heat oven to 400°F. Roll dough to form 18x8-inch rectangle. Line 14x4½-inch tart pan* with dough. Trim dough

Apple Galette with Puff Pastry

Crisp layers of buttery puff pastry hold a spiral of sliced Golden Delicious apples to make a simple yet elegant dessert.

- ⅓ cup apricot preserves
- 2 teaspoons water
- 1 (17.3-oz.) pkg. frozen puff pastry sheets
- 4 medium Golden Delicious apples (about 1¾ lb.), peeled, thinly sliced
- 1 tablespoon fresh lemon juice
- ¼ cup sugar
- 2 tablespoons unsalted butter

1. Heat oven to 400°F.
2. In small saucepan, combine preserves and water; cook over low heat until mixture comes to a simmer. Strain through fine strainer into small bowl.

Apple Galette with Puff Pastry

Set aside. Allow puff pastry to thaw at room temperature 20 to 30 minutes before rolling.

3. On floured pastry cloth or work surface, place 1 sheet puff pastry. Place second sheet puff pastry directly over first sheet. Roll layered sheets together into 14-inch square. Prick with fork at 1-inch intervals. Place dough in 11-inch tart pan. DO NOT STRETCH DOUGH. Trim with scissors, leaving 1-inch overhang.

4. Brush overhang with ice water. Fold overhang inside pan; press gently to seal dough. Refrigerate at least 15 minutes.

5. Brush bottom of pastry shell with 2 tablespoons of the strained preserves. Place half of apples over bottom of tart. Arrange remaining apples over pastry in concentric circles with rounded sides to outside edge of tart pan. Sprinkle apples with lemon juice and sugar; dot with butter.

6. Place tart in oven. Place baking sheet or foil on rack below tart to catch juices. Bake 55 to 60 minutes or until crust is browned and juices are bubbly.

Cover with foil if browning too quickly. Cool on wire rack 5 minutes. Brush with remaining preserves. Remove from pan. Cool 10 minutes before slicing. (Tart is best eaten soon after baking. However, it can be reheated in 350°F. oven for 5 to 10 minutes or until warm.)

10 servings

PER SERVING: 315 calories, 21.5 g total fat (8 g saturated fat), 2 g protein, 29.5 g carbohydrate, 15 mg cholesterol, 100 mg sodium, 1.5 g fiber

Apricot-Pear Tart

Sautéed pears and caramelized apricots, accented with orange zest and Grand Marnier, peek through a sugary lattice crust. Setting the tart pan on a hot baking sheet encourages browning of the bottom crust.

PASTRY
- 3 cups all-purpose flour
- 1 teaspoon salt
- ½ teaspoon baking powder
- ⅔ cup unsalted butter, chilled, cut up
- ¼ cup shortening, chilled, cut up
- 8 to 10 tablespoons ice water

FILLING

Apricot-Pear Tart

½ cup water
10 tablespoons sugar
1 cup dried apricots, cut into
   ½-inch pieces
3 lb. firm ripe Anjou pears
   (about 6 large pears),
   peeled, cut into ¾-inch
   slices
1 tablespoon fresh lemon
   juice
2 tablespoons unsalted butter
2 teaspoons grated orange
   peel
2 tablespoons Grand Marnier
   liqueur or orange juice

1. In large bowl, combine flour, salt and baking powder; mix well. With pastry blender or fingertips, work in butter and shortening until a mixture of coarse crumbs and some pea-size pieces form.
2. Sprinkle ice water, 1 tablespoon at a time, around edge of bowl. Stir with fork until moist crumbs form.
3. Press together to form dough. All crumbs should adhere to dough and clean the bowl. If not, add a few drops of water. Divide dough in half; flatten each half into 5-inch round. Dust lightly with flour; cover with plastic wrap. Refrigerate at least 30 minutes.
4. On floured pastry cloth or work surface, roll half of dough to form 13-inch round. Line 11-inch tart pan with dough. Trim edges by pressing rolling pin across top of pan. Refrigerate while preparing filling.
5. In small heavy saucepan, combine ½ cup water and 2 tablespoons of the sugar. Bring to a boil over medium-high heat, stirring occasionally. Reduce heat to medium-low; simmer 3 minutes. Stir in apricots; continue cooking 5 to 8 minutes or until most of the liquid has been absorbed.
6. Place pears in large bowl. Sprinkle with lemon juice and 6 tablespoons of the sugar; stir gently until well mixed.
7. Melt 2 tablespoons butter in large skillet over medium heat. Stir in orange peel. Add pears; mix gently to coat fruit

with butter. Increase heat to medium-high; sauté 8 to 12 minutes or until most of liquid has evaporated, increasing heat to high, if necessary. As pears cook, shake skillet to keep them from sticking, but do not stir, as fruit is delicate and breaks easily.
8. Remove from heat. Stir in apricots and liqueur. Return to medium heat; sauté an additional 2 to 4 minutes or until most of liquid evaporates and pears begin to stick to bottom of skillet. Spread fruit in shallow pan. Cool 15 to 20 minutes.
9. Heat oven to 400°F. Place baking sheet on center oven rack to heat.
10. When fruit is cool, spoon into dough-lined pan. Roll remaining dough into 13-inch round. With fluted pastry wheel, cut 8 (1½-inch-wide) strips of dough. Arrange 4 strips evenly over fruit. Turn pan a quarter turn; weave remaining strips of dough, forming a diagonal lattice.
11. Brush lattice with cold water; sprinkle with remaining 2 tablespoons sugar. Place tart pan on preheated baking sheet; bake 45 to 50 minutes or until crust is light brown and juices are bubbly. Cool on wire rack.

10 servings

PER SERVING: 475 calories, 20.5 g total fat (10.5 g saturated fat), 5 g protein, 69.5 g carbohydrate, 40 mg cholesterol, 260 mg sodium, 5 g fiber

Port-Glazed Fig and Walnut Tartlets

We won't kid you—this recipe has numerous steps, but the results are so divine, it's worth it. From the crunchy cornmeal crust to the nutty fig topping, each bite is delectable. The tartlets make an elegant finale for a special meal.

PASTRY
1 cup all-purpose flour
6 tablespoons yellow
   cornmeal
1 tablespoon sugar
¼ teaspoon salt

9 tablespoons unsalted butter,
   chilled, cut up
1 egg white, beaten until
   frothy

TOPPING
1¼ lb. fresh figs (about
   24 small to medium figs)*
2 cups port
⅔ cup sugar
2 teaspoons fresh lemon juice
2 cups walnut halves, toasted,
   cut into large pieces**

PASTRY CREAM
3 egg yolks
¼ cup sugar
1 tablespoon cornstarch
2 teaspoons all-purpose flour
1 cup milk
½ cup whipping cream
1 tablespoon unsalted butter
1 teaspoon vanilla

1. In large bowl, combine flour, cornmeal, 1 tablespoon sugar and salt; mix well. With pastry blender or fingertips, work in butter until a mixture of coarse crumbs and some pea-size pieces form.
2. Make well in center; add egg white. Stir with fork until moist crumbs form. Press together to form dough. All crumbs should adhere to dough and clean the bowl. If not, add a few drops of water. Shape into 5-inch round. Cover with plastic wrap and refrigerate 30 minutes.
3. Divide dough into 6 pieces. Press dough onto bottom and up sides of 6 (4½-inch) tartlet pans. Prick bottoms with fork. Refrigerate 30 minutes.
4. Heat oven to 375°F. To bake tartlet shells, place on baking sheet. Cut 6 (6-inch) pieces of heavy-duty foil. Butter foil. Press foil, butter side down, into bottom and up sides of tartlet pans. Fill each with shallow layer of pie weights, dried beans or rice.
5. Bake 20 minutes. Carefully remove foil and weights; bake an additional 2 to 3 minutes or until golden brown. Cool on wire rack; set aside. (Tartlet

shells can be made up to 2 days ahead. Store in airtight container.)

6. With stems attached, quarter figs. (If using large figs, cut into ¾-inch wedges.) Set 6 wedges with stems intact aside for garnish. Remove stems from remaining figs; set aside.

7. In large saucepan, combine port and ⅔ cup sugar. Bring to a boil over medium heat. Stirring occasionally, cook 20 to 25 minutes or until thick and syrupy, reducing heat if necessary when mixture begins to thicken. Watch carefully to avoid burning.

8. Add figs and lemon juice; stir gently to coat fruit with syrup. Cook over medium-low heat 6 to 8 minutes or until figs are almost tender, stirring occasionally to avoid sticking. Gently stir in walnuts; cook an additional 5 to 7 minutes or until juices are bubbly and thickened. Let stand 30 minutes to cool.

9. To make pastry cream, in medium bowl, whisk egg yolks until slightly thickened. Whisk in ¼ cup sugar 1 tablespoon at a time. Stir in cornstarch and 2 teaspoons flour.

10. In medium saucepan, heat milk and cream over medium heat until mixture comes to a simmer. Slowly pour hot milk mixture into egg mixture, whisking constantly.

11. Return mixture to pan. Cook over medium heat until mixture comes to a boil and begins to thicken, whisking constantly. Simmer about 1 minute. Remove from heat. Stir in 1 tablespoon butter and vanilla. Cover top with buttered plastic wrap. Cool about 10 minutes.

12. Divide pastry cream evenly among tartlet shells. Place on baking sheet. Bake 10 to 12 minutes or until set. Cool 10 minutes.

13. Spoon fig mixture over pastry cream, mounding it slightly in center. Garnish with reserved figs. (*Tartlets can be made up to 2 days ahead. Cover and refrigerate. Before serving, warm tartlets in 300°F. oven for 12 to 15 minutes.*)

TIPS *If fresh figs are unavailable, substitute 24 dried figs, chopped.
**To toast nuts, spread on baking sheet; bake at 375°F. for 7 to 10 minutes or until lightly browned. Cool.
6 tartlets

PER TARTLET: 845 calories, 50 g total fat (19 g saturated fat), 12.5 g protein, 93.5 g carbohydrate, 185 mg cholesterol, 150 mg sodium, 6 g fiber

Almond-Plum Tart with Butter-Crumb Topping

A cookie crust holds fanned red plums baked on a tasty almond filling. The tart is topped with a buttery streusel that is made from the same cookie-crumb mixture used in the crust.

PASTRY
2⅓ cups all-purpose flour
⅓ cup sugar
¼ teaspoon baking powder
¼ teaspoon salt
¾ cup unsalted butter, chilled, cut up
1 egg, beaten

FILLING
1 cup sliced almonds
⅔ cup sugar
1 egg white
½ teaspoon almond extract
7 medium red plums
1 teaspoon fresh lemon juice

1. In large bowl, combine flour, ⅓ cup sugar, baking powder and salt; mix well. With pastry blender or fingertips, work in butter until a mixture of coarse crumbs and some pea-size pieces form. Reserve 1¼ cups crumb mixture for topping.

2. Make well in center of remaining crumb mixture. Add egg; stir with fork until moist crumbs form. Press together to form dough. All crumbs should adhere to dough and clean the bowl. If not, add a few drops of water.

3. Turn dough out onto floured surface. With heel of hand, push about 3 tablespoons of dough away from you about 6 to 8 inches, smearing it across work surface. Repeat process until all of dough has been worked. If hand becomes sticky, flour as needed. Gather dough together and repeat twice.

4. Flatten dough into 5-inch round. Dust lightly with flour; cover with plastic wrap. Refrigerate at least 30 minutes.

5. Place almonds and ⅓ cup sugar in food processor; process until nuts are finely chopped. Add egg white and almond extract; pulse just until blended (do not overprocess). Place in small bowl; set aside.

6. On floured pastry cloth or work surface, roll dough to form 13-inch round. Line 11-inch tart pan with dough. Trim edges by pressing rolling pin across top of pan. Spread almond filling evenly in crust. Refrigerate while preparing fruit.

7. Heat oven to 375°F. Halve and slice plums crosswise into ⅛-inch slices. Arrange plum slices over almond filling, starting at outside of pan and working towards the center. Drizzle plums with lemon juice and remaining ⅓ cup sugar. Sprinkle with reserved crumbs.

8. Bake 55 to 60 minutes or until crust and topping are golden brown and juices are bubbly. Cool on wire rack.
10 servings

PER SERVING: 405 calories, 20.5 g total fat (9.5 g saturated fat), 6.5 g protein, 50.5 g carbohydrate, 60 mg cholesterol, 85 mg sodium, 2.5 g fiber

Autumn Fruit Cradle

This rustic free-form tart holds a mixture of apples, pears and cranberries spiced with cinnamon and ginger. There's no guessing about what's inside the tart. The large opening across the top shows a colorful array of caramelized fruits. Bake free-form tarts such as this one on baking sheets without sides so that the tarts are easy to slide off after baking.

PASTRY
2 cups all-purpose flour
1 tablespoon sugar

Autumn Fruit Cradle

¾ teaspoon salt
½ teaspoon baking powder
½ cup unsalted butter, chilled, cut up
¼ cup shortening, chilled, cut up
5 to 6 tablespoons ice water

FILLING
3 Golden Delicious apples (about 1½ lb.), peeled, cut into ¼-inch slices

2 Anjou pears, peeled, cut into ½-inch slices
1 cup cranberries
2 teaspoons fresh lemon juice
½ cup plus 2 tablespoons sugar
½ cup packed dark brown sugar
2 tablespoons cornstarch
1 teaspoon ground ginger
1 teaspoon cinnamon
1 egg

1 teaspoon water
1 tablespoon unsalted butter

1. In large bowl, combine flour, 1 tablespoon sugar, salt and baking powder; mix well. With pastry blender or fingertips, work in butter and shortening until a mixture of coarse crumbs and some pea-size pieces form.
2. Sprinkle water, 1 tablespoon at a time, around edge of bowl. Stir with fork until moist crumbs form.

3. Press together to form dough. All crumbs should adhere to dough and clean the bowl. If not, add a few drops of water. Shape into 5-inch round. Dust lightly with flour; cover with plastic wrap. Refrigerate at least 45 minutes.

4. Heat oven to 400°F. Line baking sheet with parchment paper; spray with nonstick cooking spray.

5. On floured pastry cloth or work surface, roll dough into 17x12-inch oval. Place dough on baking sheet. Refrigerate while preparing filling.

6. In large bowl, combine apples, pears and cranberries; drizzle with lemon juice. In small bowl, combine 1/2 cup of the sugar, brown sugar, cornstarch, ginger and cinnamon; mix well. Add to fruit; stir gently to combine.

7. In small bowl, combine egg and water; beat lightly. Brush over dough. Spoon fruit onto dough, mounding in center to form 12x8-inch oval. Dot with 1 tablespoon butter.

8. With pastry scraper or fingers, gently lift dough over edge of fruit, folding it into pleats as needed. Fruit will be exposed in center. DO NOT PUNCTURE DOUGH WITH FRUIT. Lightly brush dough with egg mixture. Sprinkle dough with remaining 2 tablespoons sugar.

9. Place in oven. Place large sheet of foil with edges turned up on rack below baking sheet to catch running juices. Bake 50 to 55 minutes or until crust is golden brown.

10. Cool on wire rack 5 minutes. To prevent tart from sticking, slide long, thin spatula under tart to loosen bottom crust. While tart is still warm, slide onto serving platter. Serve warm with ice cream, if desired.

10 servings

PER SERVING: 380 calories, 16.5 g total fat (8 g saturated fat), 3.5 g protein, 57.5 g carbohydrate, 45 mg cholesterol, 210 mg sodium, 3 g fiber

TECHNIQUE TIPS

Preparing dough: To keep tart dough tender and flavorful, follow these tips.

• For even distribution, cut butter into 1/2-inch pieces before adding it to the flour mixture.

• When making pastry dough in warm weather, always chill the ingredients, including the flour.

• Using a pastry blender or two knives, work the fat into the dry ingredients until some of the particles are as large as peas and others are the size of crumbs. The larger particles help create

Use a pastry cloth and cover to ease rolling.

Strive for pea- and crumb-size particles.

a flakier crust; the smaller ones make the crust tender.

• For doughs that use water, add it sparingly to the crumb mixture, a tablespoon at a time. Liquid absorption varies according to the moisture con-

tent of the flour and the relative humidity.

• Avoid overworking the dough. This causes the fat to melt and results in a less flaky pastry. More flour will then be needed for rolling, causing the crust to be tough and less flavorful. If you use a large bowl for the crust ingredients, you'll be less likely to overwork the dough.

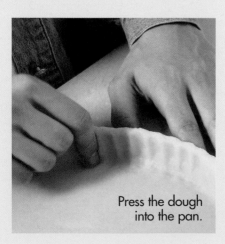
Press the dough into the pan.

PASTRY POINTERS

- Dough can be prepared ahead and stored, tightly wrapped in plastic, in the refrigerator for up to three days or the freezer for up to three months. Frozen dough should be thawed in the refrigerator overnight before using.

Rolling the dough:
Refrigerate the dough before rolling. This relaxes the dough and gives the moisture time to permeate it. Dough is properly chilled and ready to roll when a slight indentation can be made when pressing it with your fingertips. Pastry dough that is too cold is difficult to roll and will crack at the edges. Dough that is too warm is sticky.

A rolling pin cuts away the dough.

- For easier rolling, use a well-floured pastry cloth and rolling pin cover. These tools help eliminate the problem of dough sticking.

- Roll from the center toward the outer edges, turning the pastry as you go. Use even pressure on the rolling pin.

- Ease the dough into the pan. Fold the rolled dough into quarters and position it in the tart pan with the point in the center. Carefully unfold the pastry. To prevent the edge of the tart pan from cutting the dough, immediately turn the overhang towards the center. Working a small section at a time, mold the dough to the pan by pressing it against the side while gently pushing downward with your fingertips. This will ease the pastry

into the crease of the pan without stretching it and will prevent shrinkage.

- Remove excess dough with a rolling pin. Run the rolling pin across the top of the pan. The excess dough will be trimmed away by the sharp edge of the tart pan.

Controlling moisture: A juicy fruit tart is delicious, but excess juice can create soggy crusts. These steps help prevent too much juice from forming in tarts:

- When cleaning fresh fruit and berries, wash them but don't soak them in water. Place berries in a colander and rinse them with cold water. After draining, spread them in

a shallow pan lined with a double thickness of paper towels to dry.

- Don't sugar fruit until tarts are ready to be assembled and baked. Sugaring ahead of time draws out too much moisture from the fruit.

- Fill the tart right before baking. Don't let it stand before putting it in the oven.

Unmolding tarts: If juice has baked onto the rim of the pan, loosen the tart by running a small knife between the crust and the rim. To separate the outer ring from the base, place the pan on a bowl or other container small enough to allow the outer ring to slip down. Use a long, thin spatula to ease the tart from the base onto a serving platter.

Storing and reheating: Finished fruit tarts can be stored at room temperature (unless they contain dairy products, such as in Port-Glazed Fig and Walnut Tartlets). To freshen a baked tart, reheat it in a 350°F. oven for 5 to 10 minutes, depending on its size. If a tart begins to brown too much, loosely cover the top with foil.

Remove the outer ring.

SHORTCAKE

LONGINGS

Amaretti Peach Shortcakes with Chantilly Cream

Any time is the perfect
time for berries and biscuits.

Text and Recipes by Beth Hensperger

Warm biscuits. Fresh fruit. Rich cream. Shortcakes are an American passion—and an American creation, born out of home kitchens with the abundant fresh fruits of the season.

Sweet, juicy fruit and thick whipped cream are necessary components, but it's the rich, crumbly biscuit that is the hallmark of this irresistible dessert. Northerners like it unsweetened, Southerners like it with sugar. But bakers everywhere agree the best shortcake needs cold ingredients and a light hand in its creation. Beyond that, it's the cook's choice: Add flavors—vanilla, almond, cardamom, chocolate—or vary the shape—drop biscuits, heart-shaped, square or miniature. Split the biscuit and fill it with fruit and cream, or save the cream for the top only. Whatever you choose, do it now, before the fruits of summer are a fading memory.

Amaretti Peach Shortcakes with Chantilly Cream

Almonds and almond extract are natural partners with stone fruits such as peaches because of similar flavor elements. These large shortcakes have crushed amaretti cookies—Italian macaroons sold in pretty red tins by Lazzaroni—added for texture. The aroma of both the dough and the finished biscuit is heavenly.

PEACHES
- 3½ lb. slightly firm ripe peaches
- ¾ cup sugar
- 3 tablespoons fresh lemon juice

SHORTCAKES
- 1¼ cups all-purpose flour
- 1 cup cake flour
- 1 cup crushed amaretti cookies
- 3 tablespoons sugar
- 1 tablespoon baking powder
- 1¼ teaspoons salt
- 1 teaspoon baking soda
- 1 teaspoon cream of tartar
- 6 tablespoons unsalted butter, chilled, cut up
- ½ cup sour cream
- 6 tablespoons buttermilk
- 1 teaspoon almond extract

TOPPING
- 1½ teaspoons milk
- ¼ cup sliced almonds

CREAM
- 1 cup whipping cream
- 2 tablespoons sugar
- 1 teaspoon vanilla

GARNISH
Powdered sugar

1. Blanch peaches in large saucepan of boiling water 10 to 15 seconds or until skins begin to loosen. Place peaches in ice water. When cool, remove skins with fingers or paring knife. Halve, pit and cut peaches into ½-inch slices (there should be about 7 cups); place in large bowl. Sprinkle with ¾ cup sugar and lemon juice; stir to combine. Cover; refrigerate at least 2 hours.

2. Meanwhile, heat oven to 400°F. Line baking sheet with parchment paper. In large bowl, combine all-purpose flour, cake flour, cookies, 3 tablespoons sugar, baking powder, salt, baking soda and cream of tartar; mix well.

3. Add butter. Using pastry blender or 2 knives, cut in butter until mixture resembles coarse crumbs with pea-size pieces of butter. Add sour cream, buttermilk and almond extract; stir until dough forms.

4. Sprinkle work surface lightly with cake flour. Turn out dough onto flour. (Dough will be sticky.) Sprinkle flour lightly over dough. With floured hands, gently knead 8 to 10 strokes. Pat dough into square 1½ inches thick. Cut into 6 pieces; place on baking sheet. Brush tops with milk; sprinkle with almonds.

5. Bake 15 to 20 minutes or until shortcakes are firm to the touch and tops and bottoms are golden brown. Cool at least 20 minutes before serving.

6. In another large bowl, whip cream, 2 tablespoons sugar and vanilla at medium-high speed until soft peaks form. Cover; refrigerate until serving time.

7. To serve, split shortcakes in half horizontally. Place bottom halves on individual dessert plates. Top each with

peaches and their juices. Spoon cream over peaches. Cover with shortcake tops. Sprinkle with powdered sugar. Refrigerate leftovers.

6 servings

PER SERVING: 910 calories, 41 g total fat (21 g saturated fat), 12 g protein, 128 g carbohydrate, 90 mg cholesterol, 1135 mg sodium, 7 g fiber

Chocolate Shortcakes with Mixed Berries and Raspberry Sauce

Vanilla and espresso heighten the rich, chocolaty flavor in these irresistible biscuits. As an alternative to round or drop biscuits, try a large heart- or star-shaped cutter.

BERRIES
- 2 cups strawberries, quartered
- 1 cup raspberries
- ½ cup blackberries
- ¼ cup sugar
- 2 tablespoons Chambord liqueur or cranberry-raspberry juice

SHORTCAKES
- 1 cup cake flour
- ½ cup all-purpose flour
- ½ cup plus 2 teaspoons sugar
- ⅓ cup unsweetened cocoa
- 1½ teaspoons baking powder
- ½ teaspoon baking soda
- ½ teaspoon cream of tartar
- ½ teaspoon salt
- ¼ teaspoon instant espresso coffee powder
- ¼ cup unsalted butter, chilled, cut up
- ¼ cup buttermilk
- ¾ teaspoon vanilla
- 1 egg, beaten

SAUCE
- 1 (10-oz.) pkg. frozen raspberries in syrup, thawed
- 2 tablespoons Chambord

liqueur, if desired

CREAM
- 1 cup whipping cream
- 2 tablespoons sour cream
- 2 tablespoons sugar
- ¾ teaspoon vanilla

1. In large bowl, combine straw-berries, 1 cup raspberries and blackberries. Sprinkle with ¼ cup sugar and 2 table-spoons liqueur; stir until all berries are coated. Cover; refrigerate at least 3 hours.

2. Meanwhile, heat oven to 400°F. Line air-cushioned baking sheet with parchment paper, or place 2 baking sheets together and line top sheet with parchment paper. (This helps control over-browning the bottoms of these shortcakes.) In another large bowl, combine cake flour, all-purpose flour, ½ cup of the sugar, cocoa, baking powder, baking soda, cream of tartar, salt and espresso coffee powder; mix well.

3. Add butter. Using pastry blender or 2 knives, cut in butter until mixture resembles coarse crumbs with pea-size pieces of butter. Add buttermilk, 3/4 teaspoon vanilla and egg; stir until dough forms.

4. Sprinkle work surface lightly with cake flour. Turn out dough onto flour. (Dough will be sticky.) With floured hands, gently knead 12 to 14 strokes. Pat dough into round 1 inch thick.

5. Cut out shortcakes with floured 2½-inch round cutter, pressing dough scraps together when necessary. Place on baking sheet; sprinkle tops with remaining 2 teaspoons sugar.

6. Bake 14 to 16 minutes or until short-cakes are firm to the touch. Cool on wire rack at least 20 minutes.

7. Meanwhile, in food processor, combine raspberries with their syrup and 2 tablespoons liqueur; puree until smooth. Place strainer over medium bowl; pour raspberry mixture into strainer. Press mixture with back of spoon through strainer to remove seeds; discard seeds. Cover; refrigerate

until serving time.

8. In large bowl, whip cream, sour cream, 2 tablespoons sugar and ¾ teaspoon vanilla at medium-high speed until soft peaks form. Cover; refrigerate until serving time.

9. To serve, split shortcakes in half horizontally. Place bottom halves on individual dessert plates. Top with cream and berries. Cover with shortcake tops. Pour some raspberry sauce onto plates around shortcakes. Serve with remaining sauce. Refrigerate leftovers.

5 servings

PER SERVING: 845 calories, 38.5 g total fat (23 g saturated fat), 9 g protein, 118.5 g carbohydrate, 160 mg cholesterol, 560 mg sodium, 7 g fiber

Old-Fashioned Strawberry Shortcakes

No shortcake dessert comes close to the popularity of one made with strawberries. Here, the fruit mixture is spiked with a splash of balsamic vinegar, a secret flavor accent that is especially good if your berries are not perfectly ripe. Choose a good quality, sweeter vinegar.

STRAWBERRIES
- 10 cups sliced strawberries
- ¼ cup sugar
- 3 tablespoons balsamic vinegar
- 1 tablespoon packed brown sugar

SHORTCAKES
- 1¾ cups cake flour
- 1 cup all-purpose flour
- ⅓ cup packed light brown sugar
- 4 teaspoons baking powder
- 1½ teaspoons salt
- ¾ teaspoon cream of tartar
- ½ teaspoon baking soda
- ¾ cup unsalted butter, chilled, cut up
- 1 cup buttermilk, chilled

GLAZE

1½ teaspoons milk
1 teaspoon sugar

CREAM
1 cup whipping cream
3 tablespoons sugar
1 teaspoon vanilla

1. In large bowl, crush 3 cups of the strawberries with potato masher. Add remaining berries. Sprinkle with ¼ cup sugar and 1 tablespoon brown sugar; add vinegar. Stir until all berries are coated. Cover; refrigerate a minimum of 2 hours.

2. Meanwhile, heat oven to 450°F. Line baking sheet with parchment paper. In large bowl, combine cake flour, all-purpose flour, ⅓ cup brown sugar, baking powder, salt, cream of tartar and baking soda; mix well.

3. Add butter. Using pastry blender or 2 knives, cut in butter until mixture resembles coarse crumbs with pea-size pieces of butter. Add buttermilk; stir until dough forms.

4. Sprinkle work surface lightly with cake flour. Turn out dough onto flour. (Dough will be sticky.) Sprinkle flour lightly over dough. With floured hands, gently knead 8 to 10 strokes. Pat dough into round 1½ inches thick.

5. Cut out 8 shortcakes with floured 2½-inch round cutter, pressing dough scraps together when necessary. Place on baking sheet. Brush tops with milk; sprinkle with 1 teaspoon sugar.

6. Place in oven and immediately reduce oven temperature to 400°F. Bake 18 to 25 minutes or until shortcakes are firm to the touch and tops and bottoms are light brown. Cool on wire rack at least 20 minutes before serving.

7. In another large bowl, whip cream, 3 tablespoons sugar and vanilla at medium-high speed until soft peaks form. Cover; refrigerate until serving time.

8. To serve, split shortcakes in half horizontally. Place bottom halves on individual dessert plates. Top each with strawberries and their juices. Cover with shortcake tops. Spoon cream over top. Refrigerate leftovers.

8 servings

PER SERVING: 550 calories, 28.5 g total fat (17 g saturated fat), 6.5 g protein, 70.5 g carbohydrate, 80 mg cholesterol, 805 mg sodium, 5.5 g fiber

Blueberry Cornmeal Gems with Ginger Whipped Cream

Gems, popular in 19th century America, were miniature muffins that baked in special "gem" pans. Our version bakes in a muffin pan to create individual biscuits that are a bit smaller than the usual shortcake.

BLUEBERRIES
4 cups blueberries
⅓ cup sugar
¼ cup crème de cassis liqueur or cranberry-raspberry juice

GEMS
1 cup all-purpose flour
1 cup cake flour
½ cup yellow cornmeal
¼ cup plus 1 teaspoon sugar
3½ teaspoons baking powder
1 teaspoon salt
1 teaspoon cream of tartar
¾ teaspoon ground cardamom
½ teaspoon baking soda
10 tablespoons unsalted butter, chilled, cut up
1 cup buttermilk
½ teaspoon vanilla

CREAM
2 cups whipping cream
¼ cup minced crystallized ginger

1. In large bowl, combine blueberries, ⅓ cup sugar and liqueur; toss to mix. Mash slightly with potato masher or fork. Cover; refrigerate 1 hour.

2. Meanwhile, heat oven to 350°F. Spray 12 muffin cups with nonstick cooking spray. In another large bowl, combine all-purpose flour, cake flour,

Old-Fashioned Strawberry Shortcakes

cornmeal, ¼ cup of the sugar, baking powder, salt, cream of tartar, cardamom and baking soda; mix well.

3. Add butter. Using pastry blender or 2 knives, cut in butter until mixture resembles coarse crumbs with pea-size pieces of butter. Add buttermilk and vanilla. Stir until dough forms.

4. Spoon dough into muffin cups. Sprinkle with remaining 1 teaspoon sugar.

5. Bake 25 to 30 minutes or until firm to the touch and tops are light brown. Remove from muffin cups; place on wire racks. Cool at least 15 minutes before serving.

6. Meanwhile, in large bowl, whip cream at high speed until soft peaks form. Gently fold in ginger until evenly distributed. Cover; refrigerate until serving time.

7. To serve, cut gems in half horizontally. Place bottom halves on individual dessert plates. Top with blueberries and their juices. Cover with top halves. Spoon cream over top. Refrigerate leftovers.

12 servings

PER SERVING: 395 calories, 23 g total fat (14 g saturated fat), 4.5 g protein, 43.5 g carbohydrate, 70 mg cholesterol, 435 mg sodium, 2.5 g fiber

Biscuits are considered a bread, but the techniques used to create them are more akin to pastry making than bread baking. Many of the same rules you follow for pie crust apply to biscuits: Use chilled ingredients, don't overmix the dough, and handle the dough as little as possible.

Cutting in the fat: When you add the butter to the dry ingredients, the flour and fat are cut together with a pastry blender or two knives until the particles resemble coarse crumbs. Some pieces should be as large as peas; these larger particles of butter help create flakier biscuits.

Cutting in fat.

Adding liquid: Once you add the liquids to the flour and butter mixture, stir them together—with a wooden spoon, fork or even your fingers—just until the ingredients are combined. You should have a sticky dough with no large clumps of flour, but the dough will not be smooth. Be careful not to overmix the dough, which can lead to tough biscuits.

Working the dough: When the ingredients are combined, turn the dough out onto a lightly floured work surface. The kneading technique used for biscuits is far more delicate than the

Blueberry Cornmeal Gems with Ginger Whipped Cream

CONSTRUCTING A SHORTCAKE BISCUIT

kneading required when making yeast breads. The technique for biscuits is called fraiser. Here's how to do it:

• Pull the dough from the top (12 o'clock in relation to your body) over itself to make a double layer, and then, with the palm of your hand, push the dough very gently forward with the lightest of pressure to flatten some of the pieces of butter. Don't use a vigorous action or press the dough into the work surface. Make a quarter turn and repeat. Use only enough flour to make the dough manageable. You will use only 6 to 12 strokes, at one to two seconds per stroke. Then pat the dough into a rough square or round ready for shaping.

Working dough.

• Fraiser is an essential step in creating high-rising shortcake biscuits. In the heat of the oven, the fat melts and is absorbed into the dough, while steam resulting from the moisture in the dough creates pressure (with some help from chemical leaveners) between the layers and separates them from each other to make flaky shortcake biscuits. Without this step, your biscuits will be half as high.

Making shortcakes in a food processor: If you prefer to use the food

processor to make shortcakes, place the dry ingredients in a work bowl fitted with the steel blade. Process a few seconds just to aerate and mix. Remove the cover and place the butter, cut into tablespoon-size pieces, on top of the flour mixture; replace the top. Process by pulsing just until the butter is the size of peas. Do not incorporate the butter completely with the flour, or the biscuits will be tough. Add the cold liquid through the feed tube; pulse just until a moist dough is formed. Remove the dough from the work bowl, and continue to form and bake as specified in the recipe.

Shaping shortcakes: For high short-cakes that are thick enough to split, pat out the dough at least 1 inch thick. Another trick for creating high shortcakes is used by French bakers: Place the just-cut biscuit upside down on the baking sheet. The pressure from the downward cutting motion is reversed and the rise is higher.

When it comes to shaping shortcakes, you have several options.

• Shape the dough into a rectangle and cut it into squares with a sharp chef's knife.

• Cut shortcake dough into rounds with a fluted round biscuit cutter or the rim of a glass.

• Try a large star or heart.

• Create a large shortcake by pressing the dough into a greased 8-inch round cake pan or spring-form pan (for recipes with 2 cups of flour), or 9x9-inch square metal pan (for recipes with 3 cups of flour). Build up the edges slightly. Bake as

directed for 5 to 8 minutes longer than for individual short-cakes, or until a toothpick inserted into the center comes out

Try fun shapes.

clean. Cool completely in the pan on a wire rack for 10 minutes. Carefully invert to remove the shortcake from the pan; cool right side up. Split into two layers. Place the bottom on a serving plate. Spoon most of the fruit over the bottom layer; top with half of the whipped cream. Replace the top piece; spoon the remaining fruit and cream over the top. Flavoring shortcakes The biscuit recipe for Old-Fashioned Strawberry Shortcakes is a good base from which to create flavored shortcakes:

• Add 4 teaspoons of poppy seeds for Poppy Seed Shortcakes.

• Mix in a large pinch of powdered saffron for Saffron Shortcakes.

• Add 2½ teaspoons ground cinna-mon for Cinnamon Shortcakes.

• Substitute ½ cup ground pecans for the same amount of flour for Pecan Shortcakes.

• Add the grated peel of 2 large oranges for Orange Shortcakes.

ENTERTAINING

MENU

Warm Cheese with Nuts
1995 S. Anderson Napa
Valley Brut ($28)
or
Mumm Cuvée Napa
Brut Prestige
(non-vintage, $15)

❖

Spiced Butternut Squash Soup
1998 Robert Mondavi
Pinot Noir Carneros ($35)
or
1998 Saintsbury Garnet
Carneros Pinot Noir ($15)

❖

**Roast Pork Tenderloin
with Zinfandel Sauce
Dried Fruit Compote**
1998 Frog's Leap Zinfandel ($25)
or
1998 Beaulieu Vineyard
Napa Valley Zinfandel ($11)

❖

Pear-Almond Tart
1995 Grgich Hills "Violetta" ($31)
or
1997 Joseph Phelps "Eisrebe" ($19)

*If any of these wines are
not available, ask your wine
merchant to suggest a wine
with similar characteristics.*

Roast Pork Tenderloin with Zinfandel Sauce, Dried Fruit Compote

A wine and food expert turns matchmaker with this elegant menu.

Text and Recipes by Maria Lorraine Binchet

Napa Valley is relatively small, but it is home to more than 300 wineries, many of them producing some of the best wine in the world. Though wine seems to course through our veins here, we are also very, very interested in food.

When food meets a perfect match in a wine, each becomes better. And that's the reasoning behind this classic-tasting menu. Each of the four courses is paired with a different wine (listing at left), so you are able to try a few of this region's wines and learn a bit about pairing in the process. Two wine recommendations are given for each course; you may choose either one, depending on your budget.

As you enjoy the dinner, ask your guests to identify the flavors they taste. Pay special attention to how the flavors of the food and wine work together.

Roast Pork Tenderloin with Zinfandel Sauce

*Pork makes a perfect **main dish** for this menu. Brined meat has a depth of flavor, tenderness and moistness after roasting that is striking in comparison to unbrined meats. This brine, as in most brines today, is used more for flavor than curing. The salt begins to cure the pork; the apple and orange juice flavor and tenderize it.*

BRINE
- 4 cups apple juice
- ½ cup frozen orange juice concentrate, thawed
- ⅓ cup packed brown sugar
- ¼ cup kosher (coarse) salt
- 1 tablespoon freshly ground pepper
- ½ vanilla bean, split lengthwise

PORK
- 3 pork tenderloins (about 2¼ lb.)
- 2 tablespoons olive oil

SAUCE
- ¾ cup Zinfandel or any good-quality red wine
- ¾ cup reduced-sodium chicken broth
- 2 tablespoons butter, cut up, softened

Two days ahead of time:

1. In large saucepan, mix all brine ingredients. Bring to a boil over medium-high heat. Remove from heat. Cover; refrigerate until completely cooled.

2. Place pork in shallow nonreactive pan or large resealable plastic bag. Pour chilled brine over pork, making sure brine completely covers pork. Cover tightly; refrigerate 2 days.

Day of serving:

3. Heat oven to 350°F. Remove pork from brine; pat dry. Discard brine. Tuck small ends of tenderloins under so that pork is same thickness throughout.

4. Heat oil in large ovenproof roasting pan over high heat until hot. Add pork; brown on all sides.

5. Place pan with pork in oven; bake 13 to 15 minutes or until internal temperature reaches 140°F. Remove pork from pan; place on cutting board. Cover loosely with foil; let stand 10 to 15 minutes before cutting into ½-inch-thick slices.

6. Meanwhile, place roasting pan over high heat. Add Zinfandel; bring to a boil, scraping up browned bits from bottom of pan. Add broth; boil until reduced by half. When liquid has been reduced by half, whisk in butter. Serve pork with sauce and accompany it with Dried Fruit Compote.

6 servings

PER SERVING: 345 calories, 15 g total fat (5.5 g saturated fat), 38.5 g protein, 11 g carbohydrate, 115 mg cholesterol, 1015 mg sodium, 0 g fiber

Spiced Butternut Squash Soup

*Make this **soup** two to three days ahead of time to allow the flavors to marry and to free up time the day of the party. For an extra touch, warm the soup bowls.*

- 2 tablespoons olive oil
- 1 medium onion, finely chopped
- 3 garlic cloves, minced

1 (1½-lb.) butternut squash, peeled, seeded, cut into 1-inch cubes (about 3 cups)
2 carrots, sliced
4 cups reduced-sodium chicken broth, or vegetable broth
4 teaspoons grated fresh ginger
¾ teaspoon salt
½ teaspoon ground coriander
½ teaspoon curry powder
6 tablespoons sour cream or crème fraîche
⅓ cup chopped fresh cilantro

1. Heat oil in large heavy saucepan over medium heat until hot. Add onion and garlic; cover and cook about 10 minutes or until onion has softened.
2. Remove cover. Stir in squash, carrots, broth, ginger, salt, coriander and curry powder. Simmer about 30 min-utes or until vegetables are tender.
3. Puree soup in batches in food processor or blender. Cover and refrig-erate until ready to serve. (Soup will be quite thick after refrigeration.)
4. Slowly reheat soup in large saucepan over medium heat, stirring occasionally. If necessary, to thin soup, add up to an additional 1 cup broth. Ladle soup into individual soup bowls. Garnish each with sour cream and cilantro.

6 (about ¾-cup) servings

PER SERVING: 170 calories, 8.5 g total fat (2.5 g saturated fat), 5.5 g protein, 20.5 g carbohydrate, 10 mg cholesterol, 630 mg sodium, 4.5 g fiber

Warm Cheese with Nuts

*There are two delicious contrasts in this **appetizer**: the shift in texture from the cheese's crunchy crust to its soft, gooey center; and the extremes in temperature between the hot cheese just out of the oven and the chilled Champagne. A varia-tion is to make individually sized medal-lions and place them, after baking, on a salad of mixed greens tossed with a clas-sic vinaigrette.*

½ cup walnuts or hazelnuts
2 tablespoons grated lemon peel
1 tablespoon chopped fresh tarragon
12 oz. soft goat cheese
1 egg, beaten
   Crackers or bread

1. In food processor, combine walnuts, lemon peel and tarragon; pulse until finely ground. Place in shallow bowl.
2. Shape cheese into 3 (½-inch-thick) rounds.
3. Dip each cheese round in egg, then ground nut mixture, coating all sides thoroughly. Place on baking sheet. Refrigerate 30 minutes to 2 hours.
4. When ready to serve, heat oven to 375°F. Bake 10 to 12 minutes or until nuts are lightly toasted and cheese is warm. Let stand 5 to 10 minutes. Serve with crackers or bread.

6 servings

PER SERVING: 215 calories, 18 g total fat (9 g saturated fat), 10 g protein, 4.5 g carbohydrate, 75 mg cholesterol, 205 mg sodi-um, .5 g fiber

Dried Fruit Compote

The combination of the sweet dried fruit with black pepper and balsamic vinegar gives this compote a complex, mouth-awakening flavor. Make the compote a few days ahead of the party to allow the flavors to meld.

1 tablespoon butter
½ medium onion, finely chopped
½ cup dried cranberries
½ cup chopped dried apricots
½ cup chopped pitted prunes

Warm Cheese with Nuts

2 cups red wine
½ cup fresh orange juice
4 teaspoons grated orange
     peel
1 tablespoon sugar
1 teaspoon chopped fresh
     rosemary
1 teaspoon balsamic vinegar
¾ teaspoon freshly ground
     pepper

1. In medium saucepan, melt butter over medium heat. Add onion; sauté 8 to 10 minutes or until softened.

2. Reduce heat to medium-low. Add all remaining ingredients; cook 30 to 40 minutes or until nearly all liquid is absorbed.

3. Cover and refrigerate until ready to serve. (Compote is best made 2 to 3 days ahead to allow flavors to blend and pepper to mellow.) Allow compote to come to room temperature before serving.

6 (about ⅓-cup) servings

PER SERVING: 145 calories, 2 g total fat (1 g saturated fat), 1.5 g protein, 30 g carbohydrate, 5 mg cholesterol, 20 mg sodium, 2.5 g fiber

Pear-Almond Tart

*This classic tart for **dessert** consists of a simple butter cookie crust, an almond filling and any fruit in season (pears and almonds are perfect for autumn but use whatever is fresh and ripe).*

CRUST
1 cup all-purpose flour
6 tablespoons sugar
¼ teaspoon salt
6 tablespoons unsalted butter,
     chilled, cut up
1 egg yolk

FILLING
⅓ cup unsalted butter,
     softened
½ cup sugar
1 tablespoon amaretto or
     orange-flavored liqueur,
     if desired
½ teaspoon vanilla
1 egg
¾ cup ground almonds

FRUIT
2 large firm ripe pears,
     peeled, sliced

1. In food processor, combine flour, 6 tablespoons sugar and salt; pulse until mixture is combined. Add 6 tablespoons butter; pulse until mixture resembles coarse crumbs. Add egg yolk; pulse just until dough begins to form. Add water 1 teaspoon at a time if dough seems dry.

2. Place dough on lightly floured surface; shape into flat round. Wrap in plastic wrap; refrigerate at least 4 hours or overnight.

3. Heat oven to 375°F. In medium bowl, beat ⅓ cup butter and ½ cup sugar at medium speed until well blended. Add amaretto, vanilla and egg; beat until thoroughly mixed. Add almonds; beat 3 to 4 minutes or until mixture is light and fluffy.

4. On lightly floured surface, roll out chilled dough to form 12-inch round. Line 9½-inch tart pan with dough; trim edges. Spread almond filling in crust. Arrange pears over filling, overlapping slices slightly. Place tart on baking sheet.

5. Place baking sheet with tart in oven. Immediately reduce oven temperature to 350°F. Bake 45 to 50 minutes or until set. Cool on wire rack.

8 servings

PER SERVING: 425 calories, 25.5 g total fat (11 g saturated fat), 6 g protein, 46.5 g carbohydrate, 95 mg cholesterol, 85 mg sodium, 3.5 g fiber

WINE AND FOOD PAIRING TIPS

Choose wine with some of the same flavors as the food you're serving. When food and wine have similar tastes, they seem to melt seamlessly into one another in your mouth. For example, the lemon and tarragon in Warm Cheese with Nuts are similar to the subtle citrus and herbal notes of sparkling wine. Effervescence complements fat and salt, so bubbly wines are often served with smoked salmon, caviar and cheese. Here are some additional pairing tips:

- Cook the food with some of the wine you plan to serve. This is the easiest way to get a good pairing and the reason Zinfandel is added to the sauce for the pork tenderloin.

- Identify the flavors in the wine first; then use ingredients that mimic them. For example, the dark cherry, prune and black pepper tastes that are characteristic of Zinfandel were the basis for the ingredients chosen for Dried Fruit Compote.

- The dessert should be less sweet than the dessert-course wine. Otherwise, the dessert wine tastes sour in comparison. Choose fruit desserts balanced between tangy and sweet, or semisweet or bittersweet chocolate desserts.

CHRISTMAS
BUFFET

Crown Roast of Pork, Apricot-Wild Rice Stuffing

MENU

Apple-Walnut Endive Salad
with Roquefort Croutons

❖

Crown Roast of Pork

❖

Apricot-Wild Rice Stuffing

❖

Steamed Vegetables

❖

Cranberry Steamed Pudding
with Creamy Butter Sauce

❖

Butterscotch Cashew
Bread Pudding

A Pittsburgh caterer shares her menu for an elegant dinner for twelve.

Text and Recipes by Rania Harris

Planning the menu for Christmas dinner begins the same way each year for me. I agonize over what might top last year's meal. It's only when I remember to consider what my family expects to see on the buffet table that calm and reason return. If I didn't prepare Crown Roast of Pork with Apricot-Wild Rice Stuffing, there would be ashes in my stocking and no gifts under the tree. And my family would mutiny if Cranberry Steamed Pudding with Creamy Butter Sauce wasn't served for dessert.

I have no quarrel with their tastes—these are excellent dishes—but there's still room for something new. This year it's a salad of endive, apple and walnuts. Even those who shy away from anything green will gravitate to its exciting flavors. It just may become a standard with my crew, making next year's Christmas dinner that much easier to plan.

Crown Roast of Pork

The butcher can cut crown roast of pork to whatever size you need—eight ribs for eight people, 12 ribs for 12 people, and so on.

- 1 (6- to 7-lb.) crown roast of pork (12 rib chops)
- 1 teaspoon dried sage
- 1 teaspoon dried thyme
- 1 teaspoon kosher (coarse) salt
- ½ teaspoon freshly ground pepper
- ½ cup molasses
- ½ cup soy sauce
- 2 medium onions, coarsely chopped
- 2 large carrots, coarsely chopped
  Apricot-Wild Rice Stuffing (recipe follows)

1. Heat oven to 350°F. Sprinkle pork inside and out with sage, thyme, salt and pepper. Cover exposed bones with foil. Place roast in large roasting pan. Place 1 cup water in bottom of pan.
2. In small bowl, combine molasses and soy sauce; blend well. Brush over roast. Place onions and carrots around roast.
3. Bake 2 to 2¼ hours or until internal temperature reaches 155°F., basting occasionally with remaining molasses-soy mixture. (Add additional water to bottom of pan if necessary.) Place roast on platter; tent with foil. Let stand 20 minutes.
4. Strain vegetables, reserving accumulated juices; discard vegetables. Place juices in serving bowl. Remove foil and string from roast. Fill center with cooked Apricot-Wild Rice Stuffing.
12 servings

PER SERVING: 330 calories, 17 g total fat (6 g saturated fat), 31 g protein, 13 g carbohydrate, 90 mg cholesterol, 885 mg sodium, 1 g fiber

Apricot-Wild Rice Stuffing

- 1½ cups wild rice
- 1 cup chopped dried apricots
- ½ cup dry sherry
- ½ cup water
- ½ cup dried cherries
- ½ cup pine nuts, toasted*
- ¼ cup chopped fresh parsley
- ¼ teaspoon freshly grated nutmeg
- ¼ teaspoon ground cloves
- ¼ teaspoon salt
- ¼ teaspoon freshly ground pepper
- ¼ cup unsalted butter
- ¾ cup finely chopped celery
- ½ cup chopped green onions

1. Cook wild rice according to package directions.
2. Meanwhile, in medium bowl, combine apricots, sherry and water. Heat in microwave on high 1 to 2 minutes or until hot. Let stand 10 minutes; drain.
3. Heat oven to 350°F. Grease 2-quart casserole. Drain apricots and discard soaking liquid; place apricots in large bowl. Add cooked wild rice, cherries, pine nuts, parsley, nutmeg, cloves, salt and pepper.
4. Melt butter in large skillet. Add celery; cook 6 to 8 minutes or just until tender. Add green onions; cook 30

seconds. Add to wild rice mixture; mix well. Spoon into casserole.

5. Bake 30 to 40 minutes or until hot.

TIP *To toast pine nuts, place in dry medium skillet. Heat over medium heat, stirring until pine nuts begin to brown. Watch carefully to prevent burning.

12 servings

PER SERVING: 205 calories, 7 g total fat (3 g saturated fat), 4.5 g protein, 32 g carbohydrate, 10 mg cholesterol, 330 mg sodium, 5 g fiber

Apple-Walnut Endive Salad with Roquefort Croutons

DRESSING

1   red onion, thinly sliced
¼   cup balsamic vinegar
½   cup extra-virgin olive oil
¼   teaspoon salt
¼   teaspoon freshly ground
     pepper

SALAD

2   heads curly endive
2   Granny Smith apples,
     unpeeled, thinly sliced
¾   cup coarsely chopped
     walnuts, toasted

CROUTONS

4   oz. Roquefort cheese,
     softened
6   slices firm white bread,
     crusts removed, toasted
2   tablespoons finely chopped
     fresh chives

1. To prepare dressing, place onion slices in medium bowl; cover with vinegar. Let stand 20 minutes. Drain vinegar from onions into small bowl. Reserve onions. Whisk oil, salt and pepper into vinegar.

2. Meanwhile, remove tough dark outer leaves of endive, saving only pale green and white tender leaves. Tear into bite-size pieces; place in large bowl.

3. To prepare croutons, crumble cheese

over bread; spread with knife. Place on baking sheet. Broil 1 to 2 minutes or until cheese is melted and bubbly. Sprinkle toast with chives. Cut each toast into 4 triangles.

4. When ready to serve, combine endive, apples, walnuts and onions. Add dressing; toss to mix. Place on serving platter. Arrange croutons around salad.

12 servings

PER SERVING: 225 calories, 17 g total fat (3.5 g saturated fat), 5 g protein, 14.5 g carbohydrate, 5 mg cholesterol, 265 mg sodium, 3 g fiber

Cranberry Steamed Pudding with Creamy Butter Sauce

This recipe was given to me more than 20 years ago by a dear friend whose family has been making it for generations. It's the most comforting and delicious pudding I've ever eaten.

PUDDING

1   cup molasses
1   cup hot water
2⅔ cups all-purpose flour
4   teaspoons baking soda
½   teaspoon salt
4   cups fresh cranberries
1   cup chopped walnuts
     Creamy Butter Sauce
     (recipe follows)

1. Grease and flour 10- to 12-cup Bundt pan. In large bowl, combine molasses and water; mix well. Add flour, baking soda and salt; whisk just until blended. Fold in cranberries and walnuts. Pour mixture into pan. Cover with foil.

2. Place steamer basket in large pot big enough to hold steamer* and Bundt pan. Add enough water to just touch bottom of steamer. Place Bundt pan on steamer. Place lid on pot.

3. Bring water to a boil. Reduce heat to medium-low; steam 2 hours or until pudding has puffed and long skewer inserted in center comes out almost

clean. (Some pudding will stick to skewer even when it is cooked through.) During cooking, add more boiling water as needed to maintain water level.**

4. Remove Bundt pan from steamer; let cool 15 minutes. Invert onto serving plate; carefully remove pan. Serve warm with Creamy Butter Sauce. (Pudding may be made ahead. Cool completely; remove from pan. Wrap in plastic wrap; refrigerate until serving time. To reheat, unwrap and place on ovenproof serving dish; cover with foil. Heat in preheated 350°F. oven for about 30 minutes or until hot.)

TIPS *A vegetable steamer works well—the center post fits right into the center of the Bundt pan.

**To check water level, make a hole in foil in center of Bundt pan. Use a funnel inserted into center to add boiling water.

16 servings

PER SERVING: 395 calories, 17 g total fat (8 g saturated fat), 3.5 g protein, 58.5 g carbohydrate, 35 mg cholesterol, 405 mg sodium, 2 g fiber

Creamy Butter Sauce

2   cups sugar
⅔   cup unsalted butter
1   cup whipping cream
1   tablespoon vanilla

In large saucepan, combine sugar, butter and cream; blend well. Bring to a boil over medium heat. Watch carefully so mixture does not boil over. Boil 3 to 4 minutes or until slightly thickened. Remove from heat; stir in vanilla. Serve warm. (Sauce may be made up to 3 days ahead. Cool completely; store in refrigerator.)

Butterscotch-Cashew Bread Pudding

To truly gild the lily on this homey, gooey dessert, scoop some vanilla bean ice cream onto each serving of pudding

Butterscotch-Cashew Bread Pudding

before drizzling on the Butterscotch-Cashew Sauce. The bit of salt on the cashews intensifies the sauce's caramel flavor.

BREAD PUDDING
- ¼ cup butter
- 4 cups (about 8 oz.) fresh French bread cubes (¾-inch pieces)
- 2 cups milk
- ½ cup packed brown sugar
- 3 eggs, slightly beaten
- 1 teaspoon rum extract

BUTTERSCOTCH-CASHEW SAUCE

- ¼ cup butter
- ½ cup coarsely chopped salted cashews
- ½ cup light corn syrup
- ½ cup packed brown sugar
- 2 tablespoons water
- ¼ cup whipping cream

1. Heat oven to 350°F. Place butter in 2-quart casserole; melt butter in oven. Remove from oven; add bread cubes and toss to coat.

2. In medium bowl, combine milk, brown sugar, eggs and rum extract; blend well. Pour over bread cubes. Bake

55 to 60 minutes or until center is set. Serve pudding with warm Butterscotch-Cashew Sauce.

3. To prepare sauce, in medium skillet, melt butter over medium-low heat. Add cashews; sauté 3 minutes. Carefully stir in corn syrup, brown sugar and water. Cook and stir until sugar is dissolved. Stir in cream. Bring to a boil; reduce heat to low. Boil gently, uncovered, 5 minutes. Serve warm over bread pudding.

6 servings

PARTY
STARTERS

Rogan Josh Meatballs

Recipes by Janice Cole

I magine this: It's nearly midnight on New Year's Eve, but your guests don't seem to care. They have appetizers on their minds and in their hands. Between bites they praise you for your culinary skills. Suddenly the clock strikes midnight and everyone raises their glasses for a toast—but it's you they're toasting, not the new year.

That's the vision we held when we created these recipes. No matter what kind of celebration was planned—a splashy bash at Christmas or New Year's or a casual summer gathering—the food, we said, must be perfect for the occasion: new flavors in spectacular-looking dishes that don't take days to make.

While some are familiar-looking favorites, others may be newcomers to your party buffet. All of them, however, are decidedly superb in taste. The ingredients—star anise, ginger, mint, chanterelles, goat cheese and more—make these offerings worthy of any celebration.

Rogan Josh Meatballs

Rogan Josh, the spicy, rich lamb stew of northern India, was the inspiration for these meatballs. The tomato-based sauce, scented with ginger, cinnamon and cardamom and spiked with cayenne, adds authentic flavor.

- 1 lb. ground lamb
- 2 tablespoons chopped fresh cilantro
- 4 teaspoons minced fresh ginger
- 2 teaspoons ground cumin
- ½ teaspoon salt
- ½ teaspoon cinnamon
- ¼ teaspoon freshly ground black pepper
- 5 garlic cloves, minced
- 1 tablespoon olive oil
- 1 teaspoon ground cardamom
- ½ teaspoon ground red pepper (cayenne)
- 1 (14.5-oz.) can crushed tomatoes
- ½ cup water

1. In large bowl, combine lamb, cilantro, 2 teaspoons of the ginger, cumin, salt, cinnamon, black pepper and 3 of the garlic cloves; mix until blended. Shape into 36 (about 1-inch) meatballs.
2. Heat oil in deep, large skillet or nonreactive Dutch oven over medium-high heat until hot. Cook meatballs in batches until browned. Place meatballs on plate.
3. Reduce heat to medium; in same skillet, combine remaining 2 teaspoons ginger and 2 garlic cloves, cardamom and ground red pepper. Cook, stirring constantly, 1 minute. Return meatballs to skillet; add tomatoes and water. Bring mixture to a boil. Reduce heat to low; simmer 20 to 30 minutes or until meatballs are no longer pink in center and sauce is thickened. Serve warm. (Meatballs can be made up to 2 days ahead. Cover and refrigerate.)
36 meatballs

PER MEATBALL: 30 calories, 2 g total fat (1 g saturated fat), 2 g protein, 1 g carbohydrate, 10 mg cholesterol, 55 mg sodium, 0 g fiber

Star Anise Chicken Skewers with Honey-Ginger Sauce

- 2 cups orange juice
- ¼ cup hoisin sauce
- 3 tablespoons star anise
- 2 tablespoons packed brown sugar
- 2 teaspoons minced fresh ginger
- ½ teaspoon crushed red pepper flakes
- 2 large garlic cloves, minced
- 1 lb. boneless skinless chicken breast halves
- 2 tablespoons chopped fresh cilantro
  Honey-Ginger Sauce (recipe follows)

1. In medium saucepan, combine all ingredients except chicken, cilantro and Honey-Ginger Sauce; mix well. Bring to a boil over medium heat; boil 1 minute. Remove from heat; cool.
2. Meanwhile, cut chicken breasts into 3x½-inch strips. Thread chicken strips onto 32 (6-inch) bamboo skewers; place in 13x9-inch (3-quart) glass baking dish. Pour cooled orange juice mixture over chicken. Cover; refrigerate at least 8 hours or up to 24 hours to marinate.
3. When ready to cook, heat oven to 450°F. Line 15x10x1-inch pan with foil.

Star Anise Chicken Skewers with Honey-Ginger Sauce

Place wire rack on foil in pan; spray rack and foil with nonstick cooking spray. Remove chicken skewers from marinade; place skewers on rack. Discard marinade. Bake 5 to 8 minutes or until chicken is no longer pink in center. Sprinkle with cilantro. Serve warm with Honey-Ginger Sauce.

32 appetizers

PER APPETIZER: 40 calories, .5 g total fat (0 g saturated fat), 3 g protein, 6 g carbohydrate, 10 mg cholesterol, 30 mg sodium, 0 g fiber

Honey-Ginger Sauce

½ cup honey
¼ cup rice vinegar
2 teaspoons soy sauce
2 teaspoons minced fresh
     cilantro
2 teaspoons grated fresh
     ginger
½ teaspoon crushed red
     pepper flakes

In small bowl, combine all sauce ingredients; blend well. Cover; refrigerate until ready to serve. Serve at room temperature.

Vegetable Spring Rolls with Cilantro-Lime Dip

¾ cup sour cream
1 tablespoon minced shallots
1 tablespoon soy sauce
12 (6½-inch-round) sheets
     rice paper
1 carrot, cut into matchstick-
     size strips
½ cucumber, cut into
     matchstick-size strips
12 small leaves Boston or
     Bibb lettuce, center ribs
     removed
¼ cup purchased roasted red
     bell peppers, cut into strips
½ avocado, sliced lengthwise
     into thin strips
½ fresh cilantro sprigs

Cilantro-Lime Dip
(recipe follows)

1. In small bowl, combine sour cream, shallots and soy sauce; blend well. Set aside.
2. Dampen several cloth towels with water; lay one towel flat on counter. Dip 1 sheet rice paper in shallow pan of water; place on towel. Without overlapping, lay as many wet rice paper sheets as possible on towel. Cover with second towel. Continue layering remaining sheets of rice paper in towels.
3. In medium bowl, toss together carrot and cucumber strips.
4. To assemble, place 1 lettuce leaf on 1 sheet rice paper; spread with 1 tablespoon sour cream mixture. Place ¹/₁₂ each of carrot mixture, roasted bell pepper and avocado, and 1 cilantro sprig in center. Roll up by folding one edge of rice paper over vegetable mixture; fold in sides and roll tightly. Place seam side down on plate. Repeat with remaining rice paper sheets and vegetables. Cover; refrigerate until ready to serve. (Spring rolls can be made up to 8 hours ahead. Cover and refrigerate.)
5. To serve, cut rolls in half diagonally. Serve with Cilantro-Lime Dip.

24 servings

PER SERVING: 60 calories, 4.5 g total fat (2 g saturated fat), 1 g protein, 4 g carbohydrate, 10 mg cholesterol, 105 mg sodium, .5 g fiber

Vegetable Spring Rolls with Cilantro-Lime Dip

Cilantro-Lime Dip

½ cup mayonnaise
½ cup sour cream
3 tablespoons chopped fresh
   cilantro
2 teaspoons fresh lime juice
1 teaspoon fresh lime peel
⅛ teaspoon salt

Combine all ingredients in food processor. Process until well blended and smooth.

Wild Mushroom Turnovers

The combination of mushrooms lends a rich, almost smoky flavor to these turnovers.

¼ cup unsalted butter
8 oz. specialty mushrooms
   (shiitakes, portobellos,
   chanterelles or crimini),
   finely chopped
4 garlic cloves, minced
¼ cup (2 oz.) cream cheese
2 tablespoons minced
   fresh chives
½ teaspoon lemon juice
¼ teaspoon salt
⅛ teaspoon freshly ground
   pepper
1 (17.3-oz.) pkg. frozen
   puff pastry, thawed
1 egg, beaten

1. Line baking sheet with parchment paper. Melt butter in large skillet over medium heat. Add mushrooms and garlic; sauté 8 to 10 minutes or until liquid is absorbed.
2. Remove from heat. Stir in cream cheese, chives, lemon juice, salt and pepper. Cool.
3. On lightly floured surface, roll 1 sheet puff pastry to 12-inch square. Cut into 25 squares, each about 2¼ inches square. Brush lightly with egg. Place 1 teaspoon mushroom mixture in center of each square. Fold in half diagonally

Scallop Bundles

to form triangles; press edges to seal. Place on baking sheet. Repeat with remaining puff pastry sheet and mushroom mixture. Cover; refrigerate until ready to bake. (Turnovers can be made up to 2 weeks ahead. Cover and freeze. Bake directly from freezer 20 to 25 minutes.)
4. To bake, heat oven to 400°F. Bake 15 to 20 minutes or until golden brown. Serve warm.
50 turnovers

PER TURNOVER: 75 calories, 6 g total fat (2.5 g saturated fat), 1 g protein, 4 g carbohydrate, 10 mg cholesterol, 40 mg sodium, 0 g fiber

Scallop Bundles

The bundles can be prepared ahead of time and only need last-minute baking before serving.

4 garlic cloves, coarsely
   chopped
¼ teaspoon salt
6 tablespoons butter, cut up
2 tablespoons chopped fresh
   tarragon
8 sea scallops (about

1½ inches diameter),
    quartered
½ teaspoon grated lemon peel
6 sheets frozen phyllo dough,
   thawed

1. Heat oven to 400°F. Line baking sheet with parchment paper. Place garlic on cutting board; sprinkle with salt. With side of knife or fork, mash garlic and salt together. Place in small bowl.
2. Melt butter in small saucepan over low heat. Add half of garlic mixture; cook 1 minute. Remove from heat; stir in 1 tablespoon of the tarragon.
3. Add scallops to remaining garlic mixture; stir in remaining 1 tablespoon tarragon and lemon peel.
4. Place 1 sheet phyllo dough on work surface; brush lightly with butter mixture. Top with second sheet of phyllo dough; brush lightly with butter mixture. Repeat with third sheet phyllo. Cut stack of phyllo into 16 squares.
5. Place 1 scallop piece in center of each phyllo square. Bring edges up over scallop; pinch edges together to form bundle. Place on baking sheet. Repeat with remaining phyllo and scallops. (Scallop bundles can be prepared up to

Gorgonzola Apple Tart

6 hours ahead. Cover and refrigerate.)
6. Bake 10 to 13 minutes or until scallops are opaque and phyllo is golden brown.

32 appetizers

PER APPETIZER: 45 calories, 2.5 g total fat (1.5 g saturated fat), 3 g protein, 3 g carbohydrate, 10 mg cholesterol, 70 mg sodium, 0 g fiber

Gorgonzola Apple Tart

CRUST
- 1 1/4 cups all-purpose flour
- 1/4 teaspoon salt
- 1/2 cup unsalted butter, chilled, cut up
- 2 to 4 tablespoons ice water

FILLING
- 3 tablespoons unsalted butter
- 3 tablespoons minced shallots
- 1 tablespoon unseasoned dry bread crumbs
- 2 large Granny Smith apples, peeled, cut into 1/4-inch slices
- 1 egg, beaten
- 1/4 cup chopped walnuts
- 1/4 cup (1 oz.) crumbled Gorgonzola cheese
- 2 tablespoons chopped fresh Italian parsley

1. In medium bowl, combine flour and salt; mix well. Add 1/2 cup butter; with pastry blender or 2 knives, work butter into flour until mixture is the size of small peas. Add 2 tablespoons water; mix until dough forms, using additional water if necessary. Cover; refrigerate 30 minutes or until chilled.
2. Meanwhile, melt 3 tablespoons butter in small skillet over medium heat. Add shallots; sauté 1 minute. Cool.
3. Heat oven to 400°F. Line baking sheet with parchment paper. On lightly floured surface, roll out dough to 13-inch round. Place on baking sheet; brush with half of butter-shallot mixture. Sprinkle with bread crumbs. Leaving 1 1/2-inch edge on outside, arrange apples on dough, overlapping slices in concentric circles. Brush apples with remaining butter mixture. Fold dough edge over apples.
4. Bake 30 minutes. Brush crust lightly with egg; sprinkle walnuts over apples. Bake an additional 10 minutes or until tart is golden brown. Remove from oven; top with cheese. Cool slightly on wire rack. Sprinkle with parsley; serve warm or at room temperature.

24 servings

PER SERVING: 95 calories, 6.5 g total fat (3.5 g saturated fat), .5 g protein, 8 g carbohydrate, 20 mg cholesterol, 50 mg sodium, .5 g fiber

Basil-Mint Artichoke Spread

Serve this spread in a bowl set inside a hollowed-out fresh artichoke, surrounded by cut-up vegetables and French bread slices.

- 1 (14-oz.) can artichoke hearts, drained
- 2 tablespoons chopped fresh basil
- 2 tablespoons chopped fresh mint
- 1 garlic clove, minced
- 6 oz. soft goat cheese
- 1/4 teaspoon freshly ground pepper
- Dash salt

In food processor, combine artichoke hearts, basil, mint and garlic; process until artichoke hearts are coarsely chopped. Add cheese, pepper and salt; process until well blended.

1 cup

PER TABLESPOON: 35 calories, 2.5 g total fat (1.5 g saturated fat), 2 g protein, 2 g carbohydrate, 10 mg cholesterol, 100 mg sodium, 1 g fiber

Chocolate Chevre Appetizers

Chocolate Chevre Appetizers

We came across this unusual combination of goat cheese and chocolate on a recent trip to Paris, where these elegant little bites were the talk of Parisian parties.

- 8 oz. goat cheese (chèvre)*
- 2 tablespoons powdered sugar
- 8 oz. bittersweet chocolate, chopped
- ½ teaspoon finely chopped fresh rosemary
- ½ teaspoon finely chopped nuts

1. In medium bowl, combine cheese and powdered sugar; mix until well blended. Place half of cheese mixture in center of large sheet of plastic wrap. Gently pat cheese into ¾-inch-thick block. Fold plastic wrap around cheese; repeat with remaining half of cheese. Place cheese in freezer 1 hour 15 minutes to 1 hour 30 minutes or until well chilled and slightly firm.

2. Place chocolate** in small heat-resistant bowl. Bring 1 inch water to a boil in small saucepan. Remove from heat. Place bowl with chocolate over saucepan (bowl should not touch water). Let stand until chocolate is melted.

3. Line baking sheet with foil. With warm knife, cut each cheese block into 12 (¾-inch) squares. Place 1 cheese square on fork; dip into melted chocolate, covering all sides. Remove from chocolate, letting excess chocolate drip away. Place on foil-lined baking sheet; sprinkle lightly with rosemary or nuts. Dip remaining cheese squares.

4. Refrigerate about 5 minutes or until set. Store in airtight container in refrigerator.

TIPS *Look for a mild, soft goat cheese (chevre) that is not too moist.
** It is easier for novices to work with half the chocolate and half the cheese at a time. Keep remaining cheese refrigerated until ready to dip.
24 appetizers

PER APPETIZER: 75 calories, 5 g total fat (3 g saturated fat), 2 g protein, 7 g carbohydrate, 10 mg cholesterol, 35 mg sodium, .5 g fiber

Roasted Antipasto

- 2 oranges
- 1 (14-oz.) can artichoke hearts, drained, quartered
- 1 red bell pepper, cut into 1½-inch pieces
- 1 yellow bell pepper, cut into 1½-inch pieces
- ¾ cup pitted kalamata olives
- ¾ cup pitted cracked green olives or green olives
- 4 garlic cloves, minced
- ¼ cup extra-virgin olive oil
- 1 tablespoon chopped fresh rosemary
- 1 teaspoon anise seeds

1. Heat oven to 425°F. With vegetable peeler, cut long strips of orange peel from oranges, being careful not to include any of the white pith directly below the peel. Cut peel into ½-inch-wide strips.

2. In large bowl, combine orange peel, artichoke hearts, bell peppers, olives and garlic. Add oil, rosemary and anise seeds; toss to coat. Spread evenly in 15x10x1-inch pan.

3. Bake 20 to 30 minutes or until vegetables are crisp-tender and lightly browned. Cool. Serve at room temperature. (Antipasto can be made up to 1 day ahead. Cover and refrigerate.)
4 cups

PER 1/4 CUP: 60 calories, 5 g total fat (.5 g saturated fat), 1 g protein, 4 g carbohydrate, 0 mg cholesterol, 275 mg sodium, 1.5 g fiber

SEASONED WITH
HERBS

MENU

Two-Basil Sparkling
Lemonade

❖

Fresh Dill and
Flax Seed Crackers
and
Goat Cheese Spread
with Fresh Dill

❖

Grilled Stuffed Pork Chops

❖

Apricot and Lavender
Compote

Grilled Stuffed Pork Chops and Two-Basil Sparkling Lemonade (page 118)

Herbs take lead roles in a summertime menu brimming with flavor.

Text by Laurel Keser; Recipes by Monique Jamet Hooker

Cooking with fresh herbs is like directing a play. You can cast an herb in a leading role (think pesto over pasta). Or you can give an herb a supporting role by merely accenting a flavor—dill with salmon, for instance, or chives with sour cream. When gardens and produce markets are brimming with fresh herbs, it's the perfect time to set the scene at your table with a cast of herbal characters. These versatile performers, with their bright green wardrobe, aromatic scents and countless flavors, can carry the show from appetizers to desserts. When the curtain closes, count on a standing ovation, with a little help from these talented actors.

Two-Basil Sparkling Lemonade

One of the most common herbs is used in an uncommon way here—to flavor a tangy lemonade. If you grow one of the hundreds of flavored basil varieties, now's your chance to use it. I've suggested pairing cinnamon, lemon or opal basil with the sweet basil, but you can use another variety or a combination of basils.

    1   cup sugar
    1½ cups water
    ⅓   cup honey
    ½   cup chopped fresh basil
    ¼   cup chopped fresh
          cinnamon, lemon or opal
          basil
    3   tablespoons finely grated
          lemon peel
    2   cups fresh lemon juice
    10 cups plain or lemon-

    flavored sparkling water
    1   cup tequila, pastis or dry
          vermouth, if desired
        Lemon slices
        Basil sprigs

1. In medium saucepan, combine sugar, water and honey; mix well. Cook over medium heat until sugar has dissolved, stirring occasionally.
2. Add basil, cinnamon basil and lemon peel. Bring to a boil. Remove from heat; cover and let stand 30 minutes. Strain; discard basil and lemon peel. Stir in lemon juice.
3. In large pitcher, combine lemon juice mixture, sparkling water and tequila; stir gently to mix.* Serve over ice. Garnish with lemon slices and basil sprigs.

TIP *To make individual servings, combine 1 part lemon juice mixture and 2 parts sparkling water.

10 (1½-cup) servings

PER SERVING: 125 calories, 0 g total fat (0 g saturated fat), .5 g protein, 33 g carbohydrate, 0 mg cholesterol, 60 mg sodium, .5 g fiber

Fresh Dill and Flax Seed Crackers

Rather than breaking the crackers apart ahead of time, serve this whole and let guests break off their own pieces.

    3   cups all-purpose flour
    ¼   teaspoon salt
    1   (¼-oz.) pkg. active dry yeast
    5   tablespoons chopped fresh
           dill
    3   tablespoons flax seeds
    3   medium garlic cloves,
           minced
    1¼   cups warm water
           (110°F. to 115°F.)

1. In large bowl, combine flour, salt and yeast; mix well. Stir in dill, flax seeds and garlic.
2. Make well in center of flour mixture. Add water; stir until dough forms.
3. Turn dough out onto lightly floured surface. Knead 2 to 3 minutes or until dough forms a soft ball. (Do not overknead or crackers will be chewy.) Place dough in lightly oiled bowl. Cover; let rise in warm place until double in size, about 45 minutes.
4. Meanwhile, heat oven to 350°F. Turn dough out onto lightly floured surface; knead gently to deflate. Divide dough into 3 pieces. Roll each piece very thin, about ¹⁄₁₆ inch thick. Place on ungreased baking sheet. Prick entire surface with fork. With knife, score dough for shape and size of crackers desired. (Do not cut through dough.)
5. Bake 16 to 20 minutes or until lightly browned. (Do not overbake. Crackers will crisp as they cool.) Cool. Cut on score lines. (Crackers can be made up to 2 days ahead. Store in an airtight container in a cool, dry place.)
5 to 6 dozen crackers

Apricot and Lavender Compote

Goat Cheese Spread with Fresh Dill

The fresh dill and pungent goat cheese beautifully complement the baked dill crackers.

- 12 oz. soft goat cheese, room temperature
- ½ cup sour cream
- ¼ cup chopped fresh dill
- 1 tablespoon paprika
- 1 tablespoon balsamic vinegar
- 1 tablespoon olive oil
- ½ teaspoon grated lemon peel
- ⅛ teaspoon salt
- ⅛ teaspoon freshly ground pepper
  Fresh dill sprigs

1. In medium bowl or food processor, combine all ingredients except dill sprigs; mix until well blended. (Spread can be made up to 2 days ahead. Cover and refrigerate. Bring to room temperature before serving.)
2. To serve, spoon into serving bowl. Garnish with dill sprigs.

2 cups

Grilled Stuffed Pork Chops

A cilantro-oregano pesto, roasted with fresh tomatoes, is stuffed into thick, juicy pork chops and grilled.

PORK CHOPS
- 1 cup chopped fresh cilantro
- ¼ cup chopped fresh oregano
- 2 tablespoons pine nuts
- 3 large garlic cloves
- ¼ cup olive oil
- 6 medium plum tomatoes, halved
- 6 boneless center-cut pork chops (1 inch thick)
- ½ cup crushed blue corn chips

GLAZE
- 6 tablespoons honey
- 1 tablespoon mustard
- ¼ teaspoon salt
- ¼ teaspoon freshly ground pepper

1. Heat oven to 425°F. Line 15x10x1-inch pan with foil. Soak 6 wooden toothpicks or bamboo skewers in cold water.
2. In food processor, combine cilantro, oregano, pine nuts, garlic and oil; process until well blended. Set aside.
3. Set small strainer over small bowl; squeeze tomatoes over strainer to collect juices. Reserve ¼ cup juice.* Place tomatoes on pan; spoon cilantro mixture into cavity of each tomato half.
4. Bake 20 minutes. Cool. (Tomatoes can be roasted up to 2 days ahead. Cover and refrigerate.)
5. Heat grill. Holding pork chop flat on work surface, cut opening in center of one side to form pocket. Sprinkle tomatoes with corn chips. Insert 2 tomato halves into each pocket; secure with toothpick or bamboo skewer.
6. In small bowl, combine honey, mustard and ¼ cup reserved tomato juice; mix well. Brush each pork chop with glaze; sprinkle with salt and pepper.
7. Place pork chops on gas grill over

medium heat or on charcoal grill 4 to 6 inches from medium coals. Cook 12 to 15 minutes or until pork is no longer pink in center, turning once and brushing with glaze.

TIP *If tomatoes do not yield ¼ cup juice, add tomato juice to measure ¼ cup.

6 servings

PER SERVING: 490 calories, 26.5 g total fat (39 g saturated fat), 25 g protein, 26.5 g carbohydrate, 105 mg cholesterol, 245 mg sodium, 1.5 g fiber

Apricot and Lavender Compote

When using lavender for the first time, add it gradually as it can be very strong, depending on the weather conditions under which it was grown. (You can always add more at the end of cooking or while cooling.) Lavender's flavor is stronger when it's been heated and after it has been stored for a few days. This compote also works well over sponge, pound or angel food cake.

1 lb. ripe apricots, quartered
¼ cup sugar
¼ cup honey
2 to 4 tablespoons fresh lavender flowers, coarsely chopped
1 vanilla bean, split lengthwise
1 quart vanilla ice cream

1. In large saucepan, combine all ingredients except ice cream; mix well. Cook over medium heat 6 to 8 minutes or until apricots are very soft and some of the juice has been reduced (a thick applesauce-like consistency).
2. Remove vanilla bean. Cool compote to room temperature. Serve over ice cream.

6 (2-cup) servings

PER SERVING: 285 calories, 10 g total fat (6 g saturated fat), 4 g protein, 48.5 g carbohydrate, 40 mg cholesterol, 70 mg sodium, 1.5 g fiber

HERBS IN THE SPOTLIGHT

Sweet basil is, to Italians, a symbol of love. What most of us love is basil's pungent, spicy-clove flavor and aroma. One of the most popular herbs, basil can find its way into nearly anything. Basil is the classic pesto herb, it serves as tomato's sidekick, and it adds another dimension to beef and lamb. It punches up a tossed salad and brightens oranges and grapefruit. Basil is native to India, Africa, Iran and Asia, and it seasons cuisines of the Mediterranean, especially Italian.

Lemon basil has a strong lemon scent popular in Indonesia. It's used in salads, marinades and desserts. It gives zip to rice, fish and poultry and makes a soothing tea.

Opal basil has iridescent purple leaves and a more pungent spicy-ginger taste than sweet basil. It's one of the most popular basils for herb vinegar and is also used to make jelly and pesto, and to season grilled vegetables.

Cinnamon basil has a spicy cinnamon flavor and is used in rice, marinades, butters, fruit salads and tea.

Cilantro is the leaf of the coriander plant, which also produces coriander seed. It's one of a handful of herbs that is totally edible from its roots to its flowers and seeds. Cilantro is popular in Asian and Mexican cuisines.

Dill, one of the oldest herbs, is a native of southern Europe and western Asia. Its feathery fronds frequently season potatoes, carrots, green beans, cucumbers and fish, as well as egg and cheese dishes. It's a savory addition to salads. Dill is commonly found in Jewish, Russian and eastern European stews and broths.

Lavender is used most often in desserts and teas but also lends its smoky, floral flavor to meats, fish, seafood and roasted vegetables. Lavender honey is a gourmet treat, and vinegar infused with lavender will add mystery to salad greens. Native to Greece, Italy, Northern Africa and Yugoslavia, lavender is grown extensively in Provence, France. Although the leaves are edible, it's the flowers that are most often called for in a recipe.

Oregano, best known for its place atop pizza, also partners well with mushrooms, broccoli, lamb, eggs, poultry, fish and beef. Salads, sauces and marinades, as well as soups, stews and breads, benefit from a sprinkle of oregano. Greek is the variety most prized for culinary purposes. It's also the one reportedly created by the Greek goddess Aphrodite as a symbol of happiness.

MEALS
IN
MINUTES

PICK-UP
PASTA

Pasta Niçoise

Fresh produce pairs with pasta for dishes that are almost as fast as take-out.

Text and Recipes by Mary Evans

It's a perfect and warm evening, too nice to linger in the kitchen preparing dinner. Or maybe there's a meeting or event to make, but you really want to cook something good. So set the pasta pot over high heat to bring water rapidly to a boil, then cook some noodles while you make a simple sauce. In the time it takes to cook the pasta al dente, you can make a sauce—cooked or uncooked—that boasts the season's freshest fare.

Team spinach and lemon with chicken in a sauce served over fettuccine. Pair linguine with a no-cook sauce of sun-dried tomatoes and feta cheese. Or combine a variety of grilled vegetables with a basil-and-oil sauce and serve over rotini. These pasta dishes are quick to make, and fast cooking preserves the fresh flavors of the ingredients. Enjoy, then go!

Pasta Niçoise

Look for pencil-thin green beans to use in this dish. The French call them haricots verts; they are in season throughout the warm weather months.

- 8 oz. farfalle (bow tie pasta)
- ½ lb. thin green beans, cut in half crosswise
- ¼ cup olive oil
- 4 garlic cloves, minced
- 4 cups chopped plum tomatoes
- ½ cup halved pitted kalamata olives
- 1 (9-oz.) can white albacore tuna packed in water, drained
- ¾ cup coarsely chopped fresh basil

1. Cook farfalle according to package directions, adding green beans during last 5 minutes of cooking time. Drain thoroughly.
2. Meanwhile, heat oil in large skillet over medium heat until hot. Add garlic; sauté 30 to 60 seconds or until garlic is fragrant.
3. Increase heat to medium-high. Add tomatoes, olives and tuna; cook an additional 2 to 3 minutes or until tomatoes are hot and slightly soft.
4. Toss farfalle with tuna mixture and basil.

4 (2-cup) servings

PER SERVING: 495 calories, 17.5 g total fat (2.5 g saturated fat), 26.5 g protein, 59 g carbohydrate, 20 mg cholesterol, 615 mg sodium, 6 g fiber

Grilled Vegetable Pasta Estivi

Estivi means summer in Italian. This dish is full of nature's bounty and makes a perfect meatless main course but can also be served as a side dish to grilled meat or fish.

- ½ small eggplant, cut into ½ -inch slices
- 2 medium zucchini, cut lengthwise into ½-inch slices
- 1 medium red onion, cut into ½ -inch slices
- 1 red bell pepper, cut into wedges
- ½ cup plus 2 tablespoons olive oil
- 8 oz. rotini (spiral-shaped pasta)
- ¼ cup chopped fresh basil
- 3 tablespoons red wine vinegar
- 1 teaspoon minced garlic
- 1 teaspoon Dijon mustard
- ¼ teaspoon salt
- ¼ teaspoon freshly ground pepper
- 1¼ cups freshly grated Parmesan cheese

1. Heat grill. Brush vegetables with 2 tablespoons of the olive oil.
2. Place vegetables on gas grill over medium-low heat or on charcoal grill 4 to 6 inches from medium-low coals. Cook 15 to 20 minutes or until vegetables are lightly browned and crisp-tender, turning every 5 minutes. Remove vegetables from grill; coarsely chop.
3. Meanwhile, cook rotini according to package directions. Reserve 2 tablespoons pasta water; drain rotini thoroughly.
4. While rotini is cooking, place remaining ½ cup oil, basil, vinegar, garlic, mustard, salt and pepper in blender; blend well. Add 1 cup of the cheese; blend until well mixed. Place in large bowl.

Chicken and Spinach Pasta

5. Add rotini, vegetables and reserved pasta water to bowl; toss to coat. Sprinkle with remaining ¼ cup cheese.
6 (1¾-cup) servings

PER SERVING: 475 calories, 29.5 g total fat (7 g saturated fat), 15 g protein, 37.5 g carbohydrate, 15 mg cholesterol, 645 mg sodium, 3.5 g fiber

Chicken and Spinach Pasta

Lemon adds punch to this easily prepared dish. For fast preparation, purchase chicken breasts that have been cut into strips.

1 tablespoon grated lemon peel
2 tablespoons fresh lemon juice
½ teaspoon coarsely ground pepper
1 lb. chicken breast strips
1 tablespoon olive oil
1 tablespoon minced garlic
¼ cup chicken broth
⅛ teaspoon salt

1 (10-oz.) pkg. stemmed washed spinach, coarsely chopped
1 (9-oz.) pkg. fresh spinach fettuccine
¼ cup pine nuts
4 oz. soft goat cheese

1. Combine lemon peel, lemon juice and pepper in medium bowl. Add chicken; mix well. Set aside.
2. Heat oil in large skillet over medium-high heat until hot. Add garlic; sauté 30 to 60 seconds or until fragrant. Add chicken mixture; sauté 2 minutes or until outside of chicken is no longer pink.
3. Add broth and salt; stir to blend. Add spinach; reduce heat to medium-low. Cover; cook 3 to 4 minutes or until spinach is wilted and chicken juices run clear, stirring occasionally.
4. Meanwhile, cook fettuccine according to package directions; drain thoroughly. Toss with chicken mixture. Sprinkle with pine nuts. Crumble goat cheese over pasta.

4 (1⅔-cup) servings

PER SERVING: 525 calories, 20 g total fat (7 g saturated fat), 39.5 g protein, 48 g carbohydrate, 140 mg cholesterol, 610 mg sodium, 4 g fiber

Pasta and Beans with Tomatoes and Pancetta

Pancetta is the Italian version of bacon but contains no smoky flavor. If unavailable, substitute mildly flavored bacon.

8 oz. orecchiette (small disk-shaped pasta) or shell-shaped pasta
½ cup chopped pancetta
1 small onion, chopped
2½ teaspoons chopped fresh rosemary
1 teaspoon minced garlic
2 cups coarsely chopped tomatoes
¼ cup red wine
¼ teaspoon salt
⅛ teaspoon freshly ground black pepper
   Dash crushed red pepper flakes
1 (19-oz.) can cannellini beans, drained, rinsed
2 tablespoons chopped fresh parsley

1. Cook orecchiette according to package directions.
2. Meanwhile, heat large skillet over medium-high heat until hot. Add pancetta; cook 2 to 3 minutes or until it begins to brown. Add onion; cook 2 to 3 minutes or until onion begins to soften. Add 2 teaspoons of the rosemary and garlic; cook an additional 30 seconds or until fragrant.
3. Add tomatoes, red wine, salt, pepper and red pepper flakes; mix well. Cook 4 to 5 minutes. Add beans; cook an additional 2 to 3 minutes or until sauce has thickened.
4. Add 3 to 4 tablespoons pasta cooking water to sauce to thin slightly. Drain

orecchiette thoroughly.

5. Toss orecchiette with sauce. Sprinkle with remaining ½ teaspoon rosemary and parsley.

4 (1½-cup) servings

PER SERVING: 425 calories, 4 g total fat (1 g saturated fat), 19 g protein, 78.5 g carbohydrate, 5 mg cholesterol, 700 mg sodium, 13 g fiber

Sun-Dried Tomato, Feta and Herbed Pasta

This no-cook pasta sauce is a breeze to prepare. Some brands of feta come already crumbled as an additional time-saver. Look for sun-dried tomatoes that are already julienned.

1 (8.5-oz.) jar julienne-cut sun-dried tomatoes in oil, undrained (about 1 cup)
8 oz. feta cheese, crumbled
¼ cup chopped fresh oregano
2 teaspoons chopped fresh mint
1 teaspoon minced fresh garlic
8 oz. linguine

1. In medium bowl, combine all ingredients except linguine; toss to combine. Let stand at room temperature to marinate while linguine is cooking.

2. Cook linguine according to package directions; drain thoroughly.

3. Toss linguine with tomato mixture. Let stand 1 to 2 minutes to warm topping before serving.

4 (1⅓-cup) servings

PER SERVING: 540 calories, 29.5 g total fat (11 g saturated fat), 17 g protein, 53 g carbohydrate, 50 mg cholesterol, 915 mg sodium, 3 g fiber

Thai-Style Shrimp and Peanut Pasta

Similar to pad thai, this dish substitutes readily available angel hair pasta for the more traditional rice noodles.

8 oz. capellini (angel hair pasta)
1 tablespoon vegetable oil
1 tablespoon minced garlic
1 to 2 red jalapeño chiles, chopped*
1¼ lb. shelled, deveined uncooked medium shrimp
1⅓ cups coconut milk
1 tablespoon packed brown sugar
3 tablespoons fresh lime juice
4 green onions, cut into 1½-inch matchstick-size strips
3 tablespoons fish sauce
¾ cup dry-roasted peanuts
2 tablespoons coarsely chopped fresh cilantro

1. Cook capellini according to package directions; drain thoroughly.

2. Meanwhile, heat oil in large skillet over medium heat until hot. Add garlic and chiles; sauté 1 to 2 minutes or until garlic is golden.

3. Increase heat to medium-high. Add shrimp; toss to coat. Sauté 1 to 2 minutes or until shrimp begin to turn pink.

4. Add coconut milk, brown sugar and lime juice; stir to blend. Bring to a boil. Cook 2 to 3 minutes or until shrimp turn pink. Remove from heat; stir in onions and fish sauce.

5. Toss capellini with shrimp sauce. Let stand 5 minutes to absorb some of sauce. Add peanuts and cilantro; toss gently to mix.

TIP *Remove seeds for a milder flavor.

4 (1¾-cup) servings

PER SERVING: 715 calories, 36 g total fat (18 g saturated fat), 40.5 g protein, 61.5 g carbohydrate, 200 mg cholesterol, 1110 mg sodium, 5 g fiber

Thai-Style Shrimp and Peanut Pasta

HOT
PROSPECTS

Turn leftovers from the Thanksgiving
bird into sought-after sandwiches.

Text and Recipes by Ethel G. Hofman

At Thanksgiving, roast turkey is the star feature of most
holiday tables. Because it's accompanied by an abun-
dance of side dishes and desserts, there is bound to be
leftover turkey. The carcass makes a rich stock, but how do you
make the leftover meat enticing? Transform it into hot and hearty
sandwiches as succulent as the day the turkey was served.

Turkey's mild taste is the perfect foil for a myriad of accompa-
nying flavors, from sweet and savory to traditional and exotic.
With that in mind, it's easy to see the possibilities. Mango chutney and portobello mushrooms join turkey in a grilled sandwich.
Apples simmered in balsamic vinegar pair with turkey and cheddar cheese between slices of crusty bread. And in a version of the
traditional muffuletta, roasted peppers and olives top turkey and
goat cheese. Now you're talking turkey!

Hot Turkey Sandwiches with Cheddar Cheese and Apples

The apples' crisp texture and tart flavor blend perfectly with the turkey and sweet sauté ingredients. Select apples that hold their shape during cooking, such as Rome, Jonathan or Gala.

- 2 tablespoons packed brown sugar
- 1 tablespoon vegetable oil
- 2 teaspoons balsamic vinegar
- 2 medium apples, unpeeled, sliced
- 1 lb. sliced cooked turkey
- ½ teaspoon dried sage
- 8 slices crusty French bread
- 4 (1-oz.) slices cheddar cheese*

1. In large skillet, combine brown sugar, oil and vinegar; cook over medium heat until bubbly. Add apples; cook about 5 minutes or just until tender, stirring occasionally. Remove apples from skillet; place in shallow bowl. Cover to keep warm.
2. Add turkey in batches to pan juices in skillet; sprinkle with sage. Cook 1 to 2 minutes or until thoroughly heated, turning once.
3. Divide turkey among 4 of the slices of bread. Top each slice with 1 slice of the cheese, ¼ of the apples and remaining bread slice.

TIP *Look for farmhouse cheddar cheeses from Vermont or New York. They are usually white in color.

4 sandwiches

PER SANDWICH: 535 calories, 19 g total fat (8.5 g saturated fat), 46 g protein, 43 g carbohydrate, 115 mg cholesterol, 550 mg sodium, 3.5 g fiber

Grilled Turkey-Portobello Sandwiches on Rye

Chutneys are a spicy Indian condiment containing fruit, vinegar, sugar and spices. They can range in texture from chunky to smooth. If yours is chunky, chop it for easier spreading.

- 2 teaspoons olive oil
- 4 small portobello mushroom caps, sliced
- 1 teaspoon lemon-pepper seasoning
- 8 slices dark rye bread
- 4 tablespoons butter, softened
- 8 tablespoons mango chutney
- 8 slices (6 oz.) Gruyère cheese
- 12 thin slices cooked turkey (12 oz.)

1. Heat oil in medium skillet over medium heat until hot. Add mushroom caps; sprinkle with lemon-pepper seasoning. Sauté 3 to 4 minutes or until tender.
2. Spread one side of each bread slice with ½ tablespoon of the butter. On the opposite side of each slice, spread 1 tablespoon of the chutney. Layer each of 4 slices of bread, chutney side up, with 1 slice of the cheese, 3 slices of the turkey, ¼ of the mushrooms and the second slice of the cheese. Cover each with slice of bread, chutney side down.
3. Heat large skillet or griddle over

Mini-Muffulettas

medium heat until hot. Place sandwiches in skillet; cook 6 to 8 minutes or until cheese is melted and bread is crisp and brown, turning once.

4 sandwiches

PER SANDWICH: 615 calories, 31 g total fat (16.5 g saturated fat), 44 g protein, 41 g carbohydrate, 135 mg cholesterol, 700 mg sodium, 4.5 g fiber

Mini-Muffulettas

Traditionally, the filling for this New Orleans-style sandwich is stuffed into a hollowed-out round loaf and cut into wedges. Using Italian rolls or mini-baguettes makes it easier to serve and eat.

  4 (8-inch) crusty French rolls
  2 cups (12 oz.) diced cooked

      turkey
 ½ cup sliced purchased
      roasted red bell peppers
 ½ cup sliced pitted Kalamata
      olives
 ⅓ cup Italian salad dressing
 ½ cup (2 oz.) crumbled goat
      cheese
  4 oz. thinly sliced salami

1. Heat oven to 375°F. Split rolls lengthwise. Remove inside soft bread to make cavity in each half. (Discard soft bread or reserve for another use.)
2. In medium bowl, combine turkey, bell peppers, olives and salad dressing; stir to combine.
3. For each sandwich, divide turkey mixture evenly into bottom half of each roll. Top each with ¼ of the goat cheese

and ¼ of the salami. Cover with top halves of rolls. Wrap in parchment paper or foil. Place on ungreased baking sheet.
4. Bake 12 to 15 minutes or until thoroughly heated.

4 sandwiches

PER SANDWICH: 555 calories, 30 g total fat (9.5 g saturated fat), 36.5 g protein, 34 g carbohydrate, 95 mg cholesterol, 1315 mg sodium, 2.5 g fiber

TURKEY TOPPINGS

Toppings are a quick and easy way to spice up a plain turkey sandwich—hot or cold. Here are some suggestions to get you started:

• **Madagascar Mayonnaise:** Mix 2 teaspoons curry powder, 2 teaspoons shredded coconut and 2 teaspoons warm honey into ½ cup mayonnaise. Spread mayonnaise on bread. Yield: ½ cup.

• **Olive Tapenade:** Mix ½ cup finely chopped oil-cured olives with 2 tablespoons Dijon-style mustard, 2 teaspoons capers and 2 teaspoons finely chopped chives. Top turkey with tapenade or spread it on bread. Yield: ¾ cup.

• **Pineapple Salsa:** Mix together ¼ cup medium salsa, ¼ cup drained, crushed pine-apple and 2 tablespoons chopped cilantro. Top turkey with salsa. Yield: ½ cup.

• **Cranberry-Apricot Chutney:** In a small microwave-safe bowl, mix together 2 tablespoons finely chopped dried apricots and 1 tablespoon balsamic vinegar. Microwave on high 40 seconds. Let stand for 2 minutes; then add ⅓ cup whole cranberry sauce and ⅓ cup prepared mincemeat. Stir together. Top turkey with chutney. Yield: ¾ cup.

SHRIMP

Don't wait for a special occasion to serve this quick-cooking crustacean.

Text and Recipes by Linda Gassenheimer

Shrimp is a favorite food of Americans, and it's easy to understand why—shrimp is great tasting, readily available and easy to cook. What's more, shrimp can be served in a variety of ways, from salads to stir-fries. These recipes give you three options: broiled (or grilled) in kabobs, stir-fried with vegetables and boiled for a salad. If you purchase peeled shrimp, it's easy to get dinner on the table in under 30 minutes, making shrimp dishes perfect for midweek suppers.

Red Pepper Shrimp with Bok Choy

The secret to wok cooking is to make sure your wok is very hot before using it. The oil should be shimmering in the pan. Then, when you add ingredients to the wok, wait about 20 seconds before tossing them. This gives the wok the chance to regain the heat lost when the cold ingredients are added.

- ½ cup dry sherry
- ¼ cup reduced-sodium soy sauce
- 2 tablespoons chopped fresh ginger
- 4 teaspoons cornstarch
- ¼ to ½ teaspoon crushed red pepper flakes
- 4 teaspoons sesame or vegetable oil
- 2 cups sliced onions
- 4 garlic cloves, minced
- 4 cups sliced bok choy
- 1¼ lb. shelled, deveined uncooked large shrimp

1. In small bowl, combine sherry, soy sauce, ginger, cornstarch and pepper flakes; mix well.
2. Heat oil in wok over high heat until hot. Add onions; stir-fry 1 minute. Add garlic and bok choy; stir-fry an additional minute. Add shrimp; stir-fry an additional minute.
3. Push vegetables and shrimp to sides of wok. Add sherry mixture to center of wok; bring to a boil. Toss shrimp with sauce and stir-fry 1 minute or until shrimp turn pink.

4 (1½-cup) servings

PER SERVING: 250 calories, 6 g total fat (1 g saturated fat), 24.5 g protein, 16.5 g carbohydrate, 200 mg cholesterol, 885 mg sodium, 2 g fiber

Lemon Shrimp Kabobs

Thread two skewers through the shrimp to solve the problem of trying to turn over the shrimp and having the skewers turn but not the shrimp. This recipe also can be cooked on a grill.

- 2 teaspoons grated lemon peel
- ¼ cup fresh lemon juice
- 1 tablespoon extra-virgin olive oil
- 2 garlic cloves, minced
- ½ teaspoon crushed red pepper flakes
- ½ teaspoon salt
- 1¼ lb. shelled, deveined uncooked large shrimp
- ¼ teaspoon freshly ground black pepper

1. In medium bowl, combine lemon peel, lemon juice, oil, garlic, pepper flakes and salt. Add shrimp; let stand 15 minutes to marinate.
2. Meanwhile, heat broiler. Line baking sheet with foil. Using 2 skewers per serving, thread shrimp through both skewers to keep shrimp flat; place on baking sheet.
3. Broil 3 to 4 minutes or until shrimp turn pink, turning once. Sprinkle shrimp with black pepper.

4 servings

PER SERVING: 110 calories, 2 g total fat (.5 g saturated fat), 21.5 g protein, .5 g carbohydrate, 200 mg cholesterol, 305 mg sodium, 0 g fiber

Mango-Shrimp Salad

The secret to this tangy salad is the juicy, plump shrimp. The method given for cooking shrimp is a perfect way to boil them.

SALAD
- 1¼ lb. shelled, deveined uncooked large shrimp
- 4 cups mixed salad greens
- 2 cups cubed ripe mangoes
- 1 red bell pepper, diced

DRESSING

Mango-Shrimp Salad

BUYING SHRIMP

Most shrimp sold today have been frozen and then thawed by the retailer. Much of what is sold in the United States is imported from Asia, Central America and South America. About 80 percent of imported shrimp are farm-raised and nearly all domestic shrimp are farm-raised.

Shrimp are sold according to size: small (36 to 45 per pound), medium (31 to 35), large (21 to 30), extra-large (16 to 20) and jumbo (11 to 15). The price per pound typically rises with the size. Large and extra-large shrimp give the best combination of flavor and value.

It's best to buy shrimp in their shells because it's easier to judge their quality. There should be no black spots and no yellowing, and they should smell of salt water and be firm, completely filling the shell. You can peel them at home, but to save time, ask the store to peel them for you. Many stores will do this for a slight additional cost.

There are hundreds of species of shrimp. These are some of the most common ones:

• **Black tiger:** These farm-raised shrimp from Asia are gray with black stripes. They turn pink when cooked.

• **Gulf brown:** Wild shrimp with a reddish-brown shell, they are most likely to taste of iodine, the result of the foods they eat.

• **Gulf pink:** They can be wild or farm-raised. Their shells are slightly red.

• **Gulf white:** Grayish-white in color, they're usually the most expensive shrimp, with good flavor and firm texture.

• **Rock shrimp:** These are caught off the mid-Atlantic and southern states and in the Gulf of Mexico. Because they're difficult to peel, they're usually sold peeled.

¼ **cup mayonnaise**
2 **teaspoons prepared horseradish**
⅓ **cup orange juice**
¼ **teaspoon salt**
¼ **teaspoon freshly ground pepper**

1. Place shrimp in large pot of water, making sure water covers shrimp. Bring water to a simmer. When bubbles start to appear around edges of pot and water is turning cloudy, remove from heat; let stand 1 minute or until shrimp turn pink.

2. Drain shrimp; rinse with cold water to cool. Place salad greens in large bowl; add shrimp, mangoes and bell pepper.

3. In small bowl, combine all dressing ingredients; blend well. Spoon dressing over salad; toss gently to coat.

4 servings

PER SERVING: 280 calories, 12.5 g total fat (2 g saturated fat), 23.5 g protein, 19.5 g carbohydrate, 210 mg cholesterol, 485 mg sodium, 3 g fiber

TOMATOES

IN THE RAW

Build a quick meal around juicy, garden-fresh tomatoes.

Text and Recipes by Jesse Cool

There's good reason why the tomato is nicknamed the love apple: Most people can't live without it. And the most loving way to use a fresh tomato is uncooked, or cooked as little as possible. That makes fresh tomatoes great allies when it comes to making quick, satisfying meals.

Consider the possibilities. Chop tomatoes and mix them with olive oil, fresh herbs and grated cheese; then toss the mixture with just-cooked pasta. Stack sliced tomatoes in sandwich fashion with cheese and tuna or chicken salad. Or spread slices on a platter, season with salt, pepper and garlic, and drizzle with olive oil. Then top with a mound of steamed summer vegetables.

Hollowed-out tomatoes make a perfect shell for quick stuffings, chilled or warm. I like to fill them with creamed spinach, creamed corn or even old-fashioned chicken à la king. The tomato warms slightly from the ingredients within.

Tomatoes are at their best when served with simple preparation. For fast summer fare, they're nature's own convenience food.

Albacore Tuna-Tomato Stack

This beautiful summer dish is essentially a sandwich without bread. Serve it on torn leaves of butterhead lettuce topped with a dollop of pesto or a drizzle of olive oil, and salt and pepper.

- 1 (12-oz.) can albacore tuna packed in water, drained
- 1 hard-boiled egg, finely chopped
- 2 tablespoons finely chopped celery
- 1 tablespoon finely chopped red onion
- 1 tablespoon finely chopped fresh dill
- 2 teaspoons finely grated lemon peel
- ¼ teaspoon salt
- ¼ teaspoon freshly ground pepper
- ¼ cup mayonnaise
- 4 medium beefsteak tomatoes

1. Coarsely crumble tuna into medium bowl. Add egg, celery, onion, dill, lemon peel, ⅛ teaspoon of the salt, ⅛ teaspoon of the pepper and mayonnaise; mix thoroughly.
2. Slice a thin layer off bottom of each tomato to create a flat surface. Cut each tomato horizontally into 4 slices. Sprinkle each layer evenly with remaining ⅛ teaspoon salt and pepper. Spoon tuna mixture between slices of each tomato.
4 servings

PER SERVING: 245 calories, 13.5 g total fat (2.5 g saturated fat), 24.5 g protein, 7 g carbohydrate, 85 mg cholesterol, 540 mg sodium, 1.5 g fiber

Fried Egg, Tomato and Avocado Sandwich

- 1 tablespoon unsalted butter
- 2 eggs
- ¼ teaspoon salt
- ¼ teaspoon freshly ground pepper
- 4 slices white or whole wheat bread, toasted
- 3 teaspoons mayonnaise
- 2 teaspoons Dijon mustard
- 1 medium tomato, cut into 4 slices
- ½ avocado, sliced
- 2 thin slices red onion

1. Melt butter in medium nonstick skillet over medium heat. Add eggs; cook until set. Sprinkle eggs with ⅛ teaspoon each of the salt and pepper.
2. Spread 2 slices of the toasted bread with mayonnaise; spread remaining 2 slices with mustard.
3. Top mayonnaise-spread slices with a layer of egg, tomato, avocado and onion. Sprinkle with remaining ⅛ teaspoon salt and pepper. Cover with mustard-spread slices.
2 sandwiches

PER SANDWICH: 400 calories, 25 g total fat (7.5 g saturated fat), 12 g protein, 33 g carbohydrate, 235 mg cholesterol, 740 mg sodium, 5 g fiber

Linguine with Tomatoes, Basil and Brie

Linguine with Tomatoes, Basil and Brie

The beauty of this dish is that the hot pasta warms all the other ingredients.

- 8 oz. linguine
- 2 cups chopped seeded tomatoes
- ½ cup sliced fresh basil
- ¼ cup extra-virgin olive oil
- 1 large garlic clove, minced
- 1 jalapeño chile, seeded, chopped
- 6 oz. Brie cheese, cut into ½-inch cubes
- ¼ teaspoon salt
- ¼ teaspoon freshly ground pepper
- ¼ cup (1 oz.) shaved Asiago cheese

1. Cook linguine according to package directions.
2. Meanwhile, in large bowl, combine tomatoes, basil, oil, garlic and jalapeño; stir gently to mix.
3. When linguine is cooked, drain and immediately add to tomato mixture. Add Brie cheese, salt and pepper; toss. Sprinkle with Asiago cheese.

4 servings

PER SERVING: 525 calories, 27 g total fat (9.5 g saturated fat), 20 g protein, 51.5 g carbohydrate, 35 mg cholesterol, 855 mg sodium, 3.5 g fiber

TOMATO TIPS

Storing: Don't refrigerate tomatoes. They are best when eaten at room temperature or at the temperature they would be when just picked and warmed by the sun. If tomatoes aren't quite ripe, store them in a brown paper bag for a day or two. If tomatoes are very ripe and you aren't ready to use them, refrigerate them; but before serving, bring them back to room temperature or warm them slightly to bring out maximum flavors.

Seeding: Seeding is done for aesthetics and texture. To remove seeds, cut the tomato in half crosswise and gently squeeze each half or tap each half against the counter or sink to loosen the seeds. Use a tiny spoon to scoop them out, if necessary.

Skinning: It's not necessary to skin a tomato; the skins on most ripe tomatoes are tender. If you choose to remove the skin, be sure to use firm, thick-fleshed tomatoes that will keep their shape better. Cut a small X at the blossom end of the tomato; plunge it into boiling water for 10 to 30 seconds (depending on how ripe it is), until it blisters slightly. Cool briefly in an ice bath; use a knife to pull off the skin.

Using green tomatoes: Tomatoes can be eaten in all stages, even when they're not fully mature. Unripe tomatoes are green or light-colored, hard and firm. Don't confuse them with varieties of tomatoes that are green-skinned even when ripe, such as Green Zebra. Unripe tomatoes can be pickled as you would a cucumber or used in chutneys and relishes. Dip them in flour or cornmeal and fry them in hot oil, or slather them with barbecue sauce or olive oil and toss them on the grill next to chicken or steak.

CURRIES

Authentic Indian dishes cook up fast and flavorful.

Text and Recipes by Raghavan Iyer

In India, my native country, curries—dishes with spicy sauces—are mainstay meals in every home. They're always created without recipes and vary tremendously from home to home and region to region. Seasonings, such as cumin and cayenne pepper, along with herbs, such as cilantro, form the backbone of many traditional curries.

A number of curries can be made quickly and easily, relying on herbs, spices, meats, vegetables and grains that cook fast. Even though these quick curries use just a few common spices, they are complex in taste, balancing sweet, sour, astringent, nutty and hot flavors. Techniques such as roasting chiles, popping mustard seeds and sautéing spices add rich flavor.

I serve seafood, meat or vegetable curries as main courses, accompanied by bowls of basmati rice and flatbreads, such as chappati (whole wheat bread), naan (traditional bread made in a clay-lined oven) and pappadum (crispy lentil wafers). Enjoy curries for a fast weekday meal, or serve them for a special gathering.

Coconut Shrimp Curry

The southwestern coast of India is home to many shellfish; their bountiful flavors are often enhanced by coconut milk, an essential base to many of the area's curries. The roasted chiles provide a wonderful contrast to the sweetness of coconut. Serve over basmati rice.

- 1 lb. shelled, deveined large shrimp
- ½ teaspoon salt
- 2 tablespoons lime juice
- 2 tablespoons vegetable oil
- 1 to 2 whole dried red chiles (cayenne or Thai)*
- 1 teaspoon mustard seeds**
- 1 cup thinly sliced shallots
- 1 cup unsweetened coconut milk

1. In medium bowl, combine shrimp, salt and lime juice. Let stand 5 to 10 minutes to marinate.

2. Meanwhile, heat oil in large skillet over medium heat until hot. Add chiles; sauté 30 to 60 seconds until slightly blackened. Remove chiles; let cool slightly. Finely chop; set aside.

3. Return skillet to medium heat. Add mustard seeds to hot oil; cover immediately and cook 15 to 30 seconds or until all seeds have popped.

4. Remove cover; immediately add shallots. Cook and stir 1 to 2 minutes or until partially browned. Add shrimp mixture; cook and stir 1 to 2 minutes. Add coconut milk and chiles; simmer 3 to 5 minutes or until shrimp turn pink.

TIPS *If whole dried chiles are unavailable, ½ to ¾ teaspoon crushed red pepper flakes can be used; add with shallots.

**If available, try black or brown mustard seeds. They are the only mustard seeds used in India and add an intensity of flavor not found in yellow mustard seeds.

4 servings

PER SERVING: 280 calories, 21 g total fat (12.5 g saturated fat), 20 g protein, 5 g carbohydrate, 160 mg cholesterol, 495 mg sodium, 1 g fiber

Cumin-Scented Chicken Curry

This North Indian dish derives its nutty flavor from cumin. Serve it with basmati rice.

- 3 tablespoons all-purpose flour
- 1 tablespoon grated lemon peel
- 4 teaspoons cumin seeds
- ¾ teaspoon ground red pepper (cayenne)
- ½ teaspoon salt
- 1½ lb. boneless skinless chicken tenders*
- 2 tablespoons vegetable oil

Potato-Swiss Chard Curry

heated. Garnish with cilantro.

TIP *Chicken tenders are available prepackaged in large supermarkets. If unavailable, boneless skinless chicken breasts, cut into strips, can be used.

4 servings

PER SERVING: 350 calories, 13.5 g total fat (3.5 g saturated fat), 43 g protein, 12 g carbohydrate, 100 mg cholesterol, 445 mg sodium, .5 g fiber

Potato-Swiss Chard Curry

This tomato-based, sweet-and-hot curry, balanced by a simple blend of spices, is typically found in northwestern India.

- 3 medium red-skinned potatoes, unpeeled, cut into 1-inch pieces
- 1 tablespoon vegetable oil
- 2 tablespoons sugar
- 2 teaspoons ground cumin
- ½ teaspoon salt
- ½ teaspoon ground red pepper (cayenne)
- 1 (14.5-oz.) can diced tomatoes, undrained
- 3 cups chopped Swiss chard

1. Place potatoes in large saucepan; cover with water. Bring to a boil. Boil 4 to 6 minutes or until crisp-tender. Drain.
2. Heat oil in large skillet over medium-high heat until hot. Add potatoes, sugar, cumin, salt and ground red pepper. Sauté 2 to 3 minutes.
3. Stir in tomatoes and Swiss chard. Reduce heat to medium-low; cover and simmer 4 to 6 minutes or until Swiss chard is crisp-tender.
4 servings

PER SERVING: 175 calories, 4 g total fat (.5 g saturated fat), 4 g protein, 34 g carbohydrate, 0 mg cholesterol, 505 mg sodium, 3.5 g fiber

1½ cups plain yogurt
2 tablespoons chopped fresh cilantro

1. In medium bowl, combine 2 tablespoons of the flour, lemon peel, cumin seeds, ground red pepper and salt; mix well. Add chicken; stir to coat. Let stand 5 minutes.
2. Heat oil in large skillet over medium

heat until hot. Add chicken mixture; cook 5 to 8 minutes or until lightly browned, stirring occasionally. Reduce heat to low; cover and simmer 2 to 3 minutes or until chicken is no longer pink in center.
3. In small bowl, combine yogurt and remaining 1 tablespoon flour; blend well. Add to chicken mixture; cook and stir 1 to 2 minutes or until thoroughly

CANNED
AID

Quick, hearty meals rely on diced tomatoes from a can.

Text and Recipes by Mary Evans

Roaming the canned food aisles recently, I ran into one of my students. "I wouldn't expect to find you here," she exclaimed. Explanations were in order.

As a cooking school instructor, I'm always encouraging my students to use the best of seasonal ingredients. Nevertheless, living in a northern climate, I also know that seasonal can mean preserved, so canned tomatoes can become an important ally. Their quality is excellent because the tomatoes are picked when they're ripe and juicy, then quickly canned to preserve maximum flavor. In fact, canned tomatoes are always a better choice when the fresh supermarket alternative is a pale, pinkish, tasteless thing, developed for ease in shipping and little else.

Already cut into recipe-size pieces, diced canned tomatoes become effortless assets to the home cook. Add them to soups and stews, or pastas and pizzas. Consider them a pantry staple and use them as part of the seasonless repertoire of culinary necessities.

Cajun Chicken and Sausage Sauté

This recipe is a takeoff on Louisiana's jambalaya. Serve it over rice. To make sure the recipe is done in 30 minutes, start cooking the rice before beginning the recipe. Keep covered until ready to serve.

- 1 tablespoon vegetable oil
- 1 cup chopped onion
- 1 green bell pepper, chopped
- ½ lb. andouille sausage,
  cut into ½-inch slices
- ½ lb. boneless skinless chicken breast halves, cut into 1-inch pieces
- 2 (14.5-oz.) cans diced tomatoes, undrained
- 2 to 3 teaspoons dried Cajun seasoning
- ½ teaspoon celery salt

1. Heat oil in large skillet over medium-high heat until hot. Add onion, bell pepper and sausage; cook 4 to 5 minutes or until onion and bell pepper begin to soften, stirring occasionally.
2. Add chicken; sauté 3 to 4 minutes or until outside of chicken is no longer pink. Add tomatoes, Cajun seasoning and salt; stir to combine. Reduce heat to low; cover and simmer an additional 5 to 6 minutes or until chicken is no longer pink in center.
4 servings

PER SERVING: 415 calories, 27.5 g total fat (9 g saturated fat), 28.5 g protein, 14.5 g carbohydrate, 80 mg cholesterol, 1505 mg sodium, 3 g fiber

Chipotle Pork Chili

Posole, a substantial and satisfying Mexican soup featuring pork and hominy, provides the inspiration for this chili. Unlike many quickly prepared dishes, this recipe captures a depth of flavor, thanks to the addition of smoky chipotle chiles.

- 1 tablespoon vegetable oil
- 1 cup chopped onion
- ¾ lb. pork tenderloin, cut into ¾-inch pieces
- 2 tablespoons chili powder
- 2 (8-oz.) cans tomato sauce
- 1 (15.5-oz.) can white hominy
- 1 (14.5-oz.) can diced tomatoes, undrained
- 1 tablespoon minced chipotle chiles in adobo sauce*

1. Heat oil in large pot or nonreactive Dutch oven over medium heat until hot. Add onion; sauté until tender, about 5 minutes.
2. Add pork and chili powder; stir to combine. Continue cooking and stirring an additional 5 minutes.
3. Add tomato sauce, hominy, tomatoes and chiles; mix well. Bring to a boil. Reduce heat to low; cook about 10 minutes, stirring occasionally.
TIP *If unavailable, add ¼ teaspoon ground red pepper (cayenne) and dash

Tomato, Artichoke and Herbed Feta Pasta

tional 5 minutes or until mixture is hot and bubbly.

4. Place linguine in large shallow bowl. Add tomato-artichoke mixture; toss to combine. Sprinkle with cheese. Serve immediately.

4 servings

PER SERVING: 415 calories, 15 g total fat (5.5 g saturated fat), 14 g protein, 57 g carbohydrate, 25 mg cholesterol, 930 mg sodium, 5.5 g fiber

of liquid smoke.
4 (1¼-cup) servings

PER SERVING: 300 calories, 8.5 g total fat (2 g saturated fat), 23.5 g protein, 34.5 g carbohydrate, 50 mg cholesterol, 1240 mg sodium, 7.5 g fiber

Tomato, Artichoke and Herbed Feta Pasta

Quartered, marinated artichoke hearts are another great pantry item. Add them to a variety of salads and antipasto platters, or use as a pizza topping. They are also a great accompaniment to roast chicken.

  8 oz. linguine
  1 tablespoon olive oil
  1½ teaspoons minced garlic
  1 (14.5-oz.) can diced
      tomatoes, drained
  1 (12-oz.) jar marinated
      quartered artichoke hearts
  ¼ cup water
  1 (4-oz.) pkg. crumbled
      herbed feta cheese

1. Cook linguine according to package directions. Drain.
2. Meanwhile, heat oil in large skillet over medium heat until hot. Add garlic; sauté about 1 minute. Stir in tomatoes. Cook 5 minutes, stirring occasionally.
3. Drain artichokes, reserving ¼ cup of the marinade. Add artichokes to tomato mixture; cook 2 minutes. Stir in water and reserved marinade. Reduce heat to low; cover and simmer an addi-

MORE QUICK DINNERS

In addition to the plain diced tomatoes called for in the recipes here, you'll find a bonanza of seasoned tomatoes on grocery store shelves. If you substitute one for the other, remember to adjust seasonings called for in recipes. Here are some additional quick dinner ideas:

• **Shrimp Pasta:** Use either dried or fresh pasta along with shrimp and canned diced tomatoes for a quick dinner alternative. Quickly sauté peeled, deveined shrimp with bite-size pieces of vegetables, onion and garlic. When the shrimp turn pink and begin to curl, add canned tomatoes. Cook until hot; then toss with cooked pasta.

• **Pesto Vegetable Soup:** Make a quick vegetable soup using a can of diced tomatoes and your favorite frozen vegetable blend. Add enough broth or water to get the consistency you desire. Then stir in some purchased pesto. Heat thoroughly and serve with croutons.

• **Italian Beef Sauté:** For a simple beef sauté, quickly brown cubes of tender beef with thin onion wedges. Stir in a can of diced tomatoes and a little red wine, if you like. Add dried thyme or Italian seasoning. Simmer briefly and serve.

STEAKS

Special dinners are fast and easy with tender cuts of beef.

Text and Recipes by Ethel G. Hofman

Celebrate any time with a meal of hearty steaks cooked to juicy perfection.

For busy cooks, steaks are a real bargain. In less than 30 minutes, you can cook the meat and even make a topping or sauce to accompany it. If your crew is partial to spicy fare, try strip steaks topped with chiles and mushrooms, or blackened rib-eye steaks. Or for deep, rich flavors, maybe you prefer a T-bone topped with a whiskey sauce.

Whatever your taste preferences, be sure to make the meal memorable by choosing tender, high-quality cuts of beef. Then cook them properly. Whether you're using the grill or the stove top, the key is to sear steak over high heat to obtain a crusty outside surface and then to cook it to a flavorful tenderness inside.

Barbecue-Spiced Blackened Rib-Eye Steaks

Pan searing was made famous by Paul Prudhomme and his blackened redfish. Use a cast iron skillet rather than a nonstick skillet. High heat damages the nonstick lining and may cause the skillet to warp. Make sure your exhaust fan is on to avoid setting off any smoke alarms.

- 4 teaspoons kosher (coarse) salt
- 1 tablespoon barbecue seasoning or rub
- 1 tablespoon paprika
- 4 beef rib-eye steaks (about 1 inch thick)
- 3 tablespoons chopped fresh parsley

1. In small bowl, combine salt, barbecue seasoning and paprika; mix well. Rub mixture on all sides of steaks; set aside.
2. Heat cast iron skillet over high heat 4 to 5 minutes or until very hot. Place steaks in skillet; sear 4 minutes, turning once.
3. Reduce heat to medium; cook an additional 3 to 4 minutes for medium-rare or until of desired doneness, turning once. Sprinkle with parsley.
4 servings

PER SERVING: 245 calories, 11 g total fat (4 g saturated fat), 33 g protein, 2 g carbohydrate, 85 mg cholesterol, 1640 mg sodium, .5 g fiber

Whiskey-Glazed T-Bone Steak

Deglazing is the technique where liquid is added to dissolve the browned bits of solidified, flavorful juices that have accumulated in the pan during cooking. Bourbon can be substituted for the whiskey in this recipe.

- 4 beef T-bone steaks (1 inch thick)
- 1 teaspoon salt
- 2 teaspoons freshly ground pepper
- 3 tablespoons vegetable oil
- ¾ teaspoon all-purpose flour
- ¼ cup whiskey
- 3 tablespoons water
  Dash sugar

1. Sprinkle steaks on both sides with salt and pepper. Heat oil in large skillet over high heat until hot. Add steaks; cook 4 minutes, turning once.
2. Reduce heat to medium-high; cook an additional 3 to 4 minutes for medium-rare, turning once. Remove skillet from heat; place steaks on warm platter.
3. Pour off all but 1 tablespoon of the drippings. Stir in flour; cook over medium heat 30 to 60 seconds, stirring constantly. Whisk in whiskey, water and sugar. Bring to a boil, scraping up any browned bits from bottom of skillet. Spoon sauce over steaks.
4 servings

PER SERVING: 315 calories, 17.5 g total fat (5 g saturated fat), 32.5 g protein, 1 g carbohydrate, 85 mg cholesterol, 660 mg sodium, .5 g fiber

Strip Steaks Smothered with Red-Hot Mushrooms

Mushrooms take on a fiery note to spice up tender, juicy strip steaks. Jalapeño chiles and hot pepper sauce give the

Strip Steaks Smothered with Red-Hot Mushrooms

sautéed mushrooms their kick. To save time, buy packaged sliced mushrooms, but rinse and pat them dry before using.

- 2 tablespoons unsalted butter
- 1 lb. sliced mushrooms
- 1 to 2 red jalapeño chiles, chopped*
- ¼ teaspoon salt
- ¼ teaspoon hot pepper sauce
- 4 beef strip loin steaks, about 1 inch thick
- 2 teaspoons garlic powder
- 2 teaspoons lemon-pepper seasoning

1. Melt butter in large skillet over high heat. Add mushrooms; cook 2 to 3 minutes or until browned at the edges. Add chiles, salt and hot pepper sauce; cook an additional 1 to 2 min-

utes or until chiles begin to soften. Set aside.

2. Heat grill. Sprinkle steaks on both sides with garlic powder and lemon-pepper seasoning.

3. Place steaks on gas grill over medium heat or on charcoal grill 4 to 6 inches from medium heat. Cook 8 to 10 minutes for medium-rare or until of desired doneness, turning once.

4. Warm mushroom mixture; spoon over steaks.

TIP *Crushed red pepper flakes can be substituted for the chiles. Use ½ to 1 teaspoon.

4 servings

PER SERVING: 325 calories, 17 g total fat (7.5 g saturated fat), 35.5 g protein, 8 g carbohydrate, 100 mg cholesterol, 405 mg sodium, 1.5 g fiber

TIPS FOR BUYING STEAK

Great-tasting steaks start with high-quality meat. If it's tenderness you're after, choose steaks from the short loin. The expensive tenderloin or filet mignon has a butter-like texture. Porterhouse and T-bone steaks have the bone left in. When the bone is removed, the meat is cut into steaks and labeled "boneless club," "shell" or "strip" steaks.

Rib and rib-eye steaks have more marbling, which gives a richer flavor. Flank steak is tough but flavorful; marinate it to tenderize the meat before cooking.

Beef grading is an optional marking you may find on steaks. It's paid for by the processor and regulated by the United States Department of Agriculture. Grades include:

- **Prime:** From young cattle, this grade is typically well marbled.

- **Choice:** It's less marbled than prime but is the most widely available grade.

- **Select:** It has the least amount of marbling and may not be as tender or juicy as Prime and Choice.

Look for meat that is bright red and firm to the touch, not mushy, and with no brown or gray discoloration. If packaged, the meat should be tightly wrapped with no tears in the plastic. Make sure you are purchasing the meat before the sell-by date noted on the label.

BEVERAGES

Lemon-Rosemary Iced Tea, Oolong Peach Bloom, Green Tea-Cherry Cooler and Iced Chocolate Chai

Spices, herbs, fruits and chocolate combine with an American classic for some refreshing new beverages.

Text and Recipes by Robert Wemischner

When the temperature climbs, there's nothing like a tall glass of tea on the rocks to cool you down. Iced tea in its simplest form has been a staple for years. It's only recently that we've begun to explore tea as a foundation for other beverages. Use the teas of India, China and other countries as a starting point, then mix them with herbs, spices, juices—even chocolate. Suddenly iced tea goes from simple to exceptional!

As with all tea beverages, the key to these drinks is to use high-grade tea brewed properly. Better quality teas produce more complex and satisfying flavors. Use these recipes to get started. Then experiment with your own ideas. Iced tea's mellow flavor makes it a perfect partner for a wide range of ingredients.

Green Tea-Cherry Cooler

This drink was inspired by a Japanese green tea flavored with black cherry. Use Sencha tea for a bright taste and a grassy freshness.

TEA
- 4 cups water
- ¼ cup green tea leaves
- 1 cup cherry juice

SYRUP
- 1 cup sugar
- 1 cup water
- 6 cinnamon sticks

1. In medium saucepan over medium heat, bring 4 cups water to just below a simmer (180°F.). Remove from heat. Add tea; let steep 4 minutes.
2. Strain mixture into pitcher. Add cherry juice. Refrigerate until cool.
3. Meanwhile, in small saucepan, bring all syrup ingredients to a boil over medium heat. Simmer 5 minutes. Refrigerate until cool.
4. Remove cinnamon sticks from syrup; add to tea mixture. Blend well. Serve over ice. If desired, garnish with cinnamon sticks.
4 servings

PER SERVING: 230 calories, .5 g total fat (0 g saturated fat), .5 g protein, 58.5 g carbohydrate, 0 mg cholesterol, 10 mg sodium, 1 g fiber

Iced Chocolate Chai

There are numerous recipes for chai tea, but this one is made to be served iced. It uses black tea and bittersweet chocolate, along with cardamom, cinnamon and allspice.

- 4 cups nonfat milk
- ½ cup sugar
- 2 tablespoons black tea leaves
- 2 oz. bittersweet chocolate, finely chopped
- 6 cardamom pods, crushed, or ¼ teaspoon ground cardamom
- 4 whole allspice, crushed
- 2 cinnamon sticks
- 1 vanilla bean, split lengthwise, or 1 teaspoon vanilla

1. In medium saucepan, combine all ingredients; bring to a boil over medium heat. Reduce heat to low; simmer 5 minutes, whisking occasionally.
2. Remove from heat; let stand 10 minutes. Strain mixture. Refrigerate until chilled.
4 servings

PER SERVING: 250 calories, 4.5 g total fat (3 g saturated fat), 9 g protein, 46 g carbohydrate, 5 mg cholesterol, 130 mg sodium, 1 g fiber

Lemon-Rosemary Iced Tea

For special occasions, serve this tea with a scoop of lemon sorbet.

- 5 cups water
- 2 cups sugar
- 12 sprigs fresh rosemary
- ¼ cup black tea leaves
- 1 cup fresh lemon juice

1. In medium saucepan over medium heat, bring water, sugar and 8 rosemary sprigs to just below a simmer (190°F.), stirring until sugar dissolves.

Remove from heat. Add tea; let steep 3 minutes.

2. Strain tea; add lemon juice. Refrigerate until cool.

3. Serve over ice. Garnish each serving with rosemary sprig.

4 servings

PER SERVING: 405 calories, 0 g total fat (0 g saturated fat), 0 g protein, 104.5 g carbohydrate, 0 mg cholesterol, 25 mg sodium, 0 g fiber

Oolong Peach Bloom

This rich-tasting but low-fat drink features oolong tea, a lightly fermented tea, the best of which comes from Taiwan.

 4 cups water
 2 tablespoons lightly packed oolong tea leaves
 1 cup fresh mint
 2 cups peach nectar
 3 tablespoons sugar
 ½ teaspoon vanilla
   Fresh peach wedges
   Fresh mint sprigs

1. In medium saucepan over medium heat, bring water to just below a simmer (190°F.). Remove from heat. Add tea and 1 cup mint; let steep 3 minutes.

2. Strain tea. Add peach nectar, sugar and vanilla; mix well. Refrigerate until chilled. Serve garnished with peach wedges and mint sprigs.

4 servings

PER SERVING: 115 calories, 0 g total fat (0 g saturated fat), .5 g protein, 29 g carbohydrate, 0 mg cholesterol, 15 mg sodium, 1 g fiber

TEA BASICS

The tea you choose and the way you brew it are important to create a full-flavored iced tea beverage. Follow these guidelines for perfect tea on the rocks.

Choosing teas: Some teas work better than others when served over ice. Typically, robust flavored teas work best. The subtle, flowery, delicate teas such as Darjeeling, from India, lose flavor when iced. But the robust Nilgiri and Assam teas, also from India, remain strong over ice. Japanese teas, from grassy Sencha to roasted Hojicha, work well. Others to consider include African teas from Kenya and Cameroon, and most Chinese teas, from black Yunnan and Keemun to green Dragonwell.

Loose, not bagged: Loose tea leaves make a more flavorful brew because some of the leaves are in large pieces and even whole. Tea leaves need to be large enough to unfurl in order to fully flavor the water. Most bagged tea is "CTC tea," meaning crushed, torn and curled. This allows tea processors to use the remnants of tea leaves in bags, rather than whole leaves, after the first processing is done.

Stronger brews: Make teas for iced drinks stronger than you do when serving those same teas hot because the ice dilutes the drink as the ice melts. Use one and one-half times the amount of tea to ensure a flavorful brew. If you have time, and at least five hours of strong sun, you can brew tea outdoors. Brewing at a cooler temperature and for a longer period of time tends to bring out the best flavors in teas without extracting any of the bitter tannic compounds. To do this, place water and tea leaves in a clean jar with a tight-fitting lid. Put the jar in a sunny spot outdoors for about 5 hours; then filter the tea and store it in the refrigerator for up to 2 days.

Water quality, temperature: For best flavor, use filtered or spring water when brewing tea. Additives in tap water may distort or completely obliterate the flavors inherent in tea. Don't scorch the tea leaves when brewing. Most black teas, such as Chinese Yunnan or Indian Assam, are best when brewed in water just under a rolling boil, about 190°F. to 205°F. Oolongs do well when water temperature is between 190°F. and 203°F.; green teas do better at about 158°F. to 180°F. Using water that has boiled and then cooled down results in flat-tasting tea because much of the oxygen is boiled out.

Shake, Strain & Pour

Text by Kelly March O'Hara; Recipe by Carole Brown

marts, garage and estate sales, and online auction sites. New designs are also available, many of which mimic the old, classic styles, including chrome and delicate glass pitchers and shakers.

Cranberry Sparklers

Choose a brut Champagne or any other dry sparkling wine for this aperitif. Don't overfill the glasses—about two thirds full is just right for sparkling wine.

- 8 tablespoons thawed cranberry juice concentrate
- 3 tablespoons orange liqueur
- 1 bottle chilled dry sparkling wine

Mix together cranberry juice concentrate and orange liqueur, divide it equally among 8 Champagne flutes. Fill glasses with sparkling wine and serve.
6 to 8 aperitifs

Cranberry Sparkler

Although food connoisseur James Beard once sniffed that "the cocktail party is an inferior form of entertainment at best," he seems to have missed the show. After all, produced with flair, mixing fancy cocktails can become pre-dinner theater.

Today countless books, movies and menus are showcasing the return of elegant, old-fashioned cocktails such as Cosmopolitans and martinis, all served up in big-bowled, thin-stemmed glasses. (The stemware keeps the drinker's hands away from the bowl, thus keeping the cocktail cold.)

Along with this resurgence in popularity of vintage drinks, classic cocktail shakers, decanters, strainers and all the various miscellany involved in producing them are becoming increasingly sought-after by collectors. While some people collect vintage barware purely for its attractive lines and elegant memories, others buy it to use. Special long spoons let you "muddle" superfine

sugar in the bottom of a glass. Chrome strainers let you keep ice out of a drink. Cocktail pitchers let you meet the request, "stirred, not shaken." (Stirring a cocktail with shaved ice in a pitcher results in a clear drink; shaking results in a colder but somewhat cloudy one.)

To discover how popular these cocktail tools are, witness a past listing on the Internet auction site eBay.com: Type in "martini," the most ubiquitous of cocktails, and a listing of hundreds of items appears. A chrome Art Deco-era cocktail shaker sells for $52. A silver "martini spike" shaped like a hypodermic needle—designed to put a hint of vermouth into a drink—brings a bid of $34. Three other bidders are busy fighting over a set of eight silver olive picks, pushing the price to more than $25.

Considering that some rare barware can fetch hundreds of dollars, today's buyers may have found bargains.

If you're interested in starting your own collection, check local antique

REACH FOR

RIESLING

Its clean, fruity notes are perfect for spring fare.

By Lisa Shara Hall

In the world of white wines, Chardonnay has reigned supreme. So consider Riesling as a refreshing alternative to that ubiquitous varietal.

No other white wine so clearly offers the pure flavors of clean, ripe fruit; Riesling almost always has elegance, power and structure, all wrapped in delicate fruit flavors. A steely backbone of acid anchors the round, fruity sweetness to create balance; moderate alcohol levels also anchor the acidity in all but the classic, lower-alcohol German style, where a kiss of sugar sweetness balances the acid. That crisp acidity makes Riesling wonderfully compatible with food, from appetizers to desserts.

Typical Riesling flavors include green apple, citrus, apricot, peaches, pineapple, honey, cinnamon and floral (grasses, honeysuckle, spring meadow) notes. For Rieslings grown in Germany and Alsace, a region in northeastern France bordering Germany, you may catch whiffs of earth, slate or wet stone.

In the New World (the term for non-European, younger wine-producing countries), Riesling is widely planted. Vineyards in Australia, New Zealand, South America, California, Oregon, Washington, upstate New York, Ontario and British Columbia show great promise. They offer a variety of styles, from sweet to dry.

RECOMMENDED BUYS

ALSACE

1995 F.E. Trimbach Riesling
Cuvée Frédérick-Emile ($33)

1997 Hugel Riesling ($14)

GERMANY

1997 Von Kesselstatt Riesling Spätlese
Mosel-Saar-Ruwer Scharzhofberger ($20)

1998 Selbach-Oster Riesling
Kabinett Mosel-Saar-Ruwer ($15)

1997 J.L. Wolf Riesling
Halbtrocken Pfalz ($10)

UNITED STATES

1998 Bonny Doon Vineyard Pacific Rim
Dry Riesling ($9)

AUSTRALIA

1998 Pike's Clare Valley ($15)

OUT OF
SOUTH AFRICA

Fine wines are now being produced from this once-restricted region.

By Mary Ewing Mulligan

Today, small wineries are increasing in number, red wine production is growing (traditionally, white grapes have dominated), and cooler areas are emerging as vineyard regions for fine wine. South Africa, approximately the size of Texas, has one-third the vineyard acreage of California. Most of it is in the southern tip of the country.

South African wines are easy to explore because most of them are named for grape varieties, just as American wines are. The one unfamiliar name is Pinotage, South Africa's own grape, born of a crossing between Pinot Noir and Cinsaut vines; Pinotage wines are red and full-bodied, with spicy-fruity flavors and sometimes an earthy note. Try one from Kanonkop ($25), Cathedral Cellars ($11) or Beyerskloof ($10). Another less familiar name is Chenin Blanc, also known as Steen, the most planted grape in South Africa. Serious Chenin Blancs are in the minority, but one fine producer, Old Vine Wine Cellars, makes Blue White Chenin Blanc ($12), a crisp, richly textured white with pear-like flavor.

Sauvignon Blanc wines from South Africa are really exciting—fresh, crisp, zingy wines with lots of flavor. Some good brands to try are Mulderbosch, Boschendal, Plasir de Merle, Thelema, Groot Constantia, Nederburg and Neil Ellis; prices range from $10 to $22. In addition, most of these producers and others, such as Cheetah Valley, make Chardonnay, which in South Africa can be either smoky and oaky, or appley and unoaked in style.

To experience the best of South African wines, though, try a Cabernet Sauvignon or a wine blended from Cabernet and Merlot, ranging from $10 to $30. Top producers include Grangehurst, Meerlust (especially Rubicon, a blend), Plasir de Merle, La Motte, Stellenryck, Zonnebloem and many more.

Winemaking in South Africa dates all the way back to 1652, but the wines have been available here for less than a decade. In fact, many of South Africa's best wineries are less than 20 years old.

Because of anti-apartheid trade sanctions against South Africa, which ended in the early 1990s, wine drinkers had no access to South African wines. And, because of government regulations, South African winemakers could not import vines, such as Chardonnay, nor did they have access to the creative stimulus gained by sampling foreign wines.

SPARKLERS

Finding a bubbly wine you like is a matter of style.

By Mary Ewing Mulligan

Do you "get no kick from Champagne?" Maybe you just haven't discovered the style that's right for you. After all, sparkling wines are definitely not a one-size-fits-all proposition.

Champagne—as well as most bubbly wine made in places other than the Champagne region of France—comes in several different sweetness styles. The most renowned, brut, is the driest. This is the category that elite brands such as Dom Pérignon and Cristal fall into. But many people find brut Champagnes a bit too dry, preferring instead a slightly sweeter style. Ironically, that style is called extra dry.

Americans particularly like extra dry Champagnes. While about 3 percent of all Champagne produced is extra dry, it represents a whopping 35 percent of all Champagne sold in the United States. The top-selling brand in the United States, Moët et Chandon White Star, is extra dry (although the label doesn't say so). You can also find extra dry from Mumm, Piper Heidsieck, Perrier-Jouët and Louis Roederer ($25 to $30). Drink them exactly as you would a drier style: before dinner, with light foods and with brunch, especially eggs.

Because extra dry Champagne is really not very sweet, its flavor can be overwhelmed by sweet foods. Another style, demi-sec, the sweetest of styles, pairs far better with desserts. Look for Veuve Clicquot, Moët et Chandon, Lanson and Louis Roederer in demi-sec ($25 to $30).

The best bet with dessert, however, is Asti—a bubbly wine from northern Italy that just brims with delicious, fruity flavor. The fresher the Asti, the better. Shop in stores with heavy turnover, and ask how long the Asti has been on the shelf; six months is about the limit for freshness. Martini & Rossi and Fontanafredda are excellent brands ($10 to $12).

VALUES IN
WINE

Moderately priced wines offer good quality and taste.

By J. Herbert Silverman

controlled cold fermentation in steel tanks instead of years in expensive oak casks are revolutionizing the ways that wines are produced.

More suppliers are entering the market, particularly those from California's Central Coast, New York State's Finger Lakes region and overseas from Chile, Southern Italy and the former Eastern bloc countries. The intensified competition results in lower costs.

Here are some good-quality, moderately priced wines, matched up with foodsthey would complement:

BEEF STEAKS
Lindemans Shiraz ($8)
or
Luis Felipe Edwards 1997 Estate
Cabernet Sauvignon ($10)

LAMB CHOPS
Carpe Diem 1997 Cabernet
Sauvignon ($9)

CHICKEN
Jekel Chardonnay ($11)
or
Sella & Mosca Sauvignon Blanc Le
Arenarie Alghero 1998 ($11)

LOBSTER
Chandon Brut Classic 196,
Vintage 1997 ($15)

PORK CHOPS
Vichon Mediterranean Merlot
Vin de Pays d'Oc ($11)

PASTA
Prosper Maufaux 1998
Côtes du Rhône ($11)

When you're looking for a nice wine to accompany a summer meal, you may be surprised to find some great buys for $15 or less. Good quality varietal wines such as Cabernet Sauvignon, Chardonnay and Merlot are readily available at affordable prices.

The presence of excellent wine at moderate prices is a result of better vineyard management, more efficient trellising and, in some cases, new irrigation technology. What's more, contemporary aging techniques and

TECHNIQUES

Lemon-Lime Meringue Pie

A food-styling trick
helps stabilize meringue pies.

All text and recipes in this techniques chapter by Janice Cole,
Cooking Pleasures Food Editor

Apple pie may get billing as the all-American dessert, but we're betting lemon meringue is a close second, judging by the number of letters we receive about the classic confection. Sweet yet tart; rich yet light—it's no wonder lemon meringue pie is so popular.

But it's also one of those desserts that can pose problems for the cook—usually because of the meringue. It doesn't whip up properly, it shrinks, it beads up or it weeps. Success lies in the technique.

To help ensure the perfect meringue, I've incorporated a food styling trick into the recipe: adding cornstarch to the egg whites to stabilize the meringue, making it less likely to bead up or shrink from the edges during baking. I learned this technique from fellow food stylists and have used it during photo shoots to produce beautiful pies. Now I use it for the pies I bake at home, too.

Lemon-Lime Meringue Pie

FILLING
- 2 eggs
- 4 egg yolks
- ¼ teaspoon salt
- 1 cup sugar
- ⅓ cup cornstarch
- 1½ cups water
- ¼ cup unsalted butter, cut up, softened
- 2 teaspoons grated lime peel
- ¼ cup fresh lime juice
- ¼ cup fresh lemon juice

MERINGUE
- ⅓ cup water
- 1 tablespoon cornstarch
- 4 egg whites
- ½ teaspoon fresh lime juice
  Dash salt
- ½ cup sugar
- 2 teaspoons grated lime peel

PIE SHELL
- 1 (9-inch) baked pie shell

1. Heat oven to 350°F. To make filling, in large bowl, whisk eggs, egg yolks and ¼ teaspoon salt until well blended. Set aside. In medium saucepan, combine 1 cup sugar and ⅓ cup cornstarch; mix well. Stir in 1½ cups water. Bring to a boil over medium heat, stirring occasionally. Boil 1 minute, stirring constantly. (Mixture will be very thick.)

2. Slowly add hot cornstarch mixture to egg mixture, whisking constantly. Return mixture to saucepan. Bring to a boil over medium heat. Boil 30 seconds, stirring constantly. Remove from heat. Add butter; stir until melted. Stir in 2 teaspoons lime peel, ¼ cup lime juice and lemon juice. Cover; let stand while making meringue.

3. To make meringue, in small saucepan, combine ⅓ cup water and 1 tablespoon cornstarch; mix well. Bring to a boil over medium heat. Boil 30 seconds, stirring constantly. Turn off heat; cover to keep warm.

4. In large bowl, combine egg whites, ½ teaspoon lime juice and dash salt; beat at medium-low speed until egg whites are frothy. Increase speed to medium; beat until egg whites hold a soft peak. With mixer running, slowly add ½ cup sugar; spoon in warm cornstarch mixture. Increase speed to medium-high; beat until mixture is glossy and egg whites hold a stiff peak. Gently fold in 2 teaspoons lime peel.

5. Heat filling over medium-high heat until very hot, stirring constantly. Immediately pour into pie shell. Spoon half of meringue evenly over hot filling, making sure meringue covers all filling and touches crust on all edges. Spoon remaining meringue onto pie and spread evenly. Add decorative swirls with back of spoon.

6. Bake 15 to 18 minutes or until meringue is dry to the touch and light brown. Place on wire rack; cool 2 hours or until room temperature. Refrigerate 3 to 4 hours or until chilled. Store in refrigerator.

8 servings

PER SERVING: 365 calories, 15 g total fat (6 g saturated fat), 6 g protein, 52.5 g carbohydrate, 175 mg cholesterol, 260 mg sodium, .5 g fiber

Lemon Meringue Pie

FILLING
- 2 eggs
- 4 egg yolks
- ¼ teaspoon salt
- 1¼ cups sugar
- ⅓ cup cornstarch
- 1½ cups water
- ¼ cup unsalted butter, cut up, softened
- 2 teaspoons grated lemon peel
- ½ cup fresh lemon juice

MERINGUE
- ⅓ cup water
- 1 tablespoon cornstarch
- 4 egg whites
- ½ teaspoon fresh lemon juice
  Dash salt
- ½ cup sugar
- 2 teaspoons grated lemon peel

PIE SHELL
- 1 (9-inch) baked pie shell

1. Heat oven to 350°F. To make filling, in large bowl, whisk eggs, egg yolks and ¼ teaspoon salt until well blended. Set aside. In medium saucepan, combine 1¼ cups sugar and ⅓ cup cornstarch; mix well. Stir in 1½ cups water. Bring to a boil over medium heat, stirring occasionally. Boil 1 minute, stirring constantly. (Mixture will be very thick.)
2. Slowly add hot cornstarch mixture to egg mixture, whisking constantly. Return mixture to saucepan. Bring to a boil over medium heat. Boil 30 seconds, stirring constantly. Remove from heat. Add butter; stir until melted. Stir in 2 teaspoons lemon peel and ½ cup lemon juice. Cover; let stand while making meringue.
3. To make meringue, in small saucepan, combine ⅓ cup water and 1 tablespoon cornstarch; mix well. Bring to a boil over medium heat. Boil 30 seconds, stirring constantly. Set aside.
4. In large bowl, combine egg whites,

½ teaspoon lemon juice and dash salt; beat at medium-low speed until egg whites are frothy. Increase speed to medium; beat until egg whites hold a soft peak. With mixer running, slowly add ½ cup sugar and cornstarch mixture. Increase speed to medium-high; beat until mixture is glossy and egg whites hold a stiff peak. Lightly fold in 2 teaspoons lemon peel.
5. Heat filling over medium-high heat until very hot, stirring constantly. Pour into pie shell. Spoon half of meringue evenly over hot filling, making sure meringue covers all filling and touches crust on all edges. Spoon remaining meringue onto pie and spread evenly. Add decorative swirls with back of spoon.
6. Bake 15 to 18 minutes or until meringue is dry to the touch and light brown. Place on wire rack; cool 2 hours or until room temperature. Refrigerate 3 to 4 hours or until chilled. Store in refrigerator.
8 servings

PER SERVING: 385 calories, 15 g total fat (6 g saturated fat), 6 g protein, 59 g carbohydrate, 175 mg cholesterol, 260 mg sodium, .5 g fiber

Making Creamy Fillings
The fillings in these pies are simple egg custards thickened with cornstarch. Whole eggs as well as egg yolks are used to add body and richness to the filling.

Whisk constantly: Use a wire whisk to stir the cornstarch, sugar and water mixture while it cooks to keep lumps from forming.

Whisk briskly.

Pour slowly: When adding the hot cornstarch mixture to the egg yolks, place the bowl on a damp towel to keep it stable while you whisk. Spoon in the hot mixture slowly. Eggs need time to adjust to heat; they curdle if they're exposed to heat too quickly.

Cook thoroughly: Once the eggs are added to the filling, they must be cooked thoroughly. This not only kills bacteria but also ensures the eggs will not break down the cornstarch and cause the filling to be runny.

Timing's important: Lemon and lime juice are added after the filling is thoroughly cooked. If they're added sooner, they can affect the cornstarch's ability to thicken.

STEPS TO PERFECT MERINGUE PIES

Make it hot: Heat the filling immediately before pouring it into the pie shell and topping with the meringue. Do not allow the filling to cool down before the meringue has been spread or the pie may "weep" because the cool filling prevents the meringue from baking completely.

Making the Meringue

The key to perfect meringue is the cornstarch-water mixture that is added to the egg whites. Cornstarch produces tender meringues that are less likely to shrink, bead or weep. Add the mixture to the egg whites a tablespoon at a time while the mixture is still warm.

Beating egg whites: For maximum volume, use room temperature egg whites.

• Begin beating the egg whites slowly, increasing speed when they are frothy and beating until soft peaks just begin to form.

• Continue beating, slowly adding the sugar and then the cornstarch mixture.

• Beat the egg whites until stiff peaks form—this takes a little time. Egg whites are ready when the beaters leave

Swirl with a spoon.

ridges in the whites and they are glossy and hold a stiff peak when the beaters are lifted out.

Spreading meringue: Spread one-half of the meringue over the hot filling, starting at the outside edge. Make sure the meringue touches the crust around the entire edge to avoid shrinkage. Pile the remaining meringue on top and swirl it with a knife or spoon.

Troubleshooting Meringue

If you have a problem with meringue, follow one of these suggestions for solving it.

Weeping: When water seeps between the filling and the meringue, the pie is weeping. This is caused by spreading the meringue over a cool filling, which prevents the meringue from baking completely.

solution: Make sure the filling is hot, even boiling, before pouring it into the pie shell. Immediately spread the meringue over the filling. The hot filling will begin to cook the meringue from the bottom, ensuring even cooking throughout.

Beading: This happens when water droplets form tiny beads on the surface of the meringue. It's caused by overbaking the meringue. When egg whites bake too long, they begin to tighten, squeezing out little drops of moisture. Over-baking also produces a tough meringue.

solution: Bake meringues just until they are light brown and dry to the touch. Egg whites need to be cooked to 160°F. but not so long that they are overdone.

Shrinkage: Meringues may shrink during baking, separating from the crust. This is caused by the meringue not clinging to the crust.

solution: Make sure the meringue is spread over the filling and touches the crust around the entire edge; do not leave any openings around the pie.

Limp or soggy: Humidity affects a meringue's texture. Damp, humid days may cause it to be limp and sticky.

solution: Ideally, meringues should be made on dry days. The cornstarch mixture used in these recipes helps them hold up under humid conditions, but to ensure success, plan to bake when it is less humid.

BOTTLING
SUMMER

Roasted Red Pepper-Rosemary Vinegar, Garlic-Ginger-Dill Vinegar, Citrus-Mint Vinegar

Herb-infused vinegars capture the season's essence.

Every year as warm weather hits, I find myself thinking of ways to capture the essence of summer. I usually have grand thoughts of preserving, drying, freezing and canning the season's bounty. Unfortunately, limited time prevents me from putting my plans into action. Making infused vinegar—vinegar flavored with fresh herbs and produce—is one way to preserve summer that doesn't take loads of time and effort. No special equipment or processing is needed. And the vinegar can be used throughout the coming months to add summertime flavors to cooking.

I usually experiment with various combinations of herbs, produce and seasonings, depending on what's available. Here are three new favorites: Roasted Red Pepper-Rosemary Vinegar, a beautiful and seductive smoky-flavored vinegar; Garlic-Ginger-Dill Vinegar, which makes a perfect all-purpose vinegar, and Citrus-Mint Vinegar, a light, almost sweet vinegar that pairs well with fruity salads. Get started today bottling the tastes of summer with these recipes, then go on to create your own.

Roasted Red Pepper-Rosemary Vinegar

Sweet red bell peppers, roasted until charred and fragrant, give this vinegar its unusually deep red color and smoky taste. Look for smooth, heavy bell peppers for roasting; the smooth surface makes it easier and quicker to roast them, resulting in firm, crisp-tender flesh. The peppers and rosemary give this vinegar enough body that it can be drizzled over salads without needing any oil.

2 large red bell peppers
¾ cup white wine vinegar
3 sprigs fresh rosemary

1. Place bell peppers over high heat on gas or electric burner. Cook, turning with tongs every 1 to 2 minutes, until skins are completely blackened. Place peppers in heavy plastic bag; close bag and let stand 15 minutes or until cool enough to handle. Peel blackened skins under running water. Slit peppers and remove veins and seeds.
2. Place bell peppers in blender. Add vinegar; blend until almost smooth. Place in sterilized glass bottle; add rosemary. Cover; refrigerate (color stays nicer in refrigerator) 7 to 14 days or until vinegar is full-flavored.
3. Remove and discard rosemary. If desired, place fresh rosemary sprig in bottle for garnish. Store in refrigerator. 1½ **cups**

PER 2 TABLESPOONS: 5 calories, 0 g total fat (0 g saturated fat), 0 g protein, 2 g carbohydrate, 0 mg cholesterol, 0 mg sodium, 0 g fiber

Garlic-Ginger-Dill Vinegar

Fresh dill asserts its flavor in this vinegar, with background hints of garlic and ginger. This is a perfect all-purpose vinegar because the fresh herb flavor combines well with many different ingredients. When preparing fresh dill, remove large stems only, leaving any small thin stems. Cut dill only until it is coarsely chopped; if it's chopped too finely, the leaves become bruised and the flavor is compromised. The vinegar in this recipe is used at room temperature, not warmed, because the delicate dill flavor can be lost if heated.

1 cup packed coarsely chopped fresh dill
¼ cup coarsely chopped fresh ginger
3 large garlic cloves, minced
1 (12.7-oz.) bottle white wine vinegar

1. In large glass jar, combine all ingredients; stir to combine. Cover; let stand at room temperature 7 to 14 days or until vinegar is full-flavored.
2. Strain vinegar; place in sterilized glass bottle. Discard dill, ginger and garlic. If desired, add fresh dill sprigs to bottle for garnish. Store at room temperature. 1½ **cups**

PER 2 TABLESPOONS: 5 calories, 0 g total fat (0 g saturated fat), 0 g protein, 2 g carbohydrate, 0 mg cholesterol, 0 mg sodium, 0 g fiber

Citrus-Mint Vinegar

Rice vinegar is milder than white wine vinegar, making it the perfect choice for this light orange-lime infused vinegar. You can vary the type of mint used, depending on what's available, or use a combination of several types, such as ginger mint, orange mint and lime mint.

- 2 large oranges
- 1 large lime
- 1 cup lightly packed fresh mint sprigs
- 1 (12-oz.) bottle rice vinegar

1. Sterilize 3-cup glass jar. With vegetable peeler, remove peel from oranges and lime, being careful not to include white pith below peel. (Reserve oranges and lime for another use.) Place orange and lime peels in jar. Add mint sprigs.
2. Heat vinegar in small saucepan over medium heat just until vinegar is warm but not hot. Pour vinegar over citrus peel and mint. Cover; let stand at room temperature 7 to 14 days or until vinegar is full-flavored.
3. Strain vinegar; place in sterilized 12-oz. bottle. Discard peels and mint. If desired, add fresh mint sprigs and large pieces of orange and lime peels to bottle for garnish. Store at room temperature.
1⅓ cups

PER 2 TABLESPOONS: 5 calories, 0 g total fat (0 g saturated fat), 0 g protein, 2 g carbohydrate, 0 mg cholesterol, 0 mg sodium, 0 g fiber

USING INFUSED VINEGARS

Try these recipe suggestions with the flavored vinegars featured here.

Roasted Red Pepper-Rosemary Vinegar

Roasted Red Pepper-Rosemary Vinaigrette: Combine 1 tablespoon Roasted Red Pepper-Rosemary Vinegar with 1 small clove of garlic, minced. Slowly whisk in 3 tablespoons of olive oil; season to taste with salt and pepper.

Marinated Red Pepper Grilled Chicken: Drizzle Roasted Red Pepper-Rosemary Vinegar over boneless skinless chicken breasts. Marinate in the refrigerator for 2 to 4 hours. Grill the chicken over medium heat. For added flavor, place rosemary stems that have been soaked in water at least 20 minutes directly on the coals while the chicken is grilling.

Garlic-Ginger-Dill Vinegar

Garlic-Ginger-Dill Vinaigrette: Combine 1 tablespoon of Garlic-Ginger-Dill Vinegar with ½ small garlic clove, minced. Slowly whisk in 3 tablespoons of olive oil; season to taste with salt and pepper.

Garlic-Ginger Roasted Tomato Linguine: Place sliced plum tomatoes in a large shallow pan. Drizzle with Garlic-Ginger-Dill Vinegar and olive oil. Bake at 425°F. for 15 minutes or until the tomatoes are tender. Toss with hot linguine, Parmesan cheese and freshly ground pepper

Citrus-Mint Vinegar

Citrus-Mint Vinaigrette: Combine 1 tablespoon Citrus-Mint Vinegar with ⅛ teaspoon Dijon mustard. Whisk in 3 tablespoons of mild olive oil or vegetable oil; season to taste with salt and pepper.

Grilled Summer Fruit Salad: Combine apricot preserves with Citrus-Mint Vinegar to make a light glaze. Brush sliced peaches, pineapple, plums, pears and/or thinly sliced apples lightly with olive oil. Grill 5 to 8 minutes or until the fruit is tender, brushing with the glaze during the last 3 minutes of cooking. Serve on a bed of mixed salad greens and garnish with coarsely chopped fresh mint.

TECHNIQUE
HOW-TO

Making flavored vinegar is very simple. Be sure to wash herbs and produce well, and sterilize jars used to infuse and store the vinegar. These additional tips will ensure success:

Herbs and seasonings: For optimum flavor, use herbs before they blossom. Choose seasonings that complement rather than dominate the flavors of the herbs and produce. Peppercorns, shallots, hot chiles, lemon peel, cinnamon sticks, edible flowers and fruit all add unique tastes to vinegar.

Vinegar: Any type can be used, but keep in mind color and acidity. Clear vinegars, such as white wine vinegar or rice vinegar, allow you to see the herbs and seasonings. But other vinegars, such as cider vinegar, red wine vinegar and sherry vinegar, can be used for interesting flavor combinations. When using delicate herbs and seasonings, use a lighter vinegar, such as rice vinegar, which has a low acidity level of 4.2 percent. White wine vinegar is a good all-purpose choice at about 5 percent acid. Brands vary in acidity so check the label before purchasing. Distilled white vinegar tends to be a little harsh for infused vinegars.

Temperature: Typically, the vinegar is heated until it's warm but not hot. The warmth begins to pull the essential oils and flavors from the herbs quicker than room temperature vinegar, so the flavor develops faster. When using delicate herbs, such as dill, or colorful herbs, such as opal basil or chive blossoms, it's better to use room temperature vinegar to protect the herbs' flavors and colors.

Containers: Use glass containers, not metal or plastic, to infuse and store vinegar. Select a wide-mouth jar for infusing so that it's easy to add herbs and seasonings. For longer term storage, transfer the vinegar to decorative bottles, if desired, or recycle vinegar containers that have been cleaned and sterilized. To sterilize jars and bottles, immerse them in a pan of boiling water for 15 minutes. Remove the pan from the heat, but let the jars stand in the hot water until ready to use.

Storage: Store vinegar at room temperature unless otherwise indicated. Flavored vinegars keep for six months to a year. After six months, the flavor may begin to dissipate.

Creating your own recipes: Use 1 to 2 cups lightly packed, coarsely chopped

fresh herbs per 12-ounce bottle of vinegar. Use less of stronger herbs, such as thyme or rosemary, and more of delicate herbs, such as basil or tarragon. If you've never made flavored vinegars, start with a single-herb vinegar; then experiment with your own special flavor combinations.

COOKING
LOBSTER

Grilled Lobster with Shallot-Red Pepper Butter

Learn how to boil it, roast it, grill it.

I grew up in a landlocked state but always had a fascination with the sea. The ocean held promise of great adventure, with endless beaches and crashing waves. I never got close to the ocean while young, but I did develop a taste for seafood. Its briny, salty flavor gave me a vicarious feeling of being on the coast.

Lobster, of course, was king. It was seldom served, but when it was, it was the epitome of elegance. We ate it plain—with a little melted butter for dipping, perhaps—content to let the lobster shine on its own. I have since discovered the joys of eating lobster in other ways. I love the smokiness of grilled lobster and the ease of do-ahead roasted lobster. And while a simple lobster tail is still enjoyable, now I usually prefer eating the whole lobster. There is something that happens when cracking the shells and prying out the meat that makes the lobster seem even sweeter. It brings me back to dreams of the ocean and the adventure that awaits.

Grilled Lobster with Shallot-Red Pepper Butter

BUTTER
- 1 cup butter
- ½ cup finely chopped shallots
- ¼ cup fresh lemon juice
- 2 teaspoons crushed red pepper flakes

LOBSTER
- 4 quarts (16 cups) water
- ¼ cup sea salt
- 4 (1¼- to 1½-lb.) lobsters

1. Melt butter in small saucepan over medium heat. Add shallots; sauté 60 to 90 seconds or until shallots are fragrant and begin to soften. Stir in lemon juice and red pepper flakes; remove from heat. Divide butter mixture in half. Set aside half of mixture to brush on lobster during grilling; reserve remaining half to serve warm with lobster.
2. Place water and salt in large pot. Cover; bring to a boil over high heat. Add lobsters; cover and return to a boil. When water boils, cook lobsters 3 to 4 minutes or until lobster shells begin to turn a mottled red. Remove lobsters from pot; immediately plunge into large bowl of ice water to stop cooking.
3. Place lobsters on cutting board; cut in half lengthwise. Remove sand sac, intestinal track and liver (see p. 161). Crack claws to allow heat from grill to penetrate. (Lobster can be made up to 3 hours ahead. Cover and refrigerate.)
4. Heat grill. Brush lobster halves with half of butter mixture. Place on gas grill over medium heat or on charcoal grill 4 to 6 inches from medium coals. Cook 6 to 8 minutes or until lobster meat is opaque, turning once and brushing occasionally with butter mixture. Heat remaining butter mixture in small saucepan until warm. Serve lobsters with warm butter mixture.

4 servings

PER SERVING: 405 calories, 29.5 g total fat (18 g saturated fat), 31 g protein, 4 g carbohydrate, 185 mg cholesterol, 1240 mg sodium, .5 g fiber

Ginger-Herb Roasted Lobster

SAUCE
- 1 cup chopped fresh Italian parsley
- ½ cup chopped fresh basil
- ½ cup chopped fresh dill
- ⅓ cup water
- 2 tablespoons chopped fresh ginger
- 2 large garlic cloves
- 2 tablespoons olive oil
- ¼ teaspoon salt
- ⅛ teaspoon freshly ground pepper

LOBSTER
- 4 quarts (16 cups) water
- ¼ cup sea salt
- 4 (1¼- to 1½-lb.) lobsters

1. In blender, combine all sauce ingredients; blend until smooth. Set aside.
2. Place water and salt in large pot. Cover; bring to a boil over high heat. Add lobsters; cover and return to a boil. When water boils, cook lobsters 3 to 4 minutes or until lobster shells begin to turn a mottled red. Remove lobsters from pot; immediately plunge into large bowl of ice water to stop cooking.
3. Place lobsters on cutting board; cut in half lengthwise. Remove sand sac, intestinal track and liver (see p. 161). Place lobsters cut side up in 2 (15x10x1-inch) pans. Spread herb sauce over lobster halves. (Lobster can be made up to 3 hours ahead. Cover

IS IT DONE YET?

To check for doneness, turn the lobster upside down and look at the tail where it joins the body. The tail meat should be firm, white and cream-colored, not translucent.

1. Place steaming rack in large pot. Add water and salt. Cover; bring to a boil over high heat.
2. Add lobsters; cover and return to a boil.
3. Once water is boiling, cook lobsters 10 to 14 minutes or until lobster meat is opaque. Serve with dipping sauces or melted butter and fresh lemon juice.
4 servings

PER SERVING: 145 calories, 1 g total fat (0 g saturated fat), 30 g protein, 2 g carbohydrate, 105 mg cholesterol, 560 mg sodium, 0 g fiber

and refrigerate.)
4. When ready to cook, arrange 2 oven racks, one above the other, in center third of oven. Heat oven to 425°F. Bake lobsters 8 to 12 minutes or until lobster meat turns opaque, switching positions of pans halfway through baking.
4 servings

PER SERVING: 215 calories, 8 g total fat (1 g saturated fat), 31 g protein, 4 g carbohydrate, 105 mg cholesterol, 1200 mg sodium, .5 g fiber

Boiled Lobster

4   quarts (16 cups) water
¼   cup sea salt
4   (1¼- to 1½-lb.) lobsters

1. Place water and salt in large pot. (There should be enough water in pot to cover lobsters, but not too much or water will boil over. Depending on size

of pot, you may need more or less water.) Cover; bring to a boil over high heat.
2. Add lobsters, head first, to boiling water; cover and return to a boil.
3. Once water returns to a boil, cook 9 to 12 minutes or until lobster meat is opaque. Remove lobsters from water, allowing excess water to drain off. Serve with dipping sauces or melted butter and fresh lemon juice.
4 servings

PER SERVING: 145 calories, 1 g total fat (0 g saturated fat), 30 g protein, 2 g carbohydrate, 105 mg cholesterol, 1045 mg sodium, 0 g fiber

Steamed Lobster

6   cups water
1   tablespoon salt
4   (1¼- to 1½-lb.) lobsters

DIPPING SAUCES

Basil-Olive Oil

½   cup coarsely chopped basil
½   cup extra-virgin olive oil
⅛   teaspoon salt
⅛   teaspoon pepper

Place all ingredients in blender. Blend until smooth.
½ cup

Thai Sweet Chili Dip

¼   cup Thai sweet chili sauce
¼   cup rice wine vinegar
2   tablespoons water
1   tablespoon chopped fresh cilantro

In medium bowl, stir together all ingredients.
⅔ cup

Buying, storing lobsters

Begin by selecting lobsters that are active. Look for tails that curl tightly and claws that hold firm, not limp. It's best to purchase and cook lobsters on the same day. However, they can be stored overnight in a cardboard box or paper bag with holes in the lowest section of the refrigerator. Never store lobsters on ice, and never hold them in fresh (tap) water.

Cooking lobsters

Some people are squeamish about cooking a lobster while it's alive, but it really is necessary: Once a lobster dies, the meat begins to deteriorate quickly and can become toxic. If you don't like handling an active lobster, you can numb it by placing it in the freezer for 1 to 2 hours. It may then be cooked according to any of the methods below.

Equipment: You'll need a very large pot to cook several lobsters at once—a large stock or canning pot will cook up to four lobsters comfortably. Or purchase a lobster pot, available in specialty stores. Don't overcrowd the pot. If you don't have a pot large enough to hold all the lobsters, cook the lobsters in batches. Lobster cooks quickly, so the wait isn't long.

Boiling: Boiling is the easiest method for cooking lobsters. Make sure the lobsters are completely submerged; cover and begin timing once the water returns to a boil.

Steaming: Some people prefer the steaming method because they believe the lobsters contain less liquid when steamed rather than boiled. I find there is not much difference between the two methods, so it is a matter of personal choice. Place lobsters on a steaming rack over the liquid, and begin timing when the liquid is at a full boil.

Parboiling: Grilled or roasted lobster should be split before being cooked. The easiest and most humane way to prepare lobsters for these methods is to partially boil them for 3 to 4 minutes rather than splitting them while alive.

Cutting lobsters in half

Place the lobster on a cutting board shell side up. Place the tip of a large chef's knife behind the head of the lobster and press firmly down. Cut through the tail portion of the lobster. Then turn the lobster and cut through the head.

Parts of a lobster

Sand sac: This is located directly behind the eyes of the lobster and is actually the stomach of the lobster. Remove the sand sac with a spoon.

Intestine: The intestine runs down the side of the tail and is often dark gray in color. It should be removed.

Tomalley: The soft light green substance found in the body of the lobster is the tomalley. It is the liver and pancreas of the lobster and acts as a filter to keep the meat wholesome. Because the tomalley can accumulate contaminants from the environment, it is currently suggested that you remove and not consume the tomalley.

Roe: Female lobsters will often contain eggs, or roe, which are located in the body cavity and are bright red in color. Many people find this a delicious prize when they split apart their lobster.

Before boiling.

After boiling.

Cutting in half.

Remove tomalley.

CARAMEL
DREAMS

Chocolate Swirl, Toasted Pecan, Ginger Cream and Buttery Soft Caramels

Master the art of these buttery, rich candies.

I've always loved soft, gooey, stick-to-your-teeth caramels. But good caramels aren't easy to find. For a time, a friend who made them kept me supplied with her rich, buttery versions. When she got too busy to make them, I decided to create my own recipes.

Now, each year as the holiday season approaches, I make a variety to share with family and friends. Everyone has their favorites, from Buttery Soft Caramels, which taste like the topping of a double-dipped caramel apple, to Ginger Creams, which leave the tangy bite of fresh ginger lingering long after the caramel is gone. Silky smooth and soft, these caramels disappear almost as quickly as I can make them.

Basic caramels are made from a few simple ingredients: butter, sugar, cream and corn syrup. The way the ingredients are combined and the temperature they're cooked to create the vast variety of caramel textures and flavors. With a watchful eye and the right equipment, they're easy to make.

Chocolate Swirl Caramels

Bittersweet chocolate pieces are sprinkled over the cooked caramel, and the heat of the caramel melts the chocolate. Make sure the chocolate is soft before running a knife through the mixture, and don't overmix.

- ½ cup unsalted butter
- 2 cups sugar
- 1½ cups whipping cream
- 1 cup light corn syrup
- 2 oz. bittersweet chocolate, finely chopped

1. Line 8-inch square pan with foil; spray with nonstick cooking spray. Melt butter in Dutch oven or heavy, large (4½- to 6-quart) saucepan over low heat. Add sugar, cream and corn syrup; stir to mix. Increase heat to medium; bring to a boil, stirring frequently.
2. Insert candy thermometer into mixture and attach to side of Dutch oven. Cook, stirring frequently, until thermometer registers 230°F. At this point, it is important to watch mixture carefully. Begin stirring constantly until thermometer registers 248°F. (firm-ball stage).
3. Immediately pour half of caramel mixture into pan. Sprinkle with half of chocolate. Pour remaining caramel mixture over chocolate; do not scrape Dutch oven. Sprinkle with remaining chocolate; let stand 2 to 3 minutes or until chocolate is melted. Run knife once through mixture to swirl. Let stand 6 to 8 hours or until cool and set.
4. Remove caramel from pan by lifting foil. Remove foil. With large knife, cut caramel into 64 pieces. Wrap each piece individually.
64 caramels

PER CARAMEL: 70 calories, 3.5 g total fat (2 g saturated fat), 0 g protein, 10.5 g carbohydrate, 10 mg cholesterol, 5 mg sodium, 0 g fiber

Toasted Pecan Caramels

These caramels are so rich, they're almost like eating a piece of dessert.

- 2½ cups pecan halves
- ½ cup butter
- 2 cups sugar
- 1½ cups whipping cream
- 1 cup light corn syrup

1. Heat oven to 375°F. Line 8-inch square pan with foil; spray with nonstick cooking spray. Place pecans on baking sheet; bake 5 to 10 minutes or until lightly toasted. Set aside ½ cup pecans. Place remaining pecans in foil-lined pan.
2. Melt butter in Dutch oven or large (4½- to 6-quart) heavy saucepan over low heat. Add sugar, cream and corn syrup; stir to mix. Increase heat to medium; bring to a boil, stirring frequently.
3. Insert candy thermometer into mixture; attach to side of Dutch oven. Cook, stirring frequently, until thermometer registers 230°F. At this point, it is important to watch mixture carefully. Begin stirring constantly until thermometer registers 248°F. (firm-ball stage).
4. Immediately pour caramel mixture into pan; do not scrape Dutch oven. Sprinkle with reserved ½ cup pecans. Let stand 6 to 8 hours or until cool and set.

5. Remove caramel from pan by lifting foil. Remove foil. With large knife, cut caramel into 64 pieces. Wrap each piece individually.
64 caramels

PER CARAMEL: 95 calories, 6 g total fat (2 g saturated fat), .5 g protein, 11 g carbohydrate, 10 mg cholesterol, 15 mg sodium, .5 g fiber

Ginger Cream Caramels

Note that these caramels are cooked to a slightly lower temperature than the other caramels. This helps keep them soft and luscious.

> 2 cups sugar
> 2 cups whipping cream
> 1 cup light corn syrup
> 1 tablespoon finely grated
>   fresh ginger

1. Line 8-inch square pan with foil; spray with nonstick cooking spray. Place all ingredients in Dutch oven or heavy, large (4½- to 6-quart) saucepan. Bring to a boil over medium heat, stirring frequently.
2. Insert candy thermometer into mixture and attach to side of Dutch oven. Cook, stirring frequently, until thermometer registers 230°F. At this point, it is important to watch mixture carefully. Begin stirring constantly until thermometer registers 245°F. (firm-ball stage).
3. Immediately pour caramel mixture into pan; do not scrape Dutch oven. Let stand 6 to 8 hours or until cool and set.
4. Remove caramel from pan by lifting foil. Remove foil. With large knife, cut caramel into 64 pieces. Wrap each piece individually.
64 caramels

PER CARAMEL: 60 calories, 2.5 g total fat (1.5 g saturated fat), 0 g protein, 10 g carbohydrate, 10 mg cholesterol, 5 mg sodium, 0 g fiber

Buttery Soft Caramels

Try to let the caramels sit overnight before cutting them. If allowed to cool completely, they will cut more easily and be less sticky.

> ½ cup unsalted butter
> 2 cups sugar
> 1½ cups whipping cream
> 1 cup light corn syrup

1. Line 8-inch square pan with foil; spray with nonstick cooking spray. Melt butter in Dutch oven or heavy, large (4½- to 6-quart) saucepan over low heat. Add sugar, cream and corn syrup; stir to mix. Increase heat to medium; bring to a boil, stirring frequently.
2. Insert candy thermometer into mixture and attach to side of Dutch oven. Cook, stirring frequently, until thermometer registers 230°F. At this point, it is important to watch mixture carefully. Begin stirring constantly until thermometer registers 248°F. (firm-ball stage).
3. Immediately pour caramel mixture into pan; do not scrape Dutch oven. Let stand 6 to 8 hours or until cool and set.
4. Remove caramel from pan by lifting foil. Remove foil. With large knife, cut caramel into 64 pieces. Wrap each piece individually.
64 caramels

PER CARAMEL: 65 calories, 3 g total fat (2 g saturated fat), 0 g protein, 10 g carbohydrate, 10 mg cholesterol, 5 mg sodium, 0 g fiber

CARAMEL EQUIPMENT

Success when making caramels depends in part on having the right tools. Here's what you need:

Large, heavy pot: Use a 4½- to 6-quart Dutch oven or saucepan. The pan must be large enough to accommodate the mixture as it rises during boiling so it doesn't boil over. A heavy pot decreases the chance of scorching or burning.

Candy thermometer: This is necessary to accurately monitor the temperature of the mixture. The higher the temperature, the firmer the caramel will be. The thermometer should clip onto the side of the pan, and it should have markings every 2 degrees. Markings every 5 degrees are not accurate enough for candy.

Wooden spoon: Because the mixture gets very hot, use a wooden spoon for stirring rather than a metal one, which conducts heat. You can also use a rubber spatula, if it is rated heat resistant.

STAGES OF COOKING CARAMELS

Cooking caramels requires patience and a watchful eye. The caramel should cook steadily, but slowly, to develop deep flavor. It takes 20 to 30 minutes for the candy to cook. During that time, the caramel should boil steadily at a medium boil. The entire surface of the mixture must be boiling for the caramel to cook evenly. As it cooks, watch the thermometer because the temperature can change quickly. Always check the temperature at eye level to get an accurate reading. Begin cooking the mixture slowly to dissolve the sugar. Here are the stages of cooking:

Stage 1: Attach the candy thermometer to the side of the pan and monitor the temperature of the mixture. It will rise quickly to 220°F., but the color doesn't change much.

Stage 2: By 230°F., the mixture is light brown in color. It's important to begin stirring constantly at this point. As the caramel reaches 240°F. to 245°F., the caramel begins to deepen in color, the bubbles get larger, and the mixture thickens. Keep stirring, especially into the edges of the pan.

Stage 3: As the caramel reaches final temperature, the color deepens to a golden brown, the mixture thickens and the bottom of the saucepan begins to appear while stirring. When the final temperature is reached, immediately pour the caramel into a prepared pan. Don't scrape the caramel from the bottom of the saucepan into the prepared pan; it may be overcooked. Instead, pour it into a small bowl—it makes a nice little treat for the cook!

Recipe Index

This index lists every recipe in The Best of Cooking Pleasures—Volume I *by name. If you're looking for a specific recipe but can't recall the exact name, turn to the General Index that starts on page 168. You can look up recipe there by ingridient(s) or cooking technique, and find what you're looking for.*

General Index

There are several ways to use this helpful index. First—you can find recipes by name. If you don't know a recipe's specific name but recall a main ingredient used, look under that heading and all the related recipes will be listed; scan for the recipe you want. If you have an ingredient in mind and want to find a great recipe for it, look under that ingredient heading as well to find a list of recipes to choose from. Finally—you can use this general index to find a summary of the recipes in each chapter of the book (beverages, main dishes, entertaining, etc.).

Recipes and Notes